T0337950

QUANTITATIVE FINANCIAL
RISK MANAGEMENT

QUANTITATIVE FINANCIAL RISK MANAGEMENT

Michael B. Miller

WILEY

Published by John Wiley & Sons, Inc., Hoboken, New Jersey.

Published simultaneously in Canada.

For general information on our other products and services or for technical support, please contact our Customer Care Department within the United States at (800) 762–2974, outside the United States at (317) 572–3993, or fax (317) 572–4002.

Wiley publishes in a variety of print and electronic formats and by print-on-demand. Some material included with standard print versions of this book may not be included in e-books or in print-on-demand. If this book refers to media such as a CD or DVD that is not included in the version you purchased, you may download this material at http://booksupport.wiley .com. For more information about Wiley products, visit www.wiley.com.

Library of Congress Cataloging-in-Publication Data

Names: Miller, Michael B. (Michael Bernard), 1973- author.
Title: Quantitative financial risk management / Michael B. Miller.
Description: Hoboken, New Jersey : Wiley, [2019] | Series: Wiley finance
    series | Includes bibliographical references and index. |
Identifiers: LCCN 2018033207 (print) | LCCN 2018044462 (ebook) | ISBN
    9781119522232 (Adobe PDF) | ISBN 9781119522263 (ePub) | ISBN 9781119522201
    | ISBN 9781119522201 (hardcover) | ISBN 9781119522232 (ePDF) | ISBN
    9781119522263 (ePub)
Subjects: LCSH: Financial risk management.
Classification: LCC HD61 (ebook) | LCC HD61 .M5373 2019 (print) | DDC
    332—dc23
LC record available at https://lccn.loc.gov/2018033207

Cover Design: Wiley
Cover Images: © Sergey Nivens/Shutterstock; © whiteMocca/Shutterstock

Printed in the United States of America

C10005024_100518

CONTENTS

PREFACE

My first book on financial risk management, *Mathematics and Statistics for Financial Risk Management*, grew out of my experience working in the hedge fund industry and my involvement with the Global Association of Risk Professionals. It was written for practitioners who may not have had the opportunity to take the advanced courses in mathematics— especially those courses in statistics—that are necessary for a deeper understanding of modern financial risk management. It was also for practitioners who had taken these courses but may have forgotten what they learned. To be honest, I often use the first book as a reference myself. Even authors forget.

As a result of that first book, I was asked to teach a graduate-level course in risk management. I realized that my students had the opposite problem of my colleagues in the hedge fund industry. My students came to the course with a very strong foundation in mathematics, but knew less about the workings of financial markets or the role of risk managers within a financial firm. This book was written for them, and I have been teaching with the material that this book is based on for a number of years now.

There is considerable overlap between the two books. Indeed, there are some sections that are almost identical. While the first book was organized around topics in mathematics, however, this book is organized around topics in risk management. In each chapter we explore a particular topic in risk management along with various mathematical tools that can be used to understand that topic. As with the first book, I have tried to provide a large number of sample problems and practical end-of-chapter questions. I firmly believe that the best way to understand financial models is to work through actual problems.

This book assumes that the reader is familiar with basic calculus, linear algebra, and statistics. When a particular topic in mathematics is central to a topic in risk management, I review the basics and introduce notation, but the pace can be quick. For example, in the first chapter we review standard deviation, but we only spend one section on what would likely be an entire chapter in an introductory book on statistics.

Risk management in practice often requires building models using spreadsheets or other financial software. Many of the topics in this book are accompanied by an icon, shown here:

These icons indicate that Excel examples can be found at John Wiley & Sons' companion website for *Quantitative Financial Risk Management,* www.wiley.com/go/millerfinancialrisk.

ABOUT THE AUTHOR

Michael B. Miller is the founder and CEO of Northstar Risk Corp. Before starting Northstar, Mr. Miller was Chief Risk Officer for Tremblant Capital and, before that, Head of Quantitative Risk Management at Fortress Investment Group.

Mr. Miller is the author of *Mathematics and Statistics for Financial Risk Management*, now in its second edition, and, along with Emanuel Derman, *The Volatility Smile*. He is also an adjunct professor at Columbia University and the co-chair of the Global Association of Risk Professional's Research Fellowship Committee. Before starting his career in finance, Mr. Miller studied economics at the American University of Paris and the University of Oxford.

QUANTITATIVE FINANCIAL
RISK MANAGEMENT

1

OVERVIEW OF FINANCIAL RISK MANAGEMENT

Imagine you are a chef at a restaurant. You've just finished preparing eggs benedict for a customer. The eggs are cooked perfectly, the hollandaise sauce has just the right mix of ingredients, and it all sits perfectly on the plate. The presentation is perfect! You're so proud of the way this has turned out that you decide to deliver the dish to the customer yourself. You place the plate in front of the customer, and she replies, "This looks great, but I ordered a filet mignon, and you forgot my drink."

Arguably, the greatest strength of modern financial risk management is that it is highly objective. It takes a scientific approach, using math and statistics to measure and evaluate financial products and portfolios. While these mathematical tools can be very powerful, they are simply that—tools. If we make unwarranted assumptions, apply models incorrectly, or present results poorly—or if our findings are ignored—then the most elegant mathematical models in the world will not help us. The eggs might be perfect, but that's irrelevant if the customer ordered a steak.

This is not a new idea, Vitruvius, a famous Roman architect wrote, "*Neque enim ingenium sine disciplina aut disciplina sine ingenio perfectum artificem potest efficere*", which roughly translates to "Neither genius without knowledge, nor knowledge without genius, will make a perfect artist." Applying this to risk management, we might say, "Neither math without knowledge of financial markets, nor knowledge of financial markets without math, will make a perfect risk manager."

Before we get to the math and statistics, then, we should take a step back and look at risk management more broadly. Before delving into the models, we explore the following questions: What is risk management? What is the proper role for a risk manager within a financial organization? What do risk managers actually do on a day-to-day basis?

We end this chapter with a brief history of risk management. As you will see, risk management has made many positive contributions to finance, but it is far from being a solved problem.

WHAT IS RISK?

Before we can begin to describe what financial risk managers *do*, we need to understand what financial risk *is*. In finance, risk arises from uncertainty surrounding future profits or returns. There are many ways to define risk, and we may change the definition slightly, depending on the task at hand.

In everyday speech, the word *risk* is associated with the possibility of negative outcomes. For something to be risky, the final outcome must be uncertain *and* there must be some possibility that the final outcome will have negative consequences. While this may seem obvious, some popular risk measures treat positive and negative outcomes equally, while others focus only negative outcomes. For this reason, in order to avoid any ambiguity when dealing specifically with negative outcomes, risk managers will often talk about *downside risk*.

Risk is often defined relative to expectations. If we have one investment with a 50/50 chance of earning $0 or $200, and a second investment with a 50/50 chance of earning $400 or $600, are both equally risky? The first investment earns $100 on average, and the second $500, but both have a 50/50 chance of being $100 above or below this expected value. Because the deviations from expectations are equal, many risk managers would consider the two investments to be equally risky. By this logic, the second investment is more attractive because it has a higher expected return, not because it is less risky.

It is also important to note that risk is about *possible* deviations from expectations. If we expect an investment to make $1 and it does make $1, the investment was not necessarily risk free. If there were any possibility that the outcome could have been something other than $1, then the investment was risky.

Absolute, Relative, and Conditional Risk

There may be no better way to understand the limits of financial risk management—why and where it may fail or succeed—than to understand the difference between absolute, relative, and conditional risk.

Financial risk managers are often asked to assign probabilities to various financial outcomes. What is the probability that a bond will default? What is the probability that an equity index will decline by more than 10% over the course of a year? These types of predictions, where risk managers are asked to assess the total or *absolute risk* of an investment, are incredibly difficult to make. As we will see, assessing the accuracy of these types of predictions, even over the course of many years, can be extremely difficult.

It is often much easier to determine relative risk than to measure risk in isolation. Bond ratings are a good example. Bond ratings can be used to assess absolute risk, but they are on much surer footing when used to assess *relative risk*. The number of defaults in a bond portfolio might be much higher or lower next year depending on the state of the economy and financial markets. No matter what happens, though, a portfolio consisting of a large number of AAA-rated bonds will almost certainly have fewer defaults than a portfolio consisting of a large number of C-rated bonds. Similarly, it is much easier to say that emerging market equities are riskier than U.S. equities, or that one hedge fund is riskier than another hedge fund.

What is the probability that the S&P 500 will be down more than 10% next year? What is the probability that a particular U.S. large-cap equity mutual fund will be down more than 8% next year? Both are very difficult questions. What is the probability that this same mutual fund will be down more than 8%, *if* the S&P 500 is down more than 10%? This last question is actually much easier to answer. What's more, these types of *conditional risk* forecasts immediately suggest ways to hedge and otherwise mitigate risk.

Given the difficulty of measuring absolute risk, risk managers are likely to be more successful if they limit themselves to relative and conditional forecasts, when possible. Likewise, when there is any ambiguity about how a risk measure can be interpreted —as with bond ratings— encouraging a relative or conditional interpretation is likely to be in a risk manager's best interest.

Intrinsic and Extrinsic Risk

Some financial professionals talk about *risk* versus *uncertainty*. A better approach might be to contrast *intrinsic* risk and *extrinsic* risk.

When evaluating financial instruments, there are some risks that we consider to be intrinsic. No matter how much we know about the financial instrument we are evaluating, there is nothing we can do to reduce this intrinsic risk (other than reducing the size of our investment).

In other circumstances risk is due only to our own ignorance. In theory, this extrinsic risk can be eliminated by gathering additional information through research and analysis.

As an example, an investor in a hedge fund may be subject to both extrinsic and intrinsic risk. A hedge fund investor will typically not know the exact holdings of a hedge fund in which they are invested. Not knowing what securities are in a fund is extrinsic risk.

For various reasons, the hedge fund manager may not want to reveal the fund's holdings, but, at least in theory, this extrinsic risk *could be* eliminated by revealing the fund's holdings to the investor. At the same time, even if the investor *did* know what securities were in the fund, the returns of the fund would still not be fully predictable because the returns of the securities in the fund's portfolio are inherently uncertain. This inherent uncertainty of the security returns represents intrinsic risk and it cannot be eliminated, no matter how much information is provided to the investor.

Interestingly, a risk manager could reduce a hedge fund investor's extrinsic risk by explaining the hedge fund's risk guidelines. The risk guidelines could help the investor gain a better understanding of what might be in the fund's portfolio, without revealing the portfolio's precise composition.

Differentiating between these two fundamental types of risk is important in financial risk management. In practice, financial risk management is as much about reducing extrinsic risk as it is about managing intrinsic risk.

Risk and Standard Deviation

At the start of this chapter, we said that risk could be defined in terms of possible deviations from expectations. This definition is very close to the definition of standard deviation in statistics. The variance of a random variable is the expected value of squared deviations from the mean, and standard deviation is just the square root of variance. This is indeed very close to our definition of risk, and in finance risk is often equated with standard deviation.

While the two definitions are similar, they are not exactly the same. Standard deviation only describes what we expect the deviations will look like on average. Two random variables can have the same standard deviation, but very different return profiles. As we will see, risk managers need to consider other aspects of the distribution of expected deviations, not just its standard deviation.

WHAT IS FINANCIAL RISK MANAGEMENT?

In finance and in this book, we often talk about *risk management*, when it is understood that we are talking about *financial risk management*. Risk managers are found in a number of fields outside of finance, including engineering, manufacturing, and medicine.

When civil engineers are designing a levee to hold back flood waters, their risk analysis will likely include a forecast of the distribution of peak water levels. An engineer will often describe the probability that water levels will exceed the height of the levee in terms similar to those used by financial risk managers to describe the probability that losses in a portfolio will exceed a certain threshold. In manufacturing, engineers will use risk management to assess the frequency of manufacturing defects. Motorola popularized the term Six Sigma to describe its goal to establish a manufacturing process where manufacturing defects were kept below 3.4 defects per million. (Confusingly the goal corresponds to 4.5 standard deviations for a normal distribution, not 6 standard deviations, but that's another story.) Similarly, financial risk managers will talk about big market moves as being three-sigma events or six-sigma events. Other areas of risk management can be valuable sources of techniques and terminology for financial risk management.

Within this broader field of risk management, though, how do we determine what is and is not financial risk management? One approach would be to define risk in terms of organizations, to say that *financial* risk management concerns itself with the risk of *financial* firms. By this definition, assessing the risks faced by Goldman Sachs or a hedge fund is financial risk management, whereas assessing the risks managed by the Army Corps of Engineers or NASA is not. A clear advantage to this approach is that it saves us from having to create a long list of activities that are the proper focus of financial risk management. The assignment is unambiguous. If a task is being performed by a financial firm, it is within the scope of financial risk management. This definition is future proof as well. If HSBC, one of the world's largest financial institutions, starts a new business line tomorrow, we do not have to ask ourselves if this new business line falls under the purview of financial risk management. Because HSBC is a financial firm, any risk associated with the new business line would be considered financial risk.

However, this approach is clearly too narrow, in that it excludes financial risks taken by nonfinancial firms. For example, auto manufacturers that provide financing for car buyers, large restaurant chains that hedge food prices with commodity futures, and municipalities that issues bonds to finance infrastructure projects all face financial risk.

This approach may also be too broad, in that it also includes risks to financial firms that have little to do with finance. For instance, most financial firms rely on large, complex computer systems. Should a financial risk manager try to assess the probability of network crashes, or the relative risk of two database platforms? The distribution of losses due to fires at bank branches? The risk of lawsuits arising from a new retail investment product? Lawsuits due to a new human resources policy? While a degree in finance might seem unlikely to prepare one to deal with these types of risk, in practice, the chief risk officer at a large financial firm often has a mandate which encompasses *all* types of risk. Similarly, regulators are concerned with risk to the financial system caused by financial firms, no matter where that risk comes from. Because of this, many would define financial risk management to include all aspects of financial firms, and the financial activities of nonfinancial firms. In recent years, the role of many financial risk professionals has expanded. Many welcome this increased responsibility, while others see it as potentially dangerous mission creep. If financial risk is defined too broadly, risk managers may take responsibility for risks for which they have little or no expertise.

Another simple way to define financial risk management would be in terms of financial instruments. Defined this way, any risk arising from the use of financial instruments is within the scope of financial risk management. By this definition, the financial risk arising from the use of an interest rate swap is within the scope of financial risk management, whether the two parties involved are financial institutions or not. This is the definition preferred by many practitioners. Readers should be aware of both possibilities: that financial risk management can be defined in terms of financial firms or financial instruments.

TYPES OF FINANCIAL RISK

Financial risk is often divided into four principal types of risk: market risk, credit risk, liquidity risk, and operational risk. To varying degrees, most financial transactions involve aspects of all four types of risk. Within financial institutions, risk management groups are often organized along these lines. Because instruments with the greatest market risk tend to have the most variable liquidity risk, market risk and liquidity risk are often managed by a single group within financial firms. In addition to market risk, credit risk, liquidity risk, and operational risk, many firms will also have an enterprise risk management group, giving us a total of five principal areas of risk management. We consider each in turn.

Market Risk

Market risk is risk associated with changing asset values. Market risk is most often associated with assets that trade in liquid financial markets, such as stocks and bonds. During trading hours, the prices of stocks and bonds constantly fluctuate. An asset's price will change as new information becomes available and investors reassess the value of that asset. An asset's value can also change due to changes in supply and demand.

All financial assets have market risk. Even if an asset is not traded on an exchange, its value can change over time. Firms that use mark-to-market accounting recognize this change explicitly. For these firms, the change in value of exchange-traded assets will be based on market prices. Other assets will either be *marked to model*—that is, their prices will be determined based on financial models with inputs that may include market prices—or their prices will be based on broker quotes—that is, their prices will be based on the price at which another party expresses their willingness to buy or sell the assets. Firms that use historical cost accounting, or book value accounting, will normally only realize a profit or a loss when an asset is sold. Even if the value of the asset is not being updated on a regular basis, the asset still has market risk. For this reason, most firms that employ historical cost accounting will reassess the value of their portfolios when they have reason to believe that there has been a significant change in the value of their assets.

For most financial instruments, we expect price changes to be relatively smooth and continuous most of the time, and large and discontinuous rarely. Because of this, market risk models often involve continuous distribution. Market risk models can also have a relatively high frequency (i.e., daily or even intraday). For many financial instruments, we will have a large amount of historical market data that we can use to evaluate market risk.

Credit Risk

Credit risk is the risk that one party in a financial transaction will fail to pay the other party. Credit risk can arise in a number of different settings. Firms may extend credit to suppliers and customers. Credit card debt and home mortgages create credit risk. One of the most common forms of credit risk is the risk that a corporation or government will fail to make interest payments or to fully repay the principal on bonds they have issued. This type of risk is known as *default risk*, and in the case of national governments it is also referred to as *sovereign risk*. Defaults occur infrequently, and the simplest models of default risk are based on discrete distributions. Although bond markets are large and credit rating agencies have been in existence for a long time, default events are rare. Because of this, we have much less historical data to work with when developing credit models, compared to market risk models.

For financial firms, counterparty credit risk is another important source of credit risk. While credit risk always involves two counterparties, when risk managers talk about counterparty credit risk they are usually talking about the risk arising from a significant long-term relationship between two counterparties. Prime brokers will often provide loans to investment firms, provide them with access to emergency credit lines, and allow them to purchase securities on margin. Assessing the credit risk of a financial firm can be difficult, time consuming, and costly. Because of this, when credit risk is involved, financial firms often enter into long-term relationships based on complex legal contracts. Counterparty risk specialists help design these contracts and play a lead role in assessing and monitoring the risk of counterparties.

Derivatives contracts can also lead to credit risk. A derivative is essentially a contract between two parties, that specifies that certain payments be made based on the value of an underlying security or securities. Derivatives include futures, forwards, swaps, and options. As the value of the underlying asset changes, so too will the value of the derivative. As the value of the derivative changes, so too will the amount of money that the counterparties owe each other. This leads to credit risk.

Another very common form of credit risk in financial markets is settlement risk. Typically, when you buy a financial asset you do not have to pay for the asset immediately. Settlement terms vary by market, but typical settlement periods are one to three days. Practitioners would describe settlement as being T+2, when payment is due two days after a trade has happened.

Liquidity Risk

Liquidity risk is the risk that you will either not be able to buy or sell an asset, or that you will not be able to buy or sell an asset in the desired quantity at the current market price. We often talk about certain markets being more or less liquid. Even in relatively liquid markets, liquidity risk can be a problem for large financial firms.

Liquidity risk can be difficult to describe mathematically, and the data needed to model liquidity risk can be difficult to obtain even under the best circumstances. Though its importance is widely recognized, liquidity risk modeling has traditionally received much less attention than market or credit risk modeling. Current approaches to liquidity risk management are often primitive. The more complex approaches that do exist are far from standard.

Operational Risk

Operational risk is risk arising from all aspects of a firm's business activities. Put simply, it is the risk that people will make mistakes and that systems will fail. Operational risk is a risk that all financial firms must deal with.

Just as the number of activities that businesses carry out is extremely large, so too are the potential sources of operational risk. That said, there are broad categories on which risk managers tend to focus. These include legal risk (most often risk arising from contracts, which may be poorly specified or misinterpreted), systems risk (risk arising from computer systems) and model risk (risk arising from pricing and risk models, which may contain errors, or may be used inappropriately).

As with credit risk, operational risk tends to be concerned with rare but significant events. Operational risk presents additional challenges in that the sources of operational risk are often difficult to identify, define, and quantify.

Enterprise Risk

The enterprise risk management group of a firm, as the name suggests, is responsible for the risk of the entire firm. At large financial firms, this often means overseeing market, credit, liquidity, and operations risk groups, and combining information from those groups into summary reports. In addition to this aggregation role, enterprise risk management tends to look at overall business risk. Large financial companies will often have a number of business units (e.g., capital markets, corporate finance, commercial banking, retail banking, asset management, etc.). Some of these business units will work very closely with risk management (e.g. capital markets, asset management), while others may have very little day-to-day interaction with risk (e.g. corporate finance). Regardless, enterprise risk management would assess how each business unit contributes to the overall profitability of the firm in order to assess the overall risk to the firm's revenue, income, and capital.

WHAT DOES A RISK MANAGER DO?

The responsibilities of a chief risk officer (CRO) can be divided into four main tasks: defining risk, monitoring risk, controlling risk, and explaining or communicating risk. Other risk professionals will be involved in some or all of these tasks.

Defining risk is the starting point of the risk management process, and possibly the most important task. Defining risk involves clearly identifying what financial variables are to be monitored and then defining acceptable behavior for those variables. Acceptable behavior is often defined in terms of averages, minimums, and maximums. For example, we might state that net equity exposure is expected to average 10% of assets under management and will not exceed 20%, or that forecasted standard deviation of daily profits will not exceed 10% for more than one day each month and will never exceed 15%. These portfolio specifications and limits are often collected in a document detailing risk management policies and procedures. This document likely outlines who is responsible for risk management, and what action will be taken in the event that a policy is breached.

Defining risk parameters in advance helps a firm manage its investments in a consistent and transparent manner. If done correctly a well-defined risk framework will make the investment process more predictable and help reduce extrinsic risk. For example, most hedge funds are allowed to invest in a wide range of financial products and to use considerable leverage. If there were no risk limits, risk levels could vary widely. By carefully defining how risk is going to be managed and communicating this to investors, we can significantly reduce extrinsic risk.

It is worth pointing out that the job of a risk manager is not necessarily to reduce risk. For an investment firm, more risk is often associated with higher potential profits. An investor might be just as worried about risk being too low as too high.

Sophisticated investors can adjust their level of risk by increasing or decreasing their exposure to a fund or by hedging. In order to do this, they need as much information as possible about the risks that the fund is taking. The risk manager can reduce extrinsic risk for these investors and help them achieve a more optimal allocation, by accurately communicating the risks that their fund is taking.

After we have defined the risk parameters of a portfolio, we need to monitor these parameters. This is the task that is most frequently associated with the role of risk management. You can imagine a CRO striding into the chief investment officer's office, to report that the firm's expected standard deviation has increased recently and is getting very close to its limit. Monitoring risk in a timely manner can often be technologically challenging.

The third, and possibly most important, task for a risk manager is to control or manage risk. Risk can be managed in a number of ways. As well as helping to enforce limits, at some investment firms the CRO will actually manage, or help manage, a hedge portfolio, which is used to control risk. At other firms, risk managers will work more closely with portfolio managers, adjusting the portfolio as necessary to increase or decrease risk.

In addition to communicating with their colleagues (e.g., back office personnel, traders, portfolio managers), an increasingly important job for risk managers is communicating with regulators and investors. In all cases, the risk manager is engaged in what we might call dimensionality reduction, taking a large set of financial instruments and market data and reducing them to small number of key statistics and insights.

A VERY BRIEF HISTORY OF RISK MANAGEMENT

Christiaan Huygens was a Dutch polymath whose interest ranged from astronomy to mathematics to engineering. Among other accomplishments Huygens discovered Titan, the largest moon of Saturn, and helped design the water fountains at the Palace of Versailles outside of Paris. But it was Huygens's publication of *De Ratiociniis in Ludo Aleae*, or *On Reason in Games of Chance*, in 1657 that is of importance to the study of risk. It was in this book that Huygens first developed the formal concept of expectations.

Like many of his contemporaries, Huygens was interested in games of chance. As he described it, if a game has a 50% probability of paying $3 and a 50% probability of paying $7, then this is, in a way, equivalent to having $5 with certainty. This is because we expect, on average, to win $5 in this game:

$$50\% \times \$3 + 50\% \times \$7 = \$5 \tag{1.1}$$

We'll have a lot more to say about expectations in Chapter 2.

As early as 1713, Daniel and Nicolas Bernoulli were beginning to doubt that human beings were quite so logical when it came to evaluating risks, and, as we will see later when we explore behavioral finance, economist still struggle with this topic. Beyond the evaluation of games of chance, the more general concept of expectations is the basis for our modern definitions for mean, variance, and many other statistical concepts. It is arguably the most important concept in modern statistics.

From the 18th century, we jump to the Crash of 1929. Even after the financial crisis of 2008 and the ensuing Great Recession, the Crash of 1929 is still considered by most experts to have been the worst financial crash in history. On October 28, 1929, Black Monday, the Dow Jones Industrial Average lost 13%. For the entire month of October the index was down 20%. The crash was likely a leading cause of the ensuing Great Depression. That the crash of the financial markets could have such a profound impact on the rest of the economy was a clear indication of the central role that financial markets play in modern economies. This potential for widespread harm is a major justification for financial regulation. In the wake of the crash, the United States government passed the Securities Act of 1933 and the Securities Exchange Act of 1934. The former would, among other things, go on to become the defining regulation for hedge funds in the United States. The later established the Securities and Exchange Commission (SEC). More recent regulatory efforts, including the Basel Accords, are direct descendants of these efforts. Today, for better or worse, regulatory compliance is a full-time job for many financial risk managers.

In 1952 *The Journal of Finance* published "Portfolio Selection" by Harry Markowitz. The article introduced the world to Modern Portfolio Theory (MPT). For this and related work, Markowitz would go on to win the Nobel Prize in Economics. The key insight of MPT is that investors are trying to get the highest returns with the least amount of risk. Given two portfolios with the same level of risk but different expected returns, a rational investor will prefer the portfolio with the higher expected return. Similarly, given two portfolios with the same expected return, but different risk levels, a rational investor will prefer the less risky portfolio. That this seems obvious—that it seems natural to frame investing in terms of risk and return—is a testament to the profound impact of MPT on finance and risk management. As mentioned previously, a risk manager's job is not necessarily to reduce risk. If we reduce risk but also reduce returns, investors may not be better off.

In his initial paper, Markowitz modeled risk in terms of variance or standard deviation. Standard deviation is still one of the most widely used measures for characterizing risk. As we will see in the next chapter, though, risk management has moved far beyond this narrow definition of risk.

On Monday October 19, 1987, stock markets around the world crashed. The Dow Jones Industrial Average lost 22%, and the S&P 500 lost 20%. This was the worst recorded one-day return in the history of both indexes. Today, when people talk about Black Monday, more often than not they are referring to this event and not the previous Black Monday from 1929. Oddly, this more recent Black Monday was a relatively isolated incident. The S&P 500 was actually up for 1987, and the economy grew both in 1987 and 1988. Contrast this to 1929, where the economy shrank by 26% over the three succeeding years. To this day, the causes of Black Monday '87 are still debated. The growing use of program trading and portfolio insurance were both possible causes. Whether or not they caused the crash, they did cause an increase in trading volume. This already high trading volume spiked on Black Monday, and many markets were unable to cope. As a result of Black Monday many exchanges upgraded their trading systems. Most financial firms that use stress testing have at least one stress test based on Black Monday '87. We will have more to say about stress testing in Chapter 4.

Long-Term Capital Management (LTCM) belongs in the history of risk management for many reasons. The failure of LTCM in 1998 was a shock to the financial community. At the time it was one of the largest, most highly regarded hedge funds in the world, with an enviable track record. It could count among its founders John Meriwether, Myron Scholes, and Robert Merton. LTCM's portfolio was so large and its network of counterparties so extensive that regulators feared its failure could devastate the larger financial community. The New York Fed called an emergency meeting of the heads of the largest investment banks to intercede and liquidate LTCM's portfolio in an orderly fashion. That a firm virtually unknown outside of the financial community, employing fewer than 200 people, could pose a risk to the entire financial system highlighted the incredible growth that had taken place throughout the 1980s and 1990s outside of traditional financial markets, most notably in derivatives and hedge funds. This is the first reason that justifies LTCM's place in the history of risk management. The second reason, which is often overlooked in the story of LTCM, is that its founders viewed risk management as a means to reduce capital requirements for both financial and nonfinancial firms. In theory, by freeing up capital for use in other endeavors, firms and the economy as a whole could become more productive. In retrospect, LTCM was clearly overleveraged and undercapitalized, but the idea that risk management can create real efficiencies for firms is still sound. The final—and perhaps most obvious—reason that LTCM belongs in the history of risk management is that its failure was in part due to its risk models and how those models were used. The risk management community took notice. The external event that precipitated LTCM's failure, Russia's default on its domestic debt, is still the basis of stress tests at many financial firms. More importantly it highlighted the limits of historically based quantitative risk models and spurred the risk management community to look for more robust solutions.

RiskMetrics is another important organization in risk management history. From its spin-off from JP Morgan in 1998 to its IPO in 2008 to its eventual acquisition by MSCI Inc. in 2010, RiskMetrics was one of the largest and most successful companies devoted entirely to risk management. Figure 1.1, which shows RiskMetrics' annual revenue, gives

FIGURE 1.1 RiskMetrics Annual Revenue

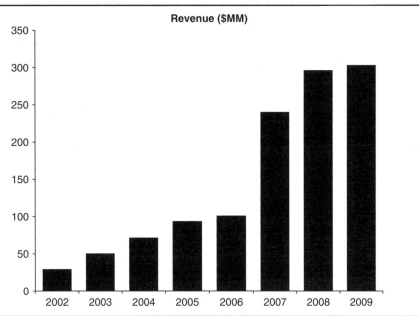

Source: Securities and Exchange Commission

an indication of just how quickly the firm grew. RiskMetrics software is still used to help manage the risk of some of the largest financial firms in the world. Despite these impressive facts, more than anything else, RiskMetrics earned its place in the history of risk management for what it gave away for free. In 1992 RiskMetrics published the *RiskMetrics Technical Document*. The document outlined RiskMetrics's approach to evaluating risk, and popularized the concept of value at risk, or VaR. Along with standard deviation, VaR is one of the most popular statistics for summarizing financial risk.

The Global Association of Risk Professionals (GARP), the world's largest nonprofit financial risk management association, was founded in 1996. As of 2018 GARP has over 150,000 members in 195 countries. In addition to hosting conferences, producing publications, and providing continuing education, GARP is the sponsor of the Financial Risk Manager (FRM) Exam.[1] The extraordinary growth of GARP's membership and of the number of people taking the FRM exam annually is an indication not only of the growth of the risk management industry, but also of the increasing importance of standards within the industry. Figure 1.2 shows the increase in FRM Exam enrollment over time. The exam was changed from a one-year to a two-year format starting in 2009, leading to a temporary spike in enrollment that year.

---

[1] Full disclosure: The author is a longstanding member of GARP and an FRM holder.

FIGURE 1.2 FRM Exam Enrollment

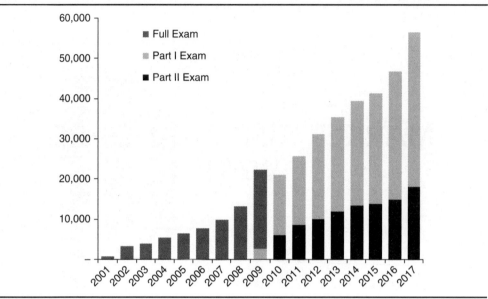

Source: Global Association of Risk Professionals

THE FUTURE OF RISK MANAGEMENT

Despite tremendous growth in recent years, financial risk management is still a young discipline. We can expect to see many changes in the roles of financial risk managers in the coming years.

The financial crisis of 2008 called into question some quantitative risk models, but it also caused many to argue for a greater role for risk managers within financial firms. While there were certainly instances when models were used incorrectly, the far greater problem was that the decision makers at large financial firms either never received the data they needed, didn't understand it, or chose to ignore it. It was not so much that we lacked the tools to properly assess risk, as it was that the tools were not being used or that the people using the tools were not being listened to.

As risk management continues to gain wider acceptance, the role of risk managers in communicating with investors and regulators will continue to grow. We are also likely to see an increasingly integrated approach to risk management and performance analysis, which are now treated as separate activities by most financial firms.

There are still important areas of risk management, such as liquidity risk, where widely accepted models and standards have yet to be developed. If history is any guide, financial markets will continue to grow in breadth, speed, and complexity. Along with this growth will come new challenges for risk managers.

The future of risk management is very bright.

2

MARKET RISK: STANDARD DEVIATION

In this chapter we will start our exploration of market risk. For the time being, we will ignore all other sources of risk, including liquidity and credit risk. We begin by examining the market risk of one security.

This is the first of six chapters on market risk. As we will see, risk managers have many statistics to choose from when trying to measure market risk. No single statistic is perfect. Each has its strengths and weaknesses. Portfolio managers, investors, and regulators depend on risk managers to choose the right statistics to report. Over the course of the next six chapters, pay special attention to: what assumptions are being made, how the various statistics compare to each other, which aspects of market risk they describe well, and which aspects of market risk they omit.

RISK AND STANDARD DEVIATION

The classical risk model equates risk solely with the standard deviation of returns. As mentioned in the previous chapter, Markowitz's market portfolio theory (MPT) assumes that investors equate standard deviation with risk. Today's risk managers have not abandoned standard deviation; rather most report standard deviation along with additional statistics, such as skewness, kurtosis, and value at risk. We will explore these other statistics eventually, but we begin with a review of standard deviation.

Standard deviation is so widely used throughout finance that we often refer to it as *volatility*, or simply *vol*. While it is important to be aware of this practice, standard deviation is a precise mathematical term, whereas volatility is a more general concept. Except for in rare instances, when we are actually referring to this more general concept of volatility, we will use *standard deviation* throughout the rest of the text.

Derivatives present a unique problem for risk management. The payout profiles of options are typically discontinuous. Small changes in the return of the underlying security have the potential to create large changes in the value of the derivative. Because of this, derivatives are often described as being nonlinear. We will explore methods for dealing with options in subsequent chapters. For the remainder of this chapter, when we refer to *security returns*, assume that we are referring to instruments such as equities, floating exchange rates, bonds, or commodity futures. Unless noted otherwise, assume that the securities are liquid, and that there is no credit risk.

Before we can formally define standard deviation, we will need to define the mean of a random variable. To this end, we begin by discussing averages, random variables, and expectations. It is assumed that the reader is familiar with probabilities, random variables, and probability density functions.[1]

AVERAGES

Everybody knows what an average is. We come across averages every day, whether they are earned run averages in baseball or grade point averages in school. In statistics there are actually three different types of averages: means, modes, and medians. By far the most commonly used in risk management is the mean.

Population and Sample Data

If you wanted to know the mean age of people working in your firm, you would simply ask every person in the firm his or her age, add the ages together, and divide by the number of people in the firm. Assuming there are n employees and a_i is the age of the ith employee, then the mean, μ, is simply

$$\mu = \frac{1}{n} \sum_{i=1}^{n} a_i = \frac{1}{n}(a_1 + a_2 + \ldots + a_{n-1} + a_n) \tag{2.1}$$

It is important for us to differentiate between population statistics and sample statistics. In this example, μ is the population mean. Assuming nobody lied about his or her age, and forgetting about rounding errors and other trivial details, we know the mean age of the

---

[1]For readers not familiar with these topics, an overview can be found in Chapter 2 of *Mathematics and Statistics for Financial Risk Management*, Miller (2014).

people in your firm *exactly*. We have a complete data set of everybody in your firm; we've surveyed the entire population.

This state of absolute certainty is, unfortunately, quite rare in finance. More often, we are faced with a situation such as this: Estimate the mean return of stock ABC, given the most recent year of daily returns. In a situation like this, we assume there is some underlying data-generating process with statistical properties that are constant over time. The underlying process has a true mean, but we cannot observe it directly. We can only estimate the true mean based on our limited data sample. In our example, assuming n returns, we estimate the mean using the same formula as before

$$\hat{\mu} = \frac{1}{n}\sum_{i=1}^{n} r_i = \frac{1}{n}(r_1 + r_2 + \ldots + r_{n-1} + r_n) \tag{2.2}$$

where $\hat{\mu}$ (pronounced "mu hat") is our *estimate* of the true mean, μ, based on our sample of n returns. We call this the sample mean.

The median and mode are also types of averages. They are used less frequently in finance, but both can be useful. The median represents the center of a group of data; within the group, half the data points will be less than the median and half will be greater. The mode is the value that occurs most frequently.

SAMPLE PROBLEM

Question:

Calculate the mean, median, and mode of the following data set:

$$-20\%, -10\%, -5\%, -5\%, 0\%, 10\%, 10\%, 10\%, 19\%$$

Answer:

$$\text{Mean} = \frac{1}{9}(-20\% - 10\% - 5\% - 5\% + 0\% + 10\% + 10\% + 10\% + 19\%) = 1\%$$

$$\text{Mode} = 10\%$$

$$\text{Median} = 0\%$$

If there is an even number of data points, the median is found by averaging the two centermost points. In the following series:

$$5\%, 10\%, 20\%, 25\%$$

the median is 15%. The median can be useful for summarizing data that is asymmetrical or contains significant outliers. Financial time series are often asymmetrical and often contain outliers. Both Black Monday events, which we mentioned in the last chapter, are examples of significant outliers.

A data set can also have more than one mode. If the maximum frequency is shared by two or more values, all of those values are considered modes. In the following series, the modes are 10% and 20%:

$$5\%, \; 10\%, \; 10\%, \; 10\%, \; 14\%, \; 16\%, \; 20\%, \; 20\%, \; 20\%, \; 24\%$$

In calculating the mean in Equations 2.1 and 2.2, each data point was counted exactly once. In certain situations, we might want to give more or less weight to certain data points. In calculating the average return of stocks in an equity index, we might want to give more weight to larger firms, perhaps weighting their returns in proportion to their market capitalizations. Given n data points, $x_i = x_1, \; x_2, \; \dots \; , \; x_n$, with corresponding weights, w_i, we can define the weighted mean, μ_w, as

$$\mu_w = \frac{\sum_{i=1}^{n} w_i x_i}{\sum_{i=1}^{n} w_i} \tag{2.3}$$

The standard mean from Equation 2.1 can be viewed as a special case of the weighted mean, where all the values have equal weight.

Discrete Random Variables

Financial markets are highly uncertain. Day-to-day changes to the price of a stock, a foreign exchange rate, or interest rates, are, in most cases, essentially random. In statistics we can model random, or *stochastic*, phenomena using random variables. There are two basic types of random variables: discrete and continuous. A discrete random variable can take on only a finite number of possible values. For example, a bond that is worth either $60 if it does default, or $100 if it does not default. A continuous random variable can take on any value within a given range. That range can be finite or infinite. For example, for a stock index, we might assume that the returns can be any value from -100% to infinity.

For a discrete random variable, we can also calculate the mean, median, and mode. For a random variable, X, with possible values, x_i, and corresponding probabilities, p_i, we define the mean, μ, as

$$\mu = \sum_{i=1}^{n} p_i x_i \tag{2.4}$$

The equation for the mean of a discrete random variable is a special case of the weighted mean, where the outcomes are weighted by their probabilities, and the sum of the weights is equal to one.

The median of a discrete random variable is the value such that the probability that a value is less than or equal to the median is equal to 50%. Working from the other end of the distribution, we can also define the median such that 50% of the values are greater than or equal to the median. For a random variable, X, if we denote the median as m, we have

$$P[X \geq m] = P[X \leq m] = 0.50 \tag{2.5}$$

For a discrete random variable, the mode is the value associated with the highest probability. As with population and sample data sets, the mode of a discrete random variable need not be unique.

SAMPLE PROBLEM

Question:

At the start of the year, a bond portfolio consists of two bonds, each worth $100. At the end of the year, if a bond defaults, it will be worth $20. If it does not default, the bond will be worth $100. The probability that both bonds default is 20%. The probability that neither bond defaults is 45%. What are the mean, median, and mode of the year-end portfolio value?

Answer:

We are given the probability for two outcomes:

$$P[V = \$40] = 20\%$$
$$P[V = \$200] = 45\%$$

At year-end, the value of the portfolio, V, can have only one of three values, and the sum of all the probabilities must equal 100%. This allows us to calculate the final probability:

$$P[V = \$120] = 100\% - 20\% - 45\% = 35\%$$

The mean of V is then $140:

$$\mu = 0.20 \times \$40 + 0.35 \times \$120 + 0.45 \times \$200 = \$140$$

The mode of the distribution is $200; this is the most likely outcome. The median of the distribution is $120; half of the outcomes are less than or equal to $120.

Continuous Random Variables

We can also define the mean, median, and mode for a continuous random variable. To find the mean of a continuous random variable, we simply integrate the product of the variable and its probability density function (PDF). This is equivalent to our approach to calculating the mean of a discrete random variable, in the limit as the number of possible outcomes approaches infinity. For a continuous random variable, X, with a PDF, $f(x)$, the mean, μ, is then

$$\mu = \int_{x_{min}}^{x_{max}} x f(x) dx \tag{2.6}$$

The median of a continuous random variable is defined exactly as it is for a discrete random variable, such that there is a 50% probability that values are less than or equal to, or greater than or equal to, the median. If we define the median as m, then

$$\int_{x_{min}}^{m} f(x) dx = \int_{m}^{x_{max}} f(x) dx = 0.50 \tag{2.7}$$

Alternatively, we can define the median in terms of the cumulative distribution function. Given the cumulative distribution function, $F(x)$, and the median, m, we have

$$F(m) = 0.50 \tag{2.8}$$

The mode of a continuous random variable corresponds to the maximum of the PDF. As before, the mode need not be unique.

SAMPLE PROBLEM

Question:

For the probability density function

$$f(x) = \frac{x}{50} \quad \text{where } 0 \leq x \leq 10$$

what are the mean, median, and mode of x?

Answer:

This probability density function is a triangle between $x = 0$ and $x = 10$, and zero everywhere else. See Figure 2.1.

For a continuous distribution, the mode corresponds to the maximum of the PDF. By inspection of the graph, we can see that the mode of $f(x)$ is equal to 10.

To calculate the median, we need to find m, such that the integral of $f(x)$ from the lower bound of $f(x)$, zero, to m is equal to 0.50. That is, we need to find

$$\int_{0}^{m} \frac{x}{50} dx = 0.50$$

First, we solve the left-hand side of the equation

$$\int_{0}^{m} \frac{x}{50} dx = \frac{1}{50} \int_{0}^{m} x dx = \frac{1}{50} \left[\frac{1}{2} x^2 \right]_{0}^{m} = \frac{1}{100}(m^2 - 0) = \frac{m^2}{100}$$

FIGURE 2.1 **Probability Density Function**

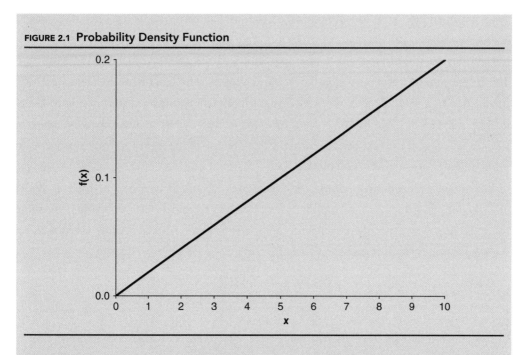

Setting this result equal to 0.50 and solving for m, we obtain our final answer,

$$\frac{m^2}{100} = 0.50$$

$$m^2 = 50$$

$$m = \sqrt{50} \approx 7.07$$

In the last step we can ignore the negative root. If we had looked at the graph without calculating the median, it might be tempting to guess that the median is 5, the midpoint of the range of the distribution. This is a common mistake. For this distribution, because lower values are less likely to occur (the PDF is lower), the median ends up being greater than 5.

The mean is approximately 6.67,

$$\mu = \int_0^{10} x\frac{x}{50}dx = \frac{1}{50}\int_0^{10} x^2 dx = \frac{1}{50}\left[\frac{1}{3}x^3\right]_0^{10} = \frac{1000}{150} \approx 6.67$$

As with the median, it is a common mistake, based on inspection of the PDF, to guess that the mean is 5.

EXPECTATIONS

On January 15, 2005, the *Huygens* space probe landed on the surface of Titan, the largest moon of Saturn. This was the culmination of a seven-year-long mission. During its descent and for over an hour after touching down on the surface, *Huygens* sent back detailed images, scientific readings, and even sounds from a strange world. There are liquid oceans on Titan, the landing site was littered with rocks made of ice, and the weather includes methane rain. The *Huygens* probe was named after Christiaan Huygens, who first discovered Titan in 1655. In addition to astronomy and physics, Huygens interests included probability theory. Originally published in Latin in 1657, *De Ratiociniis in Ludo Aleae*, or *On Reason in Games of Chance*, was one of the first texts to formally explore one of the most important concepts in probability theory, namely expectations.

Like many of his contemporaries, Huygens was interested in games of chance. As he described it, if a game has a 50% probability of paying $3 and a 50% probability of paying $7, it is, in a way, equivalent to having $5 with certainty. This is because we *expect*, on average, to win $5 in this game

$$0.50 \times 3 + 0.50 \times 7 = 5 \tag{2.9}$$

As you can already see, the concepts of expectations and averages are very closely linked. In the current example, if we play the game only once, there is no chance of winning exactly $5; we can win only $3 or $7. Still, even if we play the game only once, we say that the expected value of the game is $5. That we are talking about the mean of all the potential payouts is understood.

We can express the concept of expectations more formally using the expectation operator. We could state that the random variable, X, has an expected value of $5 as follows:

$$E[X] = 0.50 \times 3 + 0.50 \times 7 = 5 \tag{2.10}$$

where E[] is the expectation operator.[2]

In this example, the mean and the expected value have the same numeric value, $5. The same is true for discrete and continuous random variables. The expected value of a random variable is equal to the mean of the random variable.

While the value of the mean and the expected value may be the same in many situations, the two concepts are not exactly the same. In many situations in finance and risk management, the terms can be used interchangeably. The difference is often subtle.

As the name suggests, expectations are often thought of as being forward looking. Pretend we have a financial asset for which next year's mean annual return is known to be equal

---

[2]Those of you with a background in physics might be more familiar with the term *expectation value* and the notation <*X*> rather than E[*X*]. This is a matter of convention. Throughout this book we use the term *expected value* and E[*X*], which are currently more popular in finance and econometrics. Risk managers should be familiar with both conventions.

to 15%. This is not an estimate; in this hypothetical scenario, we actually know that the mean *is* 15%. We say that the expected value of the return next year is 15%. We expect the return to be 15%, because the probability-weighted mean of all the possible outcomes is 15%.

Now pretend that we don't actually *know* what the mean return of the asset is, but we have 10 years' worth of historical data for which the mean is 15%. In this case, the expected value may or may not be 15%. *If* we decide that the expected value is equal to 15%, based on the mean of the data, then we are making two assumptions. First, we are assuming that the returns in our sample were generated by the same random process over the entire historical sample period. Second, we are assuming that the returns will continue to be generated by this same process in the future. These are very strong assumptions. *If* we have other information that leads us to believe that one or both of these assumptions are false, then we may decide that the expected value is something other than 15%. In finance and risk management, we often assume that financial variables can be represented by a consistent, unchanging process. Testing the validity of this assumption can be an important part of risk management in practice.

The expectation operator, can also be used to derive the expected value of functions of random variables. As we will see in subsequent sections, the concept of expectations underpins the definitions of other statistics (e.g., variance, skewness, kurtosis), and is important in understanding regression analysis and time-series analysis. In these cases, even when we could use the mean to describe a calculation, in practice we tend to talk exclusively in terms of expectations.

SAMPLE PROBLEM

Question:

You are asked to determine the expected value of a bond in one year's time. The bond has a notional of $100. You believe there is a 20% chance that the bond will default, in which case it will be worth $40 at the end of the year. There is also a 30% chance that the bond will be downgraded, in which case it will be worth $90 in a year's time. If the bond does not default and is not downgraded, it will be worth $100.

Answer:

We need to determine the expected future value of the bond—that is, the expected value of the bond in one year's time. We are given the following,

$$P[V_{t+1} = \$40] = 0.20$$
$$P[V_{t+1} = \$90] = 0.30$$

Because there are only three possible outcomes, the probability of no downgrade and no default must be 50%,

$$P[V_{t+1} = \$100] = 0.50$$

The expected value of the bond in one year is then $85,

$$E[V_{t+1}] = 0.20 \times 40 + 0.30 \times 90 + 0.50 \times 100 = 85$$

The expectation operator is linear. That is, for two random variables, X and Y, and a constant, c, the following two equations are true:

$$E[X + Y] = E[X] + E[Y]$$

$$E[cX] = cE[X] \tag{2.11}$$

If the expected value of stock A is $10, and the expected value of stock B is $20, then the expected value of a portfolio containing A and B is $30, and the expected value of a portfolio containing five shares of A is $5 \times \$10 = \$50$.

Be very careful, though; the expectation operator is not multiplicative. The expected value of the product of two random variables is not necessarily the same as the product of their expected values,

$$E[XY] \neq E[X]E[Y] \tag{2.12}$$

Imagine we have two binary options. Each pays either $100 or nothing, depending on the value of some underlying asset at expiration. The probability of receiving $100 is 50% for both options. Furthermore, assume that it is always the case that if the first option pays $100, the second pays $0, and vice versa. The expected value of each option separately is clearly $50. If we denote the payout of the first option as X and the payout of the second as Y, we have

$$E[X] = E[Y] = 0.50 \times 100 + 0.50 \times 0 = 50 \tag{2.13}$$

In each possible outcome, though, one option is always worth zero, so the product of the payouts is always zero: $\$100 \times \$0 = \$0 \times \$100 = \$0$. The expected value of the product of the two option payouts is

$$E[XY] = 0.50 \times (100 \times 0) + 0.50 \times (0 \times 100) = 0 \tag{2.14}$$

The product of the expected values, however is $2,500, $E[X]E[Y] = \$50 \times \$50 = \$2,500$. In this case, the product of the expected values and the expected value of the products are clearly not equal. As well see in a following chapter, there are special cases when $E[XY] = E[X]E[Y]$, such as when X and Y are independent.

We have established that the expected value of the product of two variables does not necessarily equal the product of the expectations of those variables. Naturally, it follows that the expected value of the product of a variable with itself does not necessarily equal the product of the expectation of that variable with itself; that is,

$$E[X^2] \neq E[X]^2 \qquad (2.15)$$

Imagine we have a fair coin. Assign heads a value of $+1$ and tails a value of -1. We can write the probabilities of the outcomes as follows:

$$P[X = +1] = P[X = -1] = 0.50 \qquad (2.16)$$

The expected value of any coin flip is zero, but the expected value of X^2 is $+1$, not zero,

$$E[X] = 0.50(+1) + 0.50(-1) = 0$$

$$E[X]^2 = 0^2 = 0$$

$$E[X^2] = 0.50(+1^2) + 0.50(-1^2) = 1 \qquad (2.17)$$

As simple as this example is, this distinction is very important. As we will see, the difference between $E[X^2]$ and $E[X]^2$ is central to our definition of variance and standard deviation.

SAMPLE PROBLEM

Question:

Given the equation

$$Y = (X + 5)^3 + X^2 + 10X$$

what is the expected value of Y? Assume the following,

$$E[X] = 4$$

$$E[X^2] = 9$$

$$E[X^3] = 12$$

Answer:

Note that $E[X^2]$ and $E[X^3]$ cannot be derived from knowledge of $E[X]$. In this problem, $E[X^2] \neq E[X]^2$ and $E[X^3] \neq E[X]^3$.

To find the expected value of Y, we first expand the term $(X + 5)^3$ within the expectation operator,

$$E[Y] = E[(X + 5)^3 + X^2 + 10X] = E[X^3 + 16X^2 + 85X + 125]$$

Because the expectation operator is linear, we can separate the terms in the summation and move the constants outside the expectation operator.

$$E[Y] = E[X^3] + E[16X^2] + E[85X] + E[125]$$
$$= E[X^3] + 16E[X^2] + 85E[X] + 125$$

Note that the expected value of a constant is just the value of that constant, $E[125] = 125$.

At this point, we can substitute in the values for $E[X]$, $E[X^2]$, and $E[X^3]$, which were given at the start of the exercise,

$$E[Y] = 12 + 16 \times 9 + 85 \times 4 + 125 = 621$$

This gives us the final answer, 621.

VARIANCE AND STANDARD DEVIATION

The variance of a random variable measures how noisy or unpredictable that random variable is. Variance is defined as the expected value of the difference between the variable and its mean, squared. We can define the variance of a random variable X with mean μ, as σ^2, where

$$\sigma^2 = E[(X - \mu)^2] \tag{2.18}$$

The square root of variance, typically denoted by σ, is called standard deviation. As mentioned at the beginning of the chapter, in finance we often refer to standard deviation as volatility. This is analogous to referring to the mean as the average.

SAMPLE PROBLEM

Question:

A derivative has a 50/50 chance of being worth either +10 or −10 at expiry. What is the standard deviation of the derivative's value?

Answer:

$$\mu = 0.50 \times 10 + 50 \times (-10) = 0$$
$$\sigma^2 = 0.50(10 - 0)^2 + 0.50(-10 - 0)^2 = 100$$
$$\sigma = 10$$

In the preceding sample problem, we were calculating the population variance and standard deviation. *All* of the possible outcomes for the derivative were known.

To calculate the sample variance of a random variable X based on n observations, $x_1, x_2, \ldots, x_n$, we can use the following formula

$$\hat{\sigma}_x^2 = \frac{1}{n-1} \sum_{i=1}^{n} (x_i - \hat{\mu}_x)^2$$

$$E[\hat{\sigma}_x^2] = \sigma_x^2$$

(2.19)

where $\hat{\mu}_x$ is the sample mean as in Equation 2.2. Given that we have n data points, it might seem odd that we are dividing the sum by $(n - 1)$ and not n. The reason has to do with the fact that $\hat{\mu}_x$ itself is an estimate of the true mean, which also contains a fraction of each x_i. We leave the proof for a problem at the end of the chapter, but it turns out that dividing by $(n - 1)$, not n, produces an unbiased estimate of σ^2. If the mean is known, or we are calculating the population variance, then we divide by n. If instead the mean is also being estimated, then we divide by $(n - 1)$.

Equation 2.18 can easily be rearranged as follows (the proof of this equation is also left as an exercise),

$$\sigma^2 = E[X^2] - \mu^2 = E[X^2] - E[X]^2$$

(2.20)

Note that variance can be nonzero only if $E[X^2] \neq E[X]^2$.

When writing computer programs, this last version of the variance formula is often useful, since it allows us to calculate the mean and the variance in a single loop.

In finance it is often convenient to assume that the mean of a random variable is equal to zero. For example, based on theory, we might expect the spread between two equity indexes to have a mean of zero in the long run. In this case, the variance is simply the mean of the squared returns.

SAMPLE PROBLEM

Question:

Assume that the mean of the Standard & Poor's (S&P) 500 Index's daily returns is zero. You observe the following returns over the course of 10 days,

| 7% | −4% | 11% | 8% | 3% | 9% | −21% | 10% | −9% | −1% |

Estimate the standard deviation of daily S&P 500 Index returns.

Answer:

The sample mean is not exactly zero, but we are told to assume that the population mean *is* zero; therefore,

$$\hat{\sigma}_r^2 = E[r^2] = \frac{1}{n} \sum_{i=1}^{n} (r_i^2)$$

$$\hat{\sigma}_r^2 = \frac{1}{10} 0.0963 = 0.00963$$

$$\hat{\sigma}_r = 0.098$$

The standard deviation is 9.8%. Note: Because we were told to assume the mean is known, we divided by $n = 10$, not $(n - 1) = 9$.

As with the mean, for a continuous random variable we can calculate the variance by integrating with the probability density function. For a continuous random variable, X, with a probability density function, $f(x)$, the variance can be calculated as:

$$\sigma^2 = \int_{x_{min}}^{x_{max}} (x - \mu)^2 f(x) dx \tag{2.21}$$

It is not difficult to prove that, for either a discrete or a continuous random variable, multiplying by a constant will increase the standard deviation by the same factor, that is

$$\sigma(cX) = c\sigma(X) \tag{2.22}$$

In other words, if you own $10 of an equity with a standard deviation of $2, then $100 of the same equity will have a standard deviation of $20.

Adding a constant to a random variable, however, does not alter the standard deviation or the variance:

$$\sigma(X + c) = \sigma(X) \tag{2.23}$$

This is because the impact of c on the mean is the same as the impact of c on any draw of the random variable, leaving the deviation from the mean for any draw unchanged. In theory, a risk-free asset should have zero variance and standard deviation. If you own a portfolio with a standard deviation of $20, and then you add $1,000 of cash to that portfolio, assuming cash is risk-free, the standard deviation of the portfolio should still be $20.

STANDARD DEVIATION WITH DECAY

Imaging that we wish to know the expected return for an equity index. We could gather historical returns, $r_t, r_{t-1}, r_{t-2}, \ldots, r_{t-n+1}$ and then calculate the sample mean of the returns as

$$\hat{\mu}_t = \frac{1}{n} \sum_{i=0}^{n-1} r_{t-i} \tag{2.24}$$

For a practitioner, this formula immediately raises the question of what value to use for n. What value to choose for n is equivalent to asking how far back in time we should look for data. Should we use 10 years of data? One year? Thirty days? A popular choice in many fields is simply to use all available data. By this logic, if we have only 20 days of data, we use 20 days; if we have 80 years, we use 80 years. While this can be a sensible approach in some circumstances, it is much less common in modern finance. Using all available data has three potential drawbacks. First, the amount of available data for different variables may vary dramatically. For example, assume we are trying to calculate the mean return for two fixed-income portfolio managers. We have 20 years of data for one but only 2 years of data for the second. If the last two years have been particularly good years for fixed-income portfolio managers, a direct comparison of the means will naturally favor the manager with only two years of data. We could limit ourselves to the length of the shortest series, but there are potential drawbacks to this approach as well.

The second problem that arises when we use all available data is that our series length changes over time. If we have 500 days of data today, we will have 501 tomorrow, 502 the day after that, and so on. This is not necessarily a bad thing—more data may lead to a more accurate forecast—but, in practice, it is often convenient to maintain a constant window length. Among other advantages, a constant window length makes it easier to compare the accuracy of models over time.

Finally, there is the problem that the world is constantly changing. The Dow Jones Industrial Average has been available since 1896. There were initially just 12 companies in the index, including American Cotton Oil Company and Distilling & Cattle Feeding Company. That same year, Utah became the 45th U.S. state and Queen Victoria became the longest-ruling monarch in British history. Forget computers; in 1896, the Model T had not yet been introduced (1908), and the Wright Brothers' famous flight at Kitty Hawk was still some years off (1903). Does it make any sense to use stock market data from 1896 to evaluate the risk of a securities portfolio today? One can reasonably argue that the world was so different in the distant past—and in finance, the distant past is not necessarily that distant—that using extremely old data makes little sense.

If we are not going to use all available data, then a logical alternative is a constant window length. This is not without its own problems. If we use Equation 2.24 with a constant window length, then in each successive period, we add the most recent point to our data set and drop the oldest. The first objection to this method is philosophical. How can it be that the oldest point in our data set is considered just as legitimate as all the other points in our data set today (they have the same weight), yet in the very next period, the oldest point becomes completely illegitimate (zero weight)?

The second objection is more practical. As extreme points enter and leave our data set, this can cause dramatic changes in our estimator. Figure 2.2 shows a sample time series. Notice the outlier in the series at time $t = 50$. Figure 2.3 shows the rolling 40-day mean for the series.

Notice how the outlier in the original time series causes a sudden rise and drop in our estimate of the mean in Figure 2.3. The initial increase in Figure 2.3 occurs at $t = 50$ when the outlier is first included in the 40-day mean. The drop at $t = 90$ occurs when the outlier leaves the calculation. Due to the shape of the graph in Figure 2.3, this phenomenon is often referred to as plateauing. Technically, there is nothing wrong with plateauing, but it does seem strange that our estimate of the mean would change so suddenly based on one data point. The initial increase is easier to understand. If the outlier was truly unexpected, then it might be reasonable for us to update our estimate of the mean in light of this new data

FIGURE 2.2 Time Series with Outlier

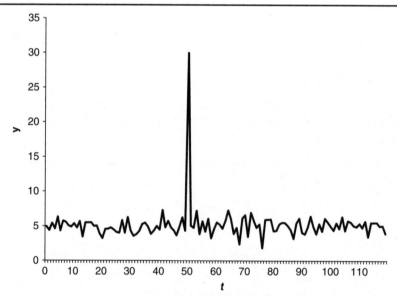

FIGURE 2.3 Rolling Mean of Time Series with Outlier

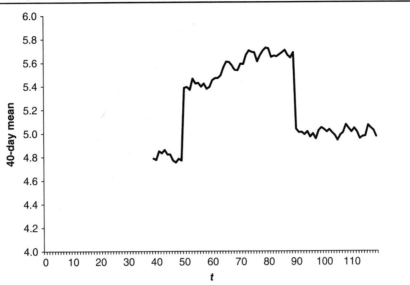

point. The sudden decrease at $t = 90$ is harder to understand. The drop occurs at $t = 90$ only because we chose a 40-day window length, and not because we received any additional information. If we are using this estimate to make financial decisions, it might seem very strange that our recommended course of action would change suddenly, when the extreme return drops out of our sample window.

In the end, the window length chosen is often arbitrary. Rarely in risk management are we presented with an obvious right choice for window length. Practitioners often choose windows that correspond to standard calendar units (e.g., one week, one month, one year) or round numbers (e.g., 100 days, 500 days). While they are convenient and widely used, it is difficult to see why these common window lengths are better than, say, one year plus five days or 142 days.

One approach that addresses many of these objections is known as an exponentially weighted moving average (EWMA). An EWMA is a weighted mean in which the weights decrease exponentially as we go back in time. The EWMA estimator of the mean can be formulated as

$$\hat{\mu}_t = \frac{1-\delta}{1-\delta^n} \sum_{i=0}^{n-1} \delta^i r_{t-i} \qquad (2.25)$$

Here, δ is a decay factor, such that $0 < \delta < 1$. For the remainder of this chapter, unless noted otherwise, assume that any decay factor, δ, is between zero and one. The term in front of the summation is the inverse of the summation of δ from 0 to $(n - 1)$.

TABLE 2.1 Example of EWMA Weights

Age	δ^i	Weight
0	1.00	15.35%
1	0.90	13.82%
2	0.81	12.44%
3	0.73	11.19%
4	0.66	10.07%
5	0.59	9.07%
6	0.53	8.16%
7	0.48	7.34%
8	0.43	6.61%
9	0.39	5.95%
Total	6.51	100.00%

In the EWMA, more weight is placed on more recent events. For example, if we have 10 sample points and a decay factor of 0.90, then the first point gets approximately 15% of the total weight, and the last point gets less than 6%. Table 2.1 shows the weights for all 10 points.

Figure 2.4 plots these weights against time, as well as the corresponding weights for the standard, equally weighted estimator.

As you can see, the EWMA weights form a smooth exponential curve that fades at a constant rate as we go back in time. Because of the shape of its chart, we often say that the equally weighted estimator is based on a rectangular window.

FIGURE 2.4 EWMA versus Rectangular Weights

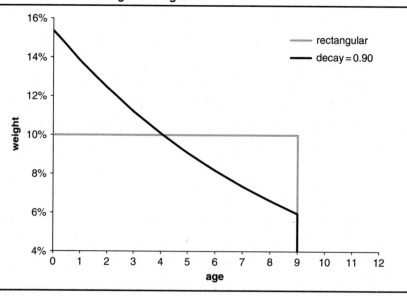

One way we can characterize an EWMA is by its half-life. Half of the weight of the mean comes before the half-life, and half after. We can find the half-life by solving for h in the equation

$$\sum_{i=0}^{h-1} \delta^i = \frac{1}{2} \sum_{i=0}^{n-1} \delta^i \tag{2.26}$$

The solution is

$$h = \frac{\ln(0.5 + 0.5\delta^n)}{\ln(\delta)} \tag{2.27}$$

For a sample of 250 data points and a decay factor of 0.98, the half-life is approximately 34. In other words, half of the weight of the estimator would be captured by the most recent 34 data points, and half in the remaining 216. A rectangular window of 250 data points, by comparison, would have a half-life of 125. Looked at another way, the EWMA with 250 data points and a decay factor of 0.98 has the same half-life as a rectangular window with 68 data points.

The EWMA can solve the problem of plateauing. The addition of an extreme data point to our data set can still cause a sudden change in our estimator, but the impact of that data point will slowly fade over time. Just before it exits the data set, the weight on the data point is likely to be so small that its removal will hardly be noticed. Figure 2.5 is based on the same series we used previously in Figure 2.2. In addition to the estimator of the mean based on an equally weighted 40-day window, we have added an estimator based on a 40-day window

FIGURE 2.5 Rolling Mean, EWMA versus Rectangular Window

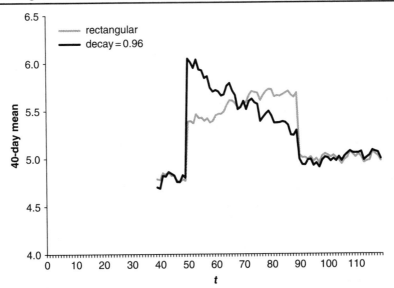

with a decay factor of 0.96. As you can see, for the series with the decay factor, the second transition is much more gradual.

Besides addressing the practical issue of plateauing, the EWMA estimator also addresses our philosophical objection to fixed windows. Rather than suddenly dropping out of the data set, the weight on any point is slowly reduced over time.

Finally, a fixed window length with a decay factor can be viewed as a compromise between a rectangular window of arbitrary length and using all available data. Because $|\delta|$ is less than one, as n goes to infinity, Equation 2.25 can be rewritten as

$$\hat{\mu}_t = (1 - \delta) \sum_{i=0}^{\infty} \delta^i r_{t-i} \tag{2.28}$$

Clearly an infinite series, if it did exist, would be using all available data. In practice, though, for reasonable decay factors, there will be very little weight on points from the distant past. Because of this, we can use a finite window length, but capture almost all of the weight of the infinite series. Mathematically,

$$\frac{\text{Weight of finite series}}{\text{Weight of infinite series}} = \frac{1-\delta^n/1-\delta}{1/1-\delta} = 1 - \delta^n \tag{2.29}$$

For a decay factor of 0.98, if our window length is 250, we would capture 99.4% of the weight of the infinite series. Ultimately, the window length is still arbitrary, but the precise choice becomes less important.

By carefully rearranging Equation 2.28, we can express the EWMA estimator as a weighted average of its previous value and the most recent observation,

$$\hat{\mu}_t = (1 - \delta) \left[r_t + \delta \sum_{i=0}^{\infty} \delta^i r_{t-i-1} \right] = (1 - \delta)r_t + \delta\hat{\mu}_{t-1} \tag{2.30}$$

Viewed this way, our EWMA is a formula for updating our beliefs about the mean over time. As new data become available, we slowly refine our estimate of the mean. This updating approach seems very logical, and could be used as a justification for the EWMA approach.

While the use of a decay factor addresses many practical problems associated with the equally weighted estimator, there may be little theoretical justification for the precise form of the EWMA estimator.

If the world is constantly changing, then the distributions of the variables we are interested in—stock returns, interest rates, and so on—will also be changing over time. It's not necessarily the case, but if the variables we are interested in are constantly changing, then the parameters that describe these variables may be more similar to their recent values than to their values in the distant past. While there is a certain logic to this justification, most formal models assume constant parameters, not parameters that slowly change over time.

Just as we used a decay factor when calculating the mean, we can use a decay factor when calculating other estimators. For an estimator of the sample variance, when the mean is known, the following is an unbiased estimator:

$$\hat{\sigma}_t^2 = \frac{1 - \delta}{1 - \delta^n} \sum_{i=0}^{n-1} \delta^i (r_{t-i} - \mu)^2 \quad 0 < \delta < 1 \tag{2.31}$$

If we imagine an estimator of infinite length, then the term δ^n goes to zero, and we have

$$\hat{\sigma}_t^2 = (1 - \delta) \sum_{i=0}^{\infty} \delta^i (r_{t-i} - \mu)^2 \tag{2.32}$$

As with our estimator of the mean, this formula can be rearranged to provide a useful updating rule,

$$\hat{\sigma}_t^2 = (1 - \delta)(r_t - \mu)^2 + \delta \hat{\sigma}_{t-1}^2 \tag{2.33}$$

In this case, the new value of our variance estimator is a weighted average of the previous estimator and the most recent squared deviation from the mean.

As mentioned in connection with the standard estimator for variance, it is not uncommon in finance for the mean to be close to zero and much smaller than the standard deviation of returns. *If* we assume the mean is zero, then our updating rule simplifies even further to

$$\hat{\sigma}_t^2 = (1 - \delta)r_t^2 + \delta \hat{\sigma}_{t-1}^2 \tag{2.34}$$

Remember that the preceding formula is valid only if we assume the mean is known and equal to zero.

In the case where the mean is unknown and must also be estimated, our estimator takes on a slightly more complicated form,

$$\hat{\sigma}_t^2 = A \sum_{i=0}^{n-1} \delta^i r_{t-i}^2 - B \hat{\mu}_t^2 \tag{2.35}$$

where $\hat{\mu}_t$ is our estimator of the sample mean, based on the same decay factor, δ, and A and B are constants defined as

$$A = \frac{S_1}{S_1^2 - S_2}$$

$$B = S_1 A$$

$$S_1 = \frac{1 - \delta^n}{1 - \delta}$$

$$S_2 = \frac{1 - \delta^{2n}}{1 - \delta^2} \tag{2.36}$$

Though these constants may look familiar, the addition of a decay factor has certainly made our variance estimator more complicated.

It is not too difficult to prove that in the limit, as δ approaches one—that is, as our estimator becomes a rectangular window—A approaches $1/(n - 1)$ and B converges to $n/(n - 1)$. Just as we would expect, in the limit, our new estimator converges to the standard variance estimator.

If we wish to know the standard deviation of a time series using a decay factor, we can simply take the square root of the appropriate estimator of the variance. No additional steps are required.

GARCH

In financial markets, variance appears to be far from constant. Both prolonged periods of high variance and prolonged periods of low variance are observed. While the transition from low to high variance can be sudden, more often we observe serial correlation in variance, with gradual mean reversion. When this is the case, periods of above-average variance are more likely to be followed by periods of above-average variance, and periods of below-average variance are likely to be followed by periods of below-average variance. For risk managers, this is one of the most important features of financial markets. It implies that, even though risk varies over time, this variation in risk is in part predictable.

Figure 2.6 shows the rolling annualized 60-day standard deviation of the S&P 500 index between 1928 and 2008. Notice how the level of the standard deviation is far

FIGURE 2.6 S&P 500, Annualized 60-Day Return Standard Deviation, 1928–2008

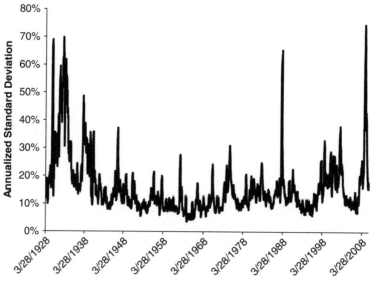

from being completely random. There are periods of sustained high volatility (e.g., 1996–2003) and periods of sustained low volatility (e.g., 1964–1969).

One of the most popular models of time-varying volatility is the autoregressive conditional heteroscedasticity (ARCH) model. We start by defining a disturbance term at time t, ε_t, in terms of an independent and identically distributed (i.i.d.)[3] standard normal variable, u_t, and a time varying standard deviation, σ_t, such that

$$\varepsilon_t = \sigma_t u_t \tag{2.37}$$

Because the standard deviation of u_t is one, the standard deviation of ε_t must be σ_t. With the exception of the degenerate case, where σ_t is constant, ε_t will not be i.i.d. In the simplest ARCH model, we can model the evolution of the variance as

$$\sigma_t^2 = \alpha_0 \bar{\sigma}^2 + \alpha_1 \sigma_{t-1}^2 u_{t-1}^2 = \alpha_0 \bar{\sigma}^2 + \alpha_1 \varepsilon_{t-1}^2 \tag{2.38}$$

where α_0 and α_1 are constants, and $\bar{\sigma}^2$ is the long-run variance. To ensure that σ^2 remains positive, we square u_{t-1} and ε_{t-1} and require $\alpha_0 > 0$, $\alpha_1 \geq 0$, and $\sigma_0^2 > 0$.

For σ^2 to be stable over time, we require that $\alpha_0 + \alpha_1 = 1$. Because u_t is standard normal, the expected value of u_{t-1}^2 is equal to 1. Because u_t is mean zero and independent of σ_t, we also know that $E[\sigma_{t-1}^2 u_{t-1}^2] = E[\sigma_{t-1}^2]E[u_{t-1}^2]$. Putting this all together, we have

$$E[\sigma_t^2] = \alpha_0 \bar{\sigma}^2 + \alpha_1 E[\sigma_{t-1}^2] \tag{2.39}$$

The requirement that $\alpha_0 + \alpha_1 = 1$ is then equivalent to requiring that the expected value of the variance equal the long-run variance, $E[\sigma_t^2] = E[\sigma_{t-1}^2] = \bar{\sigma}^2$.

In Equation 2.38, notice how σ_t is influenced by the lagged value of the disturbance term, ε_{t-1}. Because α_1 is greater than zero, if there is a large disturbance (positive or negative), then σ_t will be greater than when the disturbance is small. This leads to serial correlation in our disturbance term. High volatility begets high volatility. Equation 2.38 is typically referred to as an ARCH(1) model. By adding more lagged terms containing σ^2 and u^2, we can generalize to an ARCH(n) specification.

$$\sigma_t^2 = \alpha_0 \bar{\sigma}^2 + \sum_{i=1}^{n} \alpha_i \sigma_{t-i}^2 u_{t-i}^2 \tag{2.40}$$

Besides the additional disturbance terms, we can also add lags of σ^2 to the equation. In this form, the process is known as generalized autoregressive conditional heteroscedasticity

---

[3] We'll have a lot more to say about i.i.d. random variables in Chapter 6. In case you have not come across this terminology before, it simply means that a collection of random variables all have the same distribution and are statistically independent from each other. In the case of u_t in Equation 2.37, for each value of t, we consider u_t to be a distinct random variable, but each of the u_t have the same shaped distribution and are independent of each other.

(GARCH). The following describes a GARCH(1,1) process:

$$\sigma_t^2 = \alpha_0 \bar{\sigma}^2 + \alpha_1 \sigma_{t-1}^2 u_{t-1}^2 + \beta \sigma_{t-1}^2 \tag{2.41}$$

For the GARCH(1,1) to be stable, we require that $\alpha_0 + \alpha_1 + \beta = 1$. Just as with the ARCH model, by adding additional terms, we can build a more general GARCH(n,m) process.

MOMENTS

Earlier in the chapter, we stated that the mean of a variable X is often equated with the expected value of X, which we can write as

$$\mu = \mathrm{E}[X] \tag{2.42}$$

It turns out that we can generalize this concept as follows:

$$m_k = \mathrm{E}[X^k] \tag{2.43}$$

We refer to m_k as the kth moment of X. The mean of X is also the first moment of X.

Similarly, we can generalize the concept of variance as

$$\mu_k = \mathrm{E}[(X - \mu)^k] \tag{2.44}$$

We refer to μ_k as the kth central moment of X. We say that the moment is central because it is centered on the mean. Variance is then the second central moment.

While we can easily calculate any central moment, in risk management it is very rare that we are interested in anything beyond the fourth central moment.

SKEWNESS

The second central moment, variance, tells us how spread out a random variable is around the mean. The third central moment tells us how symmetrical the distribution is around the mean. Rather than working with the third central moment directly, by convention we first standardize the statistic. This standardized third central moment is known as *skewness*. For a random variable X, we can define the skewness as

$$\text{skewness} = \frac{\mathrm{E}[(X - \mu)^3]}{\sigma^3} \tag{2.45}$$

where σ is the standard deviation of X, and μ is the mean of X.

By standardizing the central moment, it is much easier to compare two random variables. Multiplying a random variable by a constant will not change the skewness.

A random variable that is symmetrical about its mean will have zero skewness. If the skewness of the random variable is positive, we say that the random variable exhibits positive skew. Figures 2.7 and 2.8 show examples of positive and negative skewness.

FIGURE 2.7 **Positive Skewness**

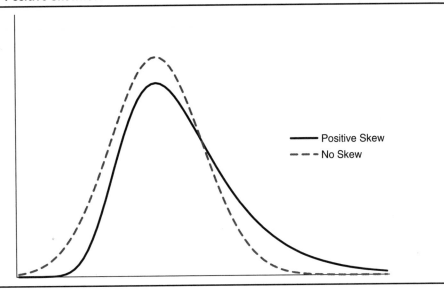

FIGURE 2.8 **Negative Skewness**

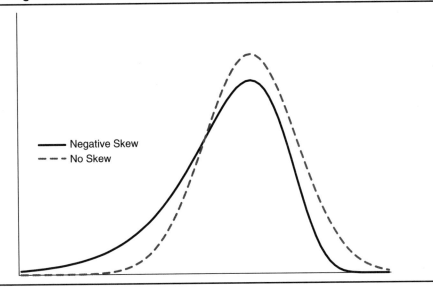

Skewness is a very important concept in risk management. If the distributions of returns of two investments are the same in all respects, with the same mean and standard deviation, but different skews, then the investment with more negative skewness is generally considered to be riskier. Historical data suggest that many financial assets exhibit negative skewness. Historically, the returns of most equity indexes have exhibited negative skewness.

As with variance, the equation for skewness differs depending on whether we are calculating the population skewness or the sample skewness. For the population statistic, the skewness of a random variable X, based on n observations, x_1, x_2, ... , x_n, can be calculated as

$$\hat{s} = \frac{1}{n} \sum_{i=1}^{n} \left(\frac{x_i - \mu}{\sigma} \right)^3 \tag{2.46}$$

where μ is the population mean and σ is the population standard deviation. Similar to our calculation of sample variance, if we are calculating the sample skewness, there is going to be an overlap with the calculation of the sample mean and sample standard deviation. We need to correct for that. The sample skewness can be calculated as

$$\tilde{s} = \frac{n}{(n-1)(n-2)} \sum_{i=1}^{n} \left(\frac{x_i - \hat{\mu}}{\hat{\sigma}} \right)^3 \tag{2.47}$$

Based on Equation 2.20, for variance, it is tempting to guess that the formula for the third central moment can be written simply in terms of $E[X^3]$ and μ. Be careful because the two sides of this equation are *not* equal:

$$E[(X - \mu)^3] \neq E[X^3] - \mu^3 \tag{2.48}$$

The correct equation for skewness is

$$E[(X - \mu)^3] = E[X^3] - 3\mu\sigma^2 - \mu^3 \tag{2.49}$$

SAMPLE PROBLEM

Question:

Prove that the left-hand side of Equation 2.49 is indeed equal to the right-hand side of the equation.

Answer:

We could start by multiplying out the terms inside the expectation. Equivalently, we could use the binomial theorem, to get

$$E[(X - \mu)^3] = E[X^3 - 3\mu X^2 + 3\mu^2 X - \mu^3]$$

Next, we separate the terms inside the expectation operator and move any constants, including μ and μ^3, outside the operator, to get

$$E[(X - \mu)^3] = E[X^3] - 3\mu E[X^2] + 3\mu^2 E[X] - \mu^3$$

$E[X]$ is simply the mean, μ. For $E[X^2]$, we reorganize our equation for variance, Equation 2.20, as follows,

$$\sigma^2 = E[X^2] - \mu^2$$

$$E[X^2] = \sigma^2 + \mu^2$$

Substituting these results into our equation and collecting terms, we arrive at the final equation:

$$E[(X - \mu)^3] = E[X^3] - 3\mu(\sigma^2 + \mu^2) + 3\mu^2\mu - \mu^3$$
$$= E[X^3] - 3\mu\sigma^2 - \mu^3$$

For many symmetrical continuous distributions, the mean, median, and mode all have the same value. Many continuous distributions with negative skew have a mean that is less than the median, which is less than the mode. For example, it might be that a certain derivative is just as likely to produce positive returns as it is to produce negative returns (the median is zero), but there are more big negative returns than big positive returns (the distribution is negatively skewed), so the mean is less than zero. As a risk manager, understanding the impact of skew on the mean relative to the median and mode can be useful. Be careful, though, because this rule of thumb does not always work. Many practitioners mistakenly believe that it is in fact always true. It is not, and it is very easy to produce a distribution that violates this rule.

KURTOSIS

The fourth central moment is similar to the second central moment, variance, in that it tells us how spread out a random variable is. However, the fourth central moment puts more weight on extreme points. As with skewness, rather than working with the fourth central moment directly, we typically work with a standardized statistic. This standardized fourth central moment is known as *kurtosis*. For a random variable X, we can define the kurtosis as K, where

$$K = \frac{E[(X - \mu)^4]}{\sigma^4} \qquad (2.50)$$

Here, σ is the standard deviation of X, and μ is its mean.

By standardizing the central moment, it is much easier to compare two random variables. As with skewness, multiplying a random variable by a constant will not change the kurtosis.

The following two populations have the same mean, variance, and skewness. The second population has a higher kurtosis.

Population 1: {−17, −17, 17, 17}
Population 2: {−23, −7, 7, 23}

Notice that, to balance out the variance, when we moved the outer two points out 6 units, we had to move the inner two points in 10 units. Because the random variable with higher

FIGURE 2.9 High Kurtosis

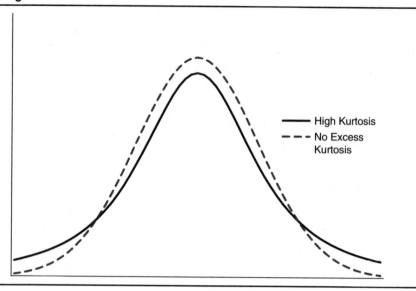

kurtosis has points further from the mean, we often refer to distribution with high kurtosis as fat-tailed. Figures 2.9 and 2.10 show examples of continuous distributions with high and low kurtosis.

Like skewness, kurtosis is an important concept in risk management. Many financial assets exhibit high levels of kurtosis. If the distribution of returns of two assets have the same mean, variance, and skewness but different kurtoses, then the distribution with the higher kurtosis will tend to have more extreme points, and will usually be considered to be riskier.

FIGURE 2.10 Low Kurtosis

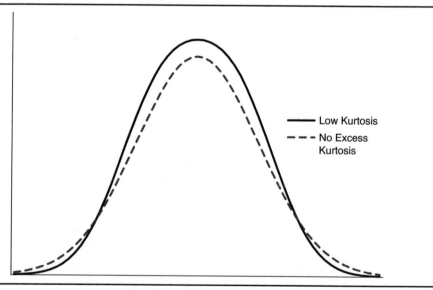

As with variance and skewness, the equation for kurtosis differs depending on whether we are calculating the population kurtosis or the sample kurtosis. For the population statistic, the kurtosis of a random variable X can be calculated as

$$\hat{K} = \frac{1}{n} \sum_{i=1}^{n} \left(\frac{x_i - \mu}{\sigma} \right)^4 \qquad (2.51)$$

where μ is the population mean and σ is the population standard deviation. Similar to our calculation of sample variance and skewness, if we are calculating the sample kurtosis there is going to be an overlap with the calculation of the sample mean and sample standard deviation. We need to correct for that. The sample kurtosis can be calculated as

$$\tilde{K} = \frac{n(n+1)}{(n-1)(n-2)(n-3)} \sum_{i=1}^{n} \left(\frac{x_i - \hat{\mu}}{\hat{\sigma}} \right)^4 \qquad (2.52)$$

It turns out that the normal distribution, has a kurtosis of exactly 3. Because normal distributions are so common, many people refer to *excess kurtosis*, which is simply the kurtosis minus 3:

$$K_{\text{excess}} = K - 3 \qquad (2.53)$$

By this convention, the normal distribution has an excess kurtosis of 0. Distributions with positive excess kurtosis are termed leptokurtotic. Distributions with negative excess kurtosis are termed platykurtotic. Be careful; by default, many applications calculate excess kurtosis, not kurtosis.

When we are also estimating the mean and variance, calculating the sample excess kurtosis is somewhat more complicated than just subtracting 3. If we have n points in our sample, then the correct formula is

$$\tilde{K}_{\text{excess}} = \tilde{K} - 3 \frac{(n-1)^2}{(n-2)(n-3)} \qquad (2.54)$$

Where $\tilde{K}$ is the sample kurtosis from Equation 2.52. As n increases, the last term on the right-hand side converges to 3.

JUMP-DIFFUSION MODEL

In the GARCH model, volatility changes gradually over time. In financial markets we do observe this sort of behavior, but we also see extreme events that seem to come out of nowhere. For example, on February 27, 2007, in the midst of otherwise calm markets, there were rumors that the Chinese central bank might raise interest rates. There was also some bad economic news in the United States. These two events contributed to what, by some measures, was a −8 standard deviation move in U.S. equity markets. A move of this many standard deviations would be extremely rare for most standard parametric distributions.

One popular way to generate this type of extreme return is to add a so-called jump term to our standard time-series model. This can be done by adding a second disturbance term, as follows

$$r_t = \alpha + \varepsilon_t + [I_t]u_t \tag{2.55}$$

Here, r_t is the market return at time t, α is a constant drift term, and ε_t is a mean zero diffusion term. As specified, our jump term has two components: $[I_t]$, an indicator variable that is either zero or one, and u_t, an additional disturbance term. Because it has a jump *and* a diffusion term, this time series model is referred to as a jump-diffusion model.

The jump-diffusion model is really just a mixture model. To get the type of behavior we want—moderate volatility punctuated by rare extreme events—we can set the standard deviation of ε_t to relatively modest levels. We then specify the probability of $[I_t]$ equaling one at some relatively low level, and set the standard deviation of u_t at a relatively high level. If we believe that extreme negative returns are more likely than extreme positive returns, we can also make the distribution of u_t asymmetrical. u_t does not have to have a mean of zero.

GARCH and jump-diffusion are not mutually exclusive. By combining GARCH and jump-diffusion, we can model and understand a wide range of market environments and dynamics.

DOLLAR STANDARD DEVIATION

In risk management, when we talk about the standard deviation of a security, we are almost always talking about the standard deviation of the returns for that security. While this is almost always the case, there will be times when we want to express standard deviation and other risk parameters in terms of dollars (or euros, yen, etc.).

In order to calculate the expected dollar standard deviation of a security, we begin by calculating the expected return standard deviation, and then multiply this value by the current dollar value of the security (or, in the case of futures, the nominal value of the contract). It's that simple. If we have $200 worth of ABC stock, and the stock's return standard deviation is 3%, then the expected dollar standard deviation is 3% × $200 = $6.

What you should *not* do is calculate the dollar standard deviation directly from past dollar returns or price changes. The difference is subtle, and it is easy to get confused. The reason that we want to calculate the return standard deviation first is that percentage returns are stable over time, whereas dollar returns rarely are. This may not be obvious in the short term, but consider what can happen to a security over a long period of time. Take, for example, IBM. In 1963, the average split-adjusted closing price of IBM was $2.00, compared to $127.53 in 2010. Even though the share price of IBM grew substantially over those 47 years, the daily return standard deviation was relatively stable, 1.00% in 1963 versus 1.12% in 2010. There may be other reasons for not wanting to use returns from as far back as 1963, but as this example makes clear, using return data from that long ago will not necessarily lead to a severe misestimation of risk. The same cannot be said about using price returns. The standard deviation of price changes in 1963 for IBM was just $0.12 versus $7.50 in 2010. If we had used the standard deviation of price changes from 1963 to estimate the risk of owning IBM in 2010, we would have severely underestimated the risk.

SAMPLE PROBLEM

Question:

You observe the following prices over 10 days for a security:

    100.00, 107.00, 119.84, 105.46, 102.30, 101.27, 108.36, 107.28, 114.79, 126.25

All prices are in dollars, and the prices are in order, with $100.00 being the oldest price, and $126.25 being the current price.
Calculate the expected return and price standard deviation for the security. Also, even though you should not use this value to forecast risk, calculate the standard deviation of the realized price changes, for comparison.

Answer:

The following table shows the prices, and the calculated price changes and returns. At the bottom we have calculated the standard deviation of the price changes and the returns.

t	P	ΔP	R
0	100.00		
1	107.00	7.00	7.00%
2	119.84	12.84	12.00%
3	105.46	−14.38	−12.00%
4	102.30	−3.16	−3.00%
5	101.27	−1.03	−1.01%
6	108.36	7.09	7.00%
7	107.28	−1.08	−1.00%
8	114.79	7.51	7.00%
9	126.25	11.48	10.00%
	std. dev.	8.62	7.67%

The expected return standard deviation is 7.67%. Given the final price of $126.25, the expected dollar standard deviation is 7.67% × $126.25 = $9.68. The realized standard deviation of the prices was only $8.62. This is lower than the expected standard deviation, because the price of the security increased over this period. Had we used this value, we would have underestimated the expected dollar standard deviation. The correct answer for the expected standard deviation in dollars is $9.68.

Note, in both cases, we calculated the sample standard deviation, not the population standard deviation. Even though it was not stated explicitly, it should have been clear from the question that these 10 prices represented a sample, upon which we were basing our estimate of the standard deviation.

When the distribution of a random variable is stable over time, we say that it is stationary. Returns for most financial assets are stationary in the long run. When the distribution of a random variable is changing over time, we say that it is non-stationary. Prices of equities and commodities are typically non-stationary.

In general, it is better to construct models using stationary variables, and to avoid non-stationary ones. If we try to construct a model directly from non-stationary data, then the parameters of our model, which should be constant over time, will not be stable. Using the example of IBM again, if we tried to construct a model that contained a parameter for the mean of IBM's price, we would find that the value of that parameter was constantly changing over time. We can calculate the mean of IBM's price over a given time period, but if the price of IBM is always growing, then it is impossible to talk about the value of the mean in general, in the long run. In theory, you might say that they mean of IBM's price is infinite in the very, very long run, but that is not very useful in practice. For similar reasons, that is why it is better to base the standard deviation calculation for equities on returns and not directly on prices.

ANNUALIZATION

Up until now, we have not said anything about the frequency of returns. Most of the examples have made use of daily data. Daily returns are widely available for many financial assets, and daily return series often serve as the starting point for risk management models. That said, in has become common practice in finance and risk management to present standard deviation as an annual number. For example, if somebody tells you that the option-implied standard deviation of a Microsoft one-month at-the-money call option is 18%—unless they specifically tell you otherwise—this will almost always mean that the annualized standard deviation is 18%. It doesn't matter that the option has one month to expiration, or that the model used to calculate the implied standard deviation used daily returns; the standard deviation quoted is annualized.

If the returns of a security meet certain requirements, namely that the returns are independently and identically distributed, converting a daily standard deviation to an annual standard deviation is simply a matter of multiplying by the square root of days in the year. For example, if we estimate the standard deviation of daily returns as 2.00%, and there are 256 business days in a year, then the expected standard deviation of annual returns is simply $32\% = 2.00\% \times \sqrt{256}$. If we have a set of non-overlapping weekly returns, we could calculate the standard deviation of weekly returns and multiply by the square root of 52 to get the expected standard deviation of annual returns. This square-root rule only works if returns are i.i.d. If the distribution of returns is changing over time, as with our GARCH model, or returns display serial correlation, which is not uncommon, then the standard deviation of annual returns could be higher or lower than the square-root rule would predict.

If returns are not i.i.d. and we are really interested in trying to predict the expected standard deviation of annual returns, then we should not use the square-root rule. We need to use a more sophisticated statistical model, or use actual annual returns as the basis of our calculation. That said, in many settings, such as quoting option-implied standard deviation or describing the daily risk of portfolio returns, annualization is mostly about presentation, and making comparison of statistics easier. In these situation, we often use the square root rule, even when returns are not i.i.d. In these settings, doing anything else would actually cause more confusion. As always, if you are unsure of the convention, it is best to clearly explain how you arrived at your calculation.

END-OF-CHAPTER QUESTIONS

1. Compute the sample mean and the standard deviation of the following returns:

7%	2%	6%	−4%	−4%	3%	0%	18%	−1%

2. Calculate the population mean, standard deviation, and skewness of each of the following two series:

Series #1	−51	−21	21	51
Series #2	−61	−7	33	35

3. Calculate the population mean, standard deviation, and kurtosis for each of the following two series:

Series #1	−23	−7	7	23
Series #2	−17	−17	17	17

4. Given the probability density function for a random variable X,

$$f(x) = \frac{x}{18} \text{ for } 0 \leq x \leq 6$$

find the variance of X.

5. For an estimator based on n data points, with a decay factor of δ, prove that the half-life, h, is given by:

$$h = \frac{\ln(0.5 + 0.5\delta^n)}{\ln(\delta)}$$

6. Using a decay factor of 0.95, calculate the mean, sample variance, and sample standard deviation of the following series. Assume $t = 7$ is the most recent data point and use all eight points:

t	0	1	2	3	4	5	6	7
x	11	84	30	73	56	58	52	35

7. Given the following set of data, calculate the mean using no decay factor (rectangular window), a decay factor of 0.99, and a decay factor of 0.90. Assume time $t = 10$ is the most recent data point and use all 11 points:

t	0	1	2	3	4	5	6	7	8	9	10
x	0.04	0.84	0.28	0.62	0.42	0.46	0.66	0.69	0.39	0.99	0.37

8. Calculate the sample standard deviation for the data set in Problem 7 using no decay factor, a decay factor of 0.99, and a decay factor of 0.90.

9. You are estimating the expected value of the annual return of a stock-market index using an EWMA estimator with a decay factor of 0.98. The current estimate of the mean is 10%. Over the next three years, the index returns 15%, −4%, and finally 8%. Recalculate the estimate of the mean in each of these three years. Assume that the window length is infinite.

10. What is the half-life for an estimator with a decay factor of 0.95 and 200 data points? What is the half-life for the same decay factor with 1,000 data points?

11. What is the half-life of an EWMA estimator with a decay factor of 0.96 and 32 data points? What is the length of a rectangular window with the most similar half-life?

12. Assume we have an EWMA estimator with a decay factor of 0.96 and 50 data points. What percentage of the weight is captured with this estimator, compared to an estimator with the same decay factor and an infinite length?

13. Assume that the mean of a data-generating process is known and equal to zero. Your initial estimate of the standard deviation is 10%, after which you observe the following returns ($t = 6$ is the most recent period). Assume that the initial estimator was generated from an infinitely long series and use a decay factor of 0.95. What is your updated estimate of the standard deviation?

t	1	2	3	4	5	6
r	–5%	18%	16%	–2%	5%	–10%

3

MARKET RISK: VALUE AT RISK

In this chapter we continue to explore how we can describe the risk of a single security. We begin by introducing the concept of value at risk (VaR). We explore several methods of calculating VaR, and end by describing how to test the accuracy of these models.

WHAT IS VALUE AT RISK?

Value at risk is one of the most widely used risk measures in finance. VaR was popularized by J.P. Morgan in the 1990s. The executives at J.P. Morgan wanted their risk managers to generate one statistic that summarized the risk of the firm's entire portfolio, at the end of each day. What they came up with was VaR.

VaR is a one-tailed confidence interval. If the 95% VaR of a portfolio is $400, then we expect the portfolio will lose $400 or less in 95% of the scenarios and lose more than $400 in 5% of the scenarios. We can define VaR for any confidence level, but 95% has become an extremely popular choice at many financial firms. The time horizon also needs to be specified for VaR. On trading desks with liquid portfolios, it is common to measure the one-day 95% VaR. In other settings, in which less liquid assets may be involved, time frames of up to one year are not uncommon.

If an actual loss equals or exceeds the predicted VaR threshold, that event is known as an *exceedance*. Another way to explain VaR is to say that for a one-day 95% VaR, the probability of an exceedance event on any given day is 5%.

Figure 3.1 provides a graphical representation of VaR at the 95% confidence level. The figure shows the probability density function for the returns of a portfolio. Because VaR is

FIGURE 3.1 Example of 95% Value at Risk

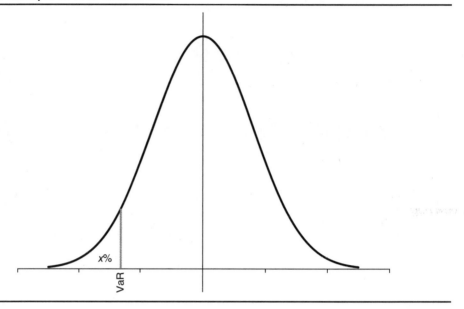

FIGURE 3.1 Example of 95% Value at Risk

being measured at the 95% confidence level, 5% of the distribution is to the left of the VaR level, and 95% is to the right.

In order to formally define VaR, we begin by defining a random variable L, which represents the loss to our portfolio. L is simply the opposite of the return to our portfolio. If the return of our portfolio is $-\$600$, then the loss, L, is $+\$600$. For a given confidence level, γ, then, value at risk is defined as

$$P[L \geq \text{VaR}_\gamma] = 1 - \gamma \qquad (3.1)$$

If a risk manager says that the one-day 95% VaR of a portfolio is $400, this means that there is a 5% probability that the portfolio will *lose* $400 or more on any given day (that L will be more than $400).

We can also define VaR directly in terms of returns. If we multiply both sides of the inequality in Equation 3.1 by -1, and replace $-L$ with R, we come up with

$$P[R \leq -\text{VaR}_\gamma] = 1 - \gamma \qquad (3.2)$$

Equations 3.1 and 3.2 are equivalent. A loss of $400 or more and a return of $-\$400$ or less are exactly the same.

While Equations 3.1 and 3.2 are equivalent, defining VaR in terms of losses as in Equation 3.1 is more common. It has the advantage that, for most portfolios for reasonable confidence levels, VaR will almost always be a positive number. That said, outside of VaR we generally work with returns. Switching back and forth between losses and returns can be confusing. In practice, rather than saying that your VaR is $400, it is often best to resolve any ambiguity by stating that your VaR is a *loss* of $400.

SAMPLE PROBLEM

Question:

The probability density function (PDF) for daily profits at Triangle Asset Management can be described by the following piecewise function (see Figure 3.2),

$$p = \frac{1}{10} + \frac{1}{100}\pi \quad \text{for } -10 \leq \pi \leq 0$$

$$p = \frac{1}{10} - \frac{1}{100}\pi \quad \text{for } 0 \leq \pi \leq 10$$

FIGURE 3.2 Triangular Probability Density Function

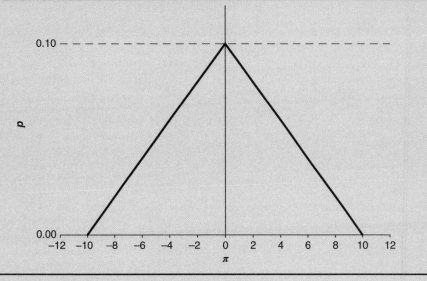

What is the one-day 95% VaR for Triangle Asset Management?

Answer:

To find the 95% VaR, we need to find a, such that

$$0.05 = \int_{-10}^{a} p \, d\pi$$

By inspection, half the distribution is below zero, so we need only bother with the first half of the function,

$$0.05 = \int_{-10}^{a} \left(\frac{1}{10} + \frac{1}{100}\pi \right) d\pi$$

$$= \left[\frac{1}{10}\pi + \frac{1}{200}\pi^2 \right]_{-10}^{a}$$

$$= \left(\frac{1}{10}a + \frac{1}{200}a^2 \right) - \left(\frac{1}{10}(-10) + \frac{1}{200}(-10)^2 \right)$$

$$= \left(\frac{1}{10}a + \frac{1}{200}a^2 \right) + 0.50$$

Rearranging terms,

$$a^2 + 20a + 90 = 0$$

Using the quadratic formula, we can solve for a,

$$a = \frac{-20 \pm \sqrt{400 - 4 \times 90}}{2} = -10 \pm \sqrt{10}$$

Because the distribution is not defined for $\pi < -10$, we can ignore the solution with $-\sqrt{10}$, giving us the final answer

$$a = -10 + \sqrt{10} = -6.84$$

The one-day 95% VaR for Triangle Asset Management is a loss of 6.84.

There are many reasons why VaR has become so popular in risk management. One of the primary appeals of VaR is its simplicity. The concept of VaR is intuitive, even to those not versed in statistics. Because it boils risk down to a single number, VaR also provides us with a convenient way to track the risk of a portfolio over time.

Another appealing feature of VaR is that is focuses on losses. This may seem like an obvious criterion for a risk measure, but variance and standard deviation treat positive and negative deviations from the mean equally. For many risk managers, VaR also seems to strike the right balance, by focusing on losses that are significant, but not too extreme. We'll have more to say about this at the end of the chapter, when we discuss backtesting.

VaR also allows us to aggregate risk across a portfolio with many different types of securities (e.g., stocks, bonds, futures, options, etc.). Prior to VaR, risk managers were often forced to evaluate different segments of a portfolio separately. For example, for the bonds in a portfolio they may have looked at the interest rate sensitivities, and for the equities they may have looked at how much exposure there was to different industries.

Finally, VaR is robust to outliers. As is true of the median or any quantile measure, a single large event in our data set (or the absence of one) will usually not change our estimate of VaR. This advantage of VaR is a direct consequence of one of its deepest flaws, that it ignores the tail of the distribution. As we will see in the next chapter, expected shortfall, a closely related measure, has exactly the opposite problem: It incorporates the tail of the distribution, but it is not robust to outliers.

DELTA-NORMAL VAR

One of the simplest and easiest ways to calculate VaR is to make what are known as delta-normal assumptions. For any underlying asset, we assume that the log returns are normally distributed and we approximate the returns of any option using its delta-adjusted exposure. The delta-normal model includes additional assumptions when multiple securities are involved, which we will cover when we begin to look at portfolio risk measures.

The delta-normal assumptions make it very easy to calculate VaR statistics even with limited computing power. This made delta-normal models a popular choice when VaR models were first introduced. Predictably, the results of such a simple model were often disappointing. A good risk manager would often be able to compensate for these deficiencies, but the basic model presented an easy target for critics. Delta-normal models are rarely used in practice today, but they are still an excellent starting point when learning about VaR models. By understanding the pros and cons of the delta-normal model, we will be able to better understand the pros and cons of more complex models. Unfortunately, many people outside of risk management believe that delta-normal models are still widely used in practice, or believe that the shortcomings of these simple models are inherent to all risk models.

To calculate the delta-normal VaR of a security, we start by calculating the standard deviation of returns for the security or, in the case of an option, for the returns of the option's underlying security. We could use any of the methods described in the previous chapter to estimate the standard deviation. For regular securities, we then multiply the return standard deviation by the absolute market value or notional of our position to get the position's standard deviation. For options we multiply by the absolute delta-adjusted exposure. The delta adjusted exposure of a single option being the underlying security's price multiplied by the option's delta. We then multiply the position's standard deviation by the appropriate factor for the inverse of the standard normal distribution (e.g. -1.64 for 95% VaR).

Notice that we have not said anything about the expected return. In practice, most VaR models assume that the distribution of returns has a mean of zero. This is almost always a very reasonable assumption at short horizons. At longer horizons this assumption may no longer be reasonable. Some practitioners will also assume that the theta for options is also zero. While this assumption may also be valid in many situations, it can fail even over short time horizons. In what follows, unless otherwise stated, assume security returns have zero mean but include theta in calculating VaR.

SAMPLE PROBLEM

Question:

You estimate the standard deviation of daily returns for XYZ Corp.'s stock at 2.00%. You own both the stock and a call option on the stock with a delta of 40% and 1-day theta of −0.01. The underlying price is $100. Calculate the one-day 95% daily VaR for each security.

Answer:

The 95% VaR corresponds to the bottom 5% of returns. For a normal distribution 5% of the distribution is less than 1.64 standard deviations below the mean. We can get this result from a lookup table, from a statistics application, or from a spreadsheet. For example, in Excel NORM.S.INV(0.05), would give us −1.64, the negative sign indicating that the result is below the mean.

For the stock, the final answer is simply: −1.64 × $100 × 2.00% = −$3.28. (If you use additional decimal places for the standard deviation, you might get −$3.29.) For the option, the final answer is only slightly more complicated: −1.64 × 40% × $100 × 2.00% − 0.01 = −$1.32.

The 1-day 95% daily VaR for the stock and option are a loss of $3.28 and $1.32, respectively.

HISTORICAL VAR

Another very simple model for estimating VaR is historical simulation or the historical method. In this approach we calculate VaR directly from past returns. For example, suppose we want to calculate the one-day 95% VaR for an equity using 100 days of data. The 95th percentile would correspond to the least worst of the worst 5% of returns. In this case, because we are using 100 days of data, the VaR simply corresponds to the fifth worst day.

Now suppose we have 256 days of data, sorted from lowest to highest as in Table 3.1. We still want to calculate the 95% VaR, but 5% of 256 is 12.8. Should we choose the 12th day? The 13th? The more conservative approach is to take the 12th point, −15.0%. Another alternative is to interpolate between the 12th and 13th points, to come up with −14.92%. Unless there is a strong justification for choosing the interpolation method, the conservative approach is recommended.

For securities with no maturity date such as stocks, the historical approach is incredibly simple. For derivatives, such as equity options, or other instruments with finite lifespans, such as bonds, it is slightly more complicated. For a derivative, we do not want to know what the actual return series was, we want to know what the return series would have been had we held exactly the same derivative in the past. For example, suppose we own an at-the-money put with two days until expiration. Two-hundred-fifty days ago, the option would have had

TABLE 3.1 95% Historical VaR Example

		R	Cum. Weight(%)
Worst	1	–34.3%	0.4%
	2	–28.9%	0.8%
	3	–25.0%	1.2%
	4	–24.9%	1.6%
	...	...	...
	10	–15.9%	3.9%
	11	–15.5%	4.3%
	12	**–15.0%**	**4.7%**
	13	**–14.9%**	**5.1%**
	...	...	...
	254	21.4%	99.2%
	255	23.0%	99.6%
Best	256	28.1%	100.0%

252 days until expiration, and it may have been far in or out of the money. We do *not* want to know what the return would have been for this option with 252 days to expiration. We want to know what the return *would have been* for an at-the-money put with two days to expiration, given conditions in the financial markets 250 days ago. Similarly, for a bond with 30 days to expiration, for risk purposes, we are interested in what the return of a bond with 30 days to maturity would have been 250 days ago, *not* what the return of a bond with 280 days to maturity was. What we need to do is to generate a constant maturity or backcast series. These constant maturity series, or backcast series, are quite common in finance. The easiest way to calculate the backcast series for an option would be to use a delta approximation. If we currently hold a put with a delta of −30%, and the underlying return 250 days ago was 5%, then our backcast return for that day would be −1.5% = −30% × 5%. A more accurate approach would be to fully reprice the option, taking into account not just changes in the underlying price, but also changes in implied volatility, the risk-free rate, the dividend yield, and time to expiration. Just as we could approximate option returns using delta, we could approximate bond returns using DV01, but a more accurate approach would be to fully reprice the bond based on changes in the relevant interest rates and credit spreads.

One advantage of historical VaR is that it is extremely simple to calculate. Another advantage is that it is easy to explain to non-risk professionals. The inputs to historical VaR should be familiar to anybody working in finance. For equities, for example, the inputs are just the historical returns. If there is ever a question about the validity of a historical VaR calculation, it is easy enough to pull up a chart of historical returns to look for a potential source of error.

The delta-normal approach is an example of what we call a *parametric model*. This is because it is based on a mathematically defined, or parametric, distribution (in this case, the normal distribution). By contrast, the historical approach is non-parametric. We have not made any assumptions about the distribution of historical returns. There are advantages and disadvantages to both approaches. The historical approach easily reproduces all the quirks that we see in historical data: changing standard deviation, skewness, kurtosis, jumps, etc. Developing a parametric model that reproduces all of the observed features of financial markets can be very difficult. At the same time, models based on distributions often make it easier to draw general conclusions. In the case of the historical approach, it is difficult to say if the data used for the model are unusual because the model does not define *usual*.

HYBRID VAR

The historical model is easy to calculate and reproduces all the quirks that we see in historical data, but it places equal weight on all data points. If risk has increased recently, then the historical model will likely underestimate current risk. The delta-normal model can place more weight on more recent data by calculating standard deviation using a decay factor. The calculation with a decay factor is somewhat more difficult, but not much. Even with the decay factor, the delta-normal model still tends to be inaccurate because of the delta and normal assumptions.

Can we combine the advantages of the historical model with the advantages of a decay factor? The hybrid approach to VaR does exactly this. Just as we did with standard deviation in Chapter 2, we can place more weight on more recent points when calculating VaR by using a decay factor. If we were calculating standard historical VaR at the 95% confidence level, then 5% of the data points would be on one side of our VaR estimate, and 95% would be on the other side. With hybrid VaR it is not the number of points that matters, but their weight. With hybrid VaR, 5% of the total weight of the data points is on one side, and 95% is on the other.

Mechanically, in order to calculate hybrid VaR, we start by assigning a weight to each data point. If our decay factor was 0.98, then we would assign a weight of 1 to the most recent date, 0.98 to the previous day, 0.98^2 to the day before that, and so on. Next, we divide these weights by the sum of all the weights, to get a percentage weight for each day. Then we sort the data based on returns. Finally, we determine our estimate of VaR, by adding up the percentage weights, starting with the worst return, until we get to the desired confidence level. If our confidence level was 95%, then we would stop when the sum of the percentage weights was equal to 5%.

Table 3.2 provides an example of how to calculate hybrid VaR. Here, we have used the same returns as in Table 3.1, and a decay factor of 0.99. We've added three columns, one for the weights, one for the weights as a percentage of the total of the weights, and one for the cumulative sum of the percentage weights. Notice how the weight of the point in the fifth row, which is only from 3 days ago, gets a much higher weight, 1.05%, than the seventh

TABLE 3.2 95% Hybrid VaR Example

		t	R	Historical Cum. Weight (%)	Hybrid Weight	Hybrid Weight (%)	Hybrid Cum. Weight (%)
Worst	1	42	−34.3%	0.4%	0.6557	0.71%	0.7%
	2	83	−28.9%	0.8%	0.4342	0.47%	1.2%
	3	10	−25.0%	1.2%	0.9044	0.98%	2.2%
	4	23	−24.9%	1.6%	0.7936	0.86%	3.0%
	5	3	−23.8%	2.0%	0.9703	1.05%	4.1%
	6	58	−20.6%	2.3%	0.5583	0.60%	4.7%
	7	**188**	**−19.7%**	**2.7%**	**0.1512**	**0.16%**	**4.8%**
	8	**103**	**−18.6%**	**3.1%**	**0.3552**	**0.38%**	**5.2%**
	9	131	−17.6%	3.5%	0.2680	0.29%	5.5%
	10	12	−15.9%	3.9%	0.8864	0.96%	6.5%
	11	116	−15.5%	4.3%	0.3117	0.34%	6.8%
	12	**245**	**−15.0%**	**4.7%**	**0.0852**	**0.09%**	**6.9%**
	13	**150**	**−14.9%**	**5.1%**	**0.2215**	**0.24%**	**7.1%**
	14	56	−13.7%	5.5%	0.5696	0.62%	7.8%
		...	...	...	...	...	...
	253	145	19.9%	98.8%	0.2329	0.25%	99.6%
	254	176	21.4%	99.2%	0.1705	0.18%	99.8%
	255	235	23.0%	99.6%	0.0942	0.10%	99.9%
Best	256	207	28.1%	100.0%	0.1249	0.14%	100.0%

row, which represents a return from 188 days ago and only gets a weight of 0.16%. In our example, we get to 5% of the total weight between the seventh and eighth rows. As before, we can be conservative and take the worst of these two points or we can interpolate between them. If we choose to be conservative, then our one-day 95% hybrid VaR with a decay factor of 0.99 would be a loss of 19.7%. Notice that our hybrid VaR, 19.7%, is greater than our standard historical VaR, 15.0%. This is because the portfolio has had more extreme negative returns recently. From the table we can see that the six worst returns all happened within the last 100 days, and two of these were within the last 10 days. In this case, hybrid VaR reflects the fact that the portfolio returns have been more volatile more recently. If the opposite had been true—if returns had been more volatile in the past and calmer more recently—then we would expect the hybrid VaR to be less than the standard historical VaR.

MONTE CARLO SIMULATION

Monte Carlo simulations are widely used throughout finance, and they can be a very powerful tool for calculating VaR. As an example of how we would calculate VaR using a Monte Carlo simulation, imagine we have a position in gold. We believe that the daily log returns of gold are normally distributed with a mean of 0.01% and a standard deviation of 1.40%. To calculate the VaR of this position, we could generate 1,000 draws from a normal distribution with a mean of 0.01% and a standard deviation of 1.40%, convert the log returns into standard returns, and then sort the returns from lowest to highest. If we are interested in our

95% VaR, we simply select the 50th worst return from the list. For this set up, the Monte Carlo simulation is very straightforward, but it is also inefficient. Because the log returns are normally distributed, we know that the 5th percentile is −1.64 standard deviations below the mean, corresponding to a log return of −2.29% = 0.01% − 1.64 × 1.40%.

The real power of Monte Carlo simulations is in more complex settings, where instruments are nonlinear, prices are path dependent, and distributions do not have well-defined inverses. Also, as we will see in subsequent chapters when we extend our VaR framework to portfolios of securities, even very simple portfolios can have very complex distributions.

Monte Carlo simulations can also be used to calculate VaR over multiple periods. In the preceding example, if instead of being interested in the one-day VaR, we wanted to know the four-day VaR, we could simply generate four one-day log returns, using the same distribution as before, and add them together to get one four-day return. We could repeat this process 1,000 times, generating a total of 4,000 one-day returns. As with the one-day example, in this particular case, there are more efficient ways to calculate the VaR statistic. That said, it is easy to imagine how multiday scenarios could quickly become very complex. What if your policy was to reduce your position by 50% every time you suffered a loss in excess of 3%? What if returns exhibited serial correlation?

Monte Carlo simulations are usually based on parametric distributions, but we could also use nonparametric methods, randomly sampling from historical returns. Continuing with our gold example, if we had 500 days of returns for gold, and we wanted to calculate the four-day VaR, we could randomly pick a number from 1 to 500, and select the corresponding historical return. We would do this four times, to create one four-day return. We can repeat this process, generating as many four-day returns as we desire. The basic idea is very simple, but there are some important details to keep in mind.

First, generating multi-period returns this way involves what we call *sampling with replacement*. Pretend that the first draw from our random number generator is a 10, and we select the 10th historical return. We don't remove that return before the next draw. If, on the second draw, our random number generator produces 10 again, then we select the same return. If we end up pulling 10 four time in a row, then our four-day return will be composed of the same 10th return repeated four times. Even though we only have 500 returns to start out with, there are 500^4, or 62.5 billion, possible four-day returns that we can generate this way. This method of estimating parameters, using sampling with replacement, is often referred to as *bootstrapping*.

The second detail that we need to pay attention to is serial correlation and changes in the distribution over time. We can only generate multi-period returns in the way just described if single-period returns are independent of each other and volatility is constant over time.

Suppose that this was not the case, and that gold tends to go through long periods of high volatility followed by long periods of low volatility. Now assume that by chance, the historical data we are using starts with 250 days of low volatility followed by 250 days of high volatility. If we randomly select returns with replacement, then the probability of getting a draw from the high-volatility period is 1/2 each time. If our random numbers are generated independently, then there is only $1/16 = (1/2)^4$ chance of drawing four returns in a row from the high period, whereas, historically, the probability was much closer to 1/2. A simple solution to this problem: Instead of generating a random number from 1 to 500, generate a random number from 1 to 497, and then select four successive returns. If our random number generator generates 125, then we create our four-day return from returns 125, 126, 127, and 128. While this method will more accurately reflect the historical behavior of volatility, and capture any serial correlation, it greatly reduces the number of possible returns from 62.5 billion to 497, which effectively reduces the Monte Carlo simulation to the historical simulation method. Another possibility is to try to normalize the data to the current standard deviation. If we believe the current standard deviation of gold is 10% and that the standard deviation on a certain day in the past was 5%, then we would simply multiply that return by two. While this approach gets us back to the full 62.5 billion possible four-day returns for our 500-day sample, it requires us to make a number of assumptions in order to calculate the standard deviation and normalize the data.

Of the three methods we have considered so far, Monte Carlo simulations are generally considered to be the most flexible. Their major drawback is speed. As computers get faster and faster, the speed of Monte Carlo simulations is becoming less of an issue. Still in some situations— a trading desk that require real-time risk numbers, for example—this speed issue may still rule out the use of Monte Carlo simulations.

CORNISH-FISHER VAR

The delta-normal VaR model assumes that underlying returns are normally distributed and that option returns can be approximated using their delta-adjusted exposure. The Cornish-Fisher VaR model maintains the first assumption, while trying to improve the approximation for options. The method relies on what is known as the Cornish-Fisher expansion. The Cornish-Fisher expansion is a general method that allows us to approximate the confidence intervals for a random variable based on the central moments of that variable. As with the delta-normal approach, the Cornish-Fisher approach can easily be extended to portfolios containing multiple securities.

To start with, we introduce some notation. Define the value of an option as V, and the value of the option's underlying security as U. Next, define the option's exposure-adjusted Black-Scholes-Merton Greeks as

$$\tilde{\Delta} = \frac{dV}{dU} U = \Delta U$$

$$\tilde{\Gamma} = \frac{d^2 V}{dU^2} U^2 = \Gamma U^2 \tag{3.3}$$

$$\theta = \frac{dV}{dt}$$

Given a return on the underlying security, R, we can approximate the change in value of the option using the exposure-adjusted Greeks as

$$dV \approx \tilde{\Delta} R + \frac{1}{2} \tilde{\Gamma} R^2 + \theta \, dt \tag{3.4}$$

If the returns of the underlying asset are normally distributed with a mean of zero and a standard deviation of σ, then we can calculate the moments of dV based on Equation 3.4. The first three central moments and skewness of dV are

$$\mu_{dV} = \mathrm{E}[dV] = \frac{1}{2} \tilde{\Gamma} \sigma^2 + \theta \, dt$$

$$\sigma_{dV}^2 = \mathrm{E}[(dV - \mathrm{E}[dV])^2] = \tilde{\Delta}^2 \sigma^2 + \frac{1}{2} \tilde{\Gamma}^2 \sigma^4 \tag{3.5}$$

$$\mu_{3,dV} = 3 \tilde{\Delta}^2 \tilde{\Gamma} \sigma^4 + \tilde{\Gamma}^3 \sigma^6$$

$$s_{dV} = \frac{\mu_{3,dV}}{\sigma_{dV}^3}$$

Where μ_{dV} is the mean of dV, σ_{dV}^2 is the variance, $\mu_{3,dV}$ is the third central moment, and s_{dV} is the skewness. Notice that even though the distribution of the underlying security's returns is symmetrical, the distribution of the change in value of the option is skewed ($s_{dV} \neq 0$). This makes sense, given the asymmetrical nature of an option payout function. That the Cornish-Fisher model captures the asymmetry of options is an advantage over the delta-normal model, which produces symmetrical distributions for options.

The central moments from Equation 3.5 can be combined to approximate a confidence interval using a Cornish-Fisher expansion, which can in turn be used to calculate an approximation for VaR. The Cornish-Fisher VaR of the an option is given by

$$VaR = -\mu_{dV} - \sigma_{dV} \left[m + \frac{1}{6}(m^2 - 1)s_{dV} \right] \tag{3.6}$$

where m corresponds to the distance in standard deviations for our VaR confidence level based on a normal distribution (e.g., $m = -1.64$ for 95% VaR).

We note three facts about Equation 3.6: First, the standard Cornish-Fisher formula includes a mean, μ_{dV}, which may be non-zero. Second, as we would expect, increasing the standard deviation, σ_{dV}, will tend to increase VaR (remember m is generally negative). Third, as we would also expect, the more negative the skew of the distribution the higher the VaR tends to be (in practice, $m^2 - 1$ will tend to be positive). Unfortunately, beyond this, the formula is far from intuitive, and its derivation is beyond the scope of this book. As is often the case, the easiest way to understand the approximation, may be to use it. The following sample problem provides an example.

SAMPLE PROBLEM

Question:

You are asked to evaluate the risk of a portfolio containing a single call option with a strike price of 110 and three months to expiration. The underlying price is 100, and the risk-free rate is 3%. The expected and implied standard deviations are both 20%. Calculate the one-day 95% VaR using both the delta-normal method and the Cornish-Fisher method. Use 365 days per year for theta and 256 days per year for standard deviation.

Answer:

To start with we need to calculate the Black-Scholes-Merton delta, gamma, and theta. These can be calculated in a spreadsheet or using other financial applications.

$$\Delta = 0.2038$$

$$\Gamma = 0.0283$$

$$\theta = -6.2415$$

The one-day standard deviation and theta can be found as follows:

$$\sigma_d = \frac{20\%}{\sqrt{256}} = 1.25\%$$

$$\theta_d = \left(\frac{-6.2415}{365} \right) = -0.0171$$

Using $m = -1.64$ for the 5% confidence level of the normal distribution, the delta-normal approximation is

$$-VaR = m\sigma_d S\Delta + \theta_d = -1.64 \times 1.25\% \times 100 \times 0.2038 - 0.0171 = -0.4361$$

For the Cornish-Fisher, approximation, we first calculate the exposure-adjusted Greeks:

$$\tilde{\Delta} = \Delta U = 0.2038 \times 100 = 20.3806$$

$$\tilde{\Gamma} = \Gamma U^2 = 0.0283 \times 100^2 = 283.1397$$

Next, we calculate the mean, standard deviation, and skewness for the change in option value:

$$\mu_{dV} = \frac{1}{2}\tilde{\Gamma}\sigma_d^2 + \theta_d = \frac{1}{2} \times 283.1379 \times (1.25\%)^2 - 0.0171 = 0.00503$$

$$\sigma_{dV}^2 = \tilde{\Delta}^2\sigma_d^2 + \frac{1}{2}\tilde{\Gamma}^2\sigma_d^4 = 20.3806^2 1.25\%^2 + \frac{1}{2}283.1397^2 1.25\%^4 = 0.06588$$

$$\sigma_{dv} = \sqrt{0.06588} = 0.256672$$

$$\mu_{3,dV} = 3\tilde{\Delta}^2\tilde{\Gamma}\sigma_d^4 + \tilde{\Gamma}^3\sigma_d^6$$

$$= 3 \times 20.3806^2 \times 283.1379 \times 1.25\%^4 + 283.1379^3 \times 1.25\%^6$$

$$= 0.0087$$

$$s_{dV} = \frac{\mu_{3,dV}}{\sigma_{dV}^3} = \frac{0.0087}{0.256672^3} = 0.51453$$

We then plug the moments into our Cornish-Fisher approximation:

$$-VaR = \mu_{dV} + \sigma_{dV}\left[m + \frac{1}{6}(m^2 - 1)s_{dV}\right]$$

$$= 0.00502 + 0.256672\left[-1.64 + \frac{1}{6}(-1.64^2 - 1)0.514528\right]$$

$$= -0.3796$$

The one-day 95% VaR for the Cornish-Fisher method is a loss of 0.3796, compared to a loss of 0.4316 for the delta-normal approximation. It turns out that in this particular case the exact answer can be found using the Black-Scholes-Merton equation. Given the assumptions of this sample problem, the actual one-day 95% VaR is 0.3759. In this sample problem, the Cornish-Fisher approximation is very close to the actual value, and provides a much better approximation than the delta-normal approach.

In certain instances, the Cornish-Fisher approximation can be extremely accurate. In practice, it is much more likely to be accurate if we do not go too far out into the tails of the distribution. If we try to calculate the 99.99% VaR using Cornish-Fisher, even for a simple portfolio, the result is unlikely to be as accurate as what we saw in the preceding sample problem. One reason is that our delta-gamma approximation will be more accurate for small returns. The other is that returns are much more likely to be well approximated by a normal distribution closer to the mean of a distribution. As we will see in the next section, there are other reasons why we might not want to calculate VaR too far out into the tails.

BACKTESTING

An obvious concern when using VaR is choosing the appropriate confidence interval. As mentioned, 95% has become a very popular choice in risk management. In some settings there may be a natural choice, but, most of the time, the specific value chosen for the confidence level is arbitrary.

A common mistake for newcomers is to choose a confidence level that is too high. Naturally, a higher confidence level sounds more conservative. A risk manager who measures one-day VaR at the 95% confidence level will, on average, experience an exceedance event every 20 days. A risk manager who measures VaR at the 99.9% confidence level expects to see an exceedance only once every 1,000 days. Is an event that happens once every 20 days really something that we need to worry about? It is tempting to believe that the risk manager using the 99.9% confidence level is concerned with more serious, riskier outcomes, and is therefore doing a better job.

The problem is that, as we go further and further out into the tail of the distribution, we become less and less certain of the shape of the distribution. In most cases, the assumed distribution of returns for our portfolio will be based on historical data. If we have 1,000 data points, then there are 50 data points to back up our 95% confidence level, but only one to back up our 99.9% confidence level. As with any parameter, the variance of our estimate of the parameter decreases with the sample size. One data point is hardly a good sample size on which to base a parameter estimate.

A related problem has to do with backtesting. Good risk managers should regularly backtest their models. Backtesting entails checking the predicted outcome of a model against actual data. Any model parameter can be backtested.

In the case of VaR, backtesting is easy. When assessing a VaR model, each period can be viewed as a Bernoulli trial. Either we observe an exceedance or we do not. In the case of one-day 95% VaR, there is a 5% chance of an exceedance event each day, and a 95% chance that there is no exceedance. In general, for a confidence level $(1 - p)$, the probability of observing an exceedance is p. If exceedance events are independent, then over the course of n days the distribution of exceedances will follow a binomial distribution

$$P[K = k] = \binom{n}{k} p^k (1 - p)^{n-k} \tag{3.7}$$

Here, n is the number of periods that we are using in our backtest, k is the number of exceedances, and $(1 - p)$ is our confidence level. The number of possible combinations of k exceedances over n days is

$$\binom{n}{k} = \frac{n!}{k!(n - k)!} \tag{3.8}$$

For example, for one-day 90% VaR, there are three possible outcomes over two days: There will be either 0, 1, or 2 exceedances. The probability of zero exceedances is the probability of no exceedance on the first day multiplied by the probability of no exceedance on the second day, or $0.90^2 = 0.81$. Similarly, the probability of two exceedances is $0.10^2 = 0.01$. There are two ways that we can have one exceedance: We can have no exceedance on the first day and an exceedance on the second day; or the opposite way around. The probability of the first combination is $0.90 \times 0.10 = 0.09$, and the probability of the second combination is $0.10 \times 0.10 = 0.09$. The probability of one exceedance is then the sum of these two combinations or 18%. We could get the same result using Equation 3.7,

$$P[K = 0] = \binom{2}{0} 0.10^0 0.90^{2-0} = \frac{2!}{0!2!} \times 1 \times 0.90^2 = 0.81$$

$$P[K = 1] = \binom{2}{1} 0.10^1 0.90^{2-1} = \frac{2!}{1!1!} \times 0.10 \times 0.90 = 0.18$$

$$P[K = 2] = \binom{2}{2} 0.10^2 0.90^{2-2} = \frac{2!}{2!0!} \times 0.10^2 \times 1 = 0.01 \tag{3.9}$$

Notice that the sum of the probabilities is equal to 100%. Over two days, one of these three combinations must happen.

SAMPLE PROBLEM

Question:

As a risk manager, you are tasked with calculating a daily 95% VaR statistic for a large fixed-income portfolio. Over the past 100 days, there have been four exceedances. How many exceedances should you have expected? What was the probability of exactly four exceedances during this time? What was the probability of four or less? Four or more?

Answer:

Remember, by convention, for a 95% VaR the probability of an exceedance is 5%, not 95%. Over 100 days, then, we would expect to see five exceedances: $(1 - 95\%) \times 100 = 5$.
The probability of exactly four exceedances is 17.81%,

$$P[K = 4] = \binom{100}{4} 0.05^4 (1 - 0.05)^{100-4} = 0.1781$$

The probability of four or fewer exceedances is 43.60%. Here, we simply do the same calculation as before, but for zero, one, two, three, and four exceedances.

It's important not to forget zero:

$$P[K \leq 4] = \sum_{k=0}^{4} \binom{100}{k} 0.05^k (1 - 0.05)^{100-k}$$

$$= 0.0059 + 0.0312 + 0.0812 + 0.1396 + 0.1781$$

$$= 0.4360$$

For the final result, we could use the brute-force approach and calculate the probabilities for $k = 4, 5, 6, \ldots, 99, 100$, a total of 97 calculations. Instead, we realize that the sum of all probabilities from 0 to 100 exceedances must be 100%. Therefore, if the probability of $K \leq 4$ is 43.60%, then the probability of $K > 4$ must be $100\% - 43.60\% = 56.40\%$. Be careful, though, we want the probability for $K \geq 4$. To get this, we simply add the probability that $K = 4$ to our previous answer to get the final answer, 74.21%,

$$P[K \geq 4] = P[K > 4] + P[K = 4]$$

$$P[K \geq 4] = 0.5640 + 0.1781 = 0.7421$$

In this case, even though we would have expected to see five exceedances, the probability of four or more exceedances or four or less exceedance is very high, 43.60% and 74.21%, respectively. Based on these results, we would be unlikely to reject our VaR model.

Backtesting VaR models is extremely easy, but what would happen if we were trying to measure one-day VaR at the 99.9% confidence level. Four years is approximately 1,000 business days, so over four years we would expect to see just one exceedance. We could easily reject the model if we observed a large number of exceedances, but what if we did not observe any? After four years, there would be a 37% probability of observing zero exceedances. Maybe our model is working fine, but maybe it is completely inaccurate and we will never see an exceedance. How long do we have to wait to reject a 99.9% VaR model if we have not seen any exceedances? Approximately 3,000 business days or 12 years. At the 99.9% confidence level, the probability of not seeing a single exceedance after 3,000 business days is a bit less than 5%. It is still possible that the model is correct at this point, but it is unlikely. Twelve years is too long to wait to know if a model is working or not. By contrast, for a 95% VaR model we could reject the model with the same level of confidence if we did not observe an exceedance after just three months. If our confidence level is too high, we will not be able to backtest our VaR model and we will not know if it is accurate.

The probability of a VaR exceedance should also be conditionally independent of all available information at the time the forecast is made. In other words, if we are calculating the 95% VaR for a portfolio, then the probability of an exceedance should always be 5%. The probability shouldn't be different because today is Tuesday, because yesterday it was sunny, or because your firm has been having a good month. Importantly, the probability should not vary because there was an exceedance the previous day or because risk levels are elevated.

A common problem with VaR models in practice is that exceedances often end up being serially correlated. When exceedances are serially correlated, you are more likely to see another exceedance in the period immediately after an exceedance. To test for serial correlation in exceedances, we can look at the periods immediately following any exceedance events. The number of exceedances in these periods should also follow a binomial distribution. For example, pretend we are calculating the one-day 95% VaR for a portfolio, and we observed 40 exceedances over the past 800 days. To test for serial correlation in the exceedances, we look at the 40 days immediately following the exceedance events and count how many of those were also exceedances. In other words, we count the number of back-to-back exceedances. Because we are calculating VaR at the 95% confidence level, of the 40 day-after days, we would expect that 2 of them (5% × 40 = 2) would also be exceedances. The actual number of these day-after exceedances should follow a binomial distribution with $n = 40$ and $p = 5\%$.

Another common problem with VaR models in practice is that exceedances tend to be correlated with the level of risk. It may seem counterintuitive, but we should be no more or less likely to see VaR exceedances in years when market volatility is high compared to when it is low. Positive correlation between exceedances and risk levels can happen when a model does not react quickly enough to changes in risk levels. Negative correlation can happen when model windows are too short, and the model over reacts. To test for correlation between exceedances and the level of risk, we can divide our exceedances into two or more buckets, based on the level of risk. As an example, pretend we have been calculating the one-day 95% VaR for a portfolio over the past 800 days. We could divide the sample period in two, placing the 400 days with the highest forecasted VaR in one bucket and the 400 days with the lowest forecasted VaR in the other. We would expect each 400-day bucket to contain 20 exceedances: 5% × 400 = 20. The actual number of exceedances in each bucket should follow a binomial distribution with $n = 400$, and $p = 5\%$.

END-OF-CHAPTER QUESTIONS

1. Prove the formula for the first Cornish-Fisher moment. That is, given

$$dV \approx \tilde{\Delta} R + \frac{1}{2}\tilde{\Gamma}R^2 + \theta dt$$

prove that

$$\mu_{dV} = E[dV] = \frac{1}{2}\tilde{\Gamma}\sigma^2 + \theta\,dt$$

Remember that R is normally distributed with a mean of zero.

2. You are the risk manager for a currency trading desk. The desk had a VaR exceedance today. What is the most likely day for the next VaR exceedance?

3. You are asked to calculate the one-day 95% VaR for a portfolio using the historical method, with a window of 256 days. The table below contains the 20 worst backcast returns for the portfolio along with the time at which the returns occurred, $t = 0, 1, 2, \ldots, 255$. The most recent date is $t = 0$, and the oldest is $t = 255$.

	t	R
1	42	−35%
2	83	−29%
3	10	−26%
4	23	−25%
5	3	−24%
6	58	−21%
7	188	−20%
8	103	−19%
9	131	−18%
10	12	−16%
11	116	−16%
12	245	−16%
13	150	−15%
14	56	−14%
15	61	−14%
16	31	−13%
17	69	−13%
18	95	−13%
19	161	−13%
20	35	−12%

4. Using the same data as in the previous question, calculate the one-day 95% VaR using the hybrid method with a window of 256 days and a decay factor of 0.99.

5. You are the risk manager for a portfolio with a mean daily return of 0.40% and a daily standard deviation of 2.3%. Assume the returns are normally distributed (not a good assumption to make, in general). What is the 95% VaR?

6. The probability density function (PDF) for daily profits at Box Asset Management can be described by the following function (see Figure 3.3),

$$p = \frac{1}{200} \quad \text{for} - 100 \leq \pi \leq 100$$

FIGURE 3.3 Probability Density Function for Box Asset Management

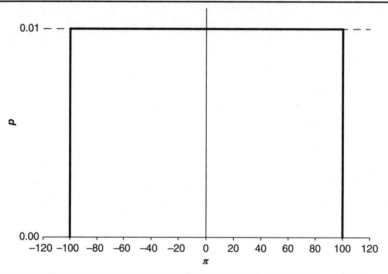

Below -100 and above 100, the PDF is zero. What is the one-day 95% VaR of Box Asset Management?

7. The probability density function (PDF) for daily profits at Pyramid Asset Management can be described by the following functions (see Figure 3.4),

$$p = \frac{3}{80} + \frac{1}{400}\pi \quad \text{for} - 15 \leq \pi \leq 5$$

$$p = \frac{5}{80} - \frac{1}{400}\pi \quad \text{for } 5 > \pi > 25$$

The density function is zero for all other values of π. What is the one-day 95% VaR for Pyramid Asset Management?

FIGURE 3.4 Probability Density Function for Pyramid Asset Management

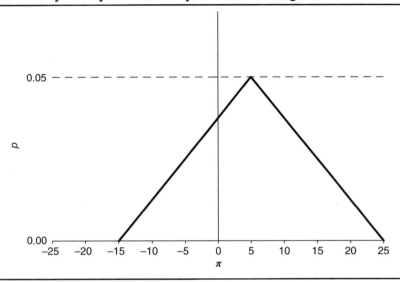

The next two questions require a basic knowledge of option pricing.

8. You estimate the standard deviation of daily returns for XYZ Corp.'s stock at 2.00%. XYZ does not pay a dividend. You own a put option and a call option on XYZ, both with one year to expiration and a strike price of $105. The delta of the call is 0.50 and the underlying price is $100. Calculate the one-day 95% daily VaR for each security and for the portfolio as a whole using the delta-normal approach. Assume theta is zero for both options (for long-dated options this may not be an unreasonable approximation).

9. This question is the same as the previous question, but rather than owning a put and call option on XYZ, you have sold a put and call on XZY. As before, the strike of both options is $105 and time to expiration is one year. As before, calculate the one-day 95% daily VaR for each security and for the portfolio as a whole using the delta-normal approach, assuming theta is zero for both options. Is the VaR less than, equal to, or greater than the VaR in the previous question? Is the risk of the two portfolios the same?

4

MARKET RISK: EXPECTED SHORTFALL, AND EXTREME VALUE THEORY

In this chapter we look at two tail-risk measures: expected shortfall, and extreme value theory. We begin with a discussion of what makes a good risk measure.

COHERENT RISK MEASURES

At this point we have introduced two widely used measures of risk, standard deviation and value at risk (VaR). Before we introduce any more, it might be worthwhile to ask what qualities a good risk measure should have.

In 1999 Philippe Artzner and his colleagues proposed a set of axioms that they felt any logical risk measure should follow. They termed a risk measure that obeyed all of these axioms *coherent*. As we will see, while VaR has a number of attractive qualities, it is not a coherent risk measure.

In addition to a number of identities, the four axioms that a coherent risk measure must obey are monotonicity, positive homogeneity, translation invariance, and subadditivity. We consider each in turn.

Monotonicity

Pretend that we have two portfolios, Portfolio A and Portfolio B. If Portfolio A loses more money than Portfolio B in all scenarios, then Portfolio A should be considered riskier. If Portfolio A loses the same amount as Portfolio B in all scenarios except one where it loses more, then Portfolio A should still be considered riskier. A risk measure that obeys this logic is said to be monotonic, or to display monotonicity.

VaR is a monotonic risk measure. Imagine again that Portfolio A loses more money than Portfolio B in all scenarios. To calculate the VaR of Portfolio B, we find the least worst of the worst 5% of scenarios for Portfolio B. Because Portfolio A loses more in all of these scenarios, we know that the VaR for Portfolio A must be greater than the VaR of Portfolio B. The other scenarios can only make the VaR worse for Portfolio A, not better. VaR correctly identifies Portfolio A as being riskier.

Standard deviation is not monotonic. As we saw in Chapter 2, adding a constant to a random variable will not change its standard deviation. Imagine that Portfolio A loses 10% more than Portfolio B in all scenarios. It follows that the mean of Portfolio A will be 10% less than the mean of Portfolio B, but in each scenario, the distance from the mean will be the same, and the standard deviation of both portfolios will be equal. Even though Portfolio A loses more than Portfolio B in all scenarios, their standard deviations are equal.

We could rescue standard deviation by redefining monotonicity in terms of unexpected losses, rather than losses. Traditionally, though, monotonicity has been defined in terms of simple losses. If we define risk in terms of simple losses, then standard deviation is not monotonic.

For an even more extreme example of why standard deviation is not monotonic, imagine that Portfolio A returns −2% in all scenarios. Now imagine that Portfolio B returns −2% in all scenarios except one, where it returns +10%. Clearly Portfolio B is the better investment, but the standard deviation of Portfolio A is zero and the standard deviation of Portfolio B is not zero.

It is hard to imagine why anybody would invest in a portfolio that always performs the same or worse than another potential investment. Arguably, in a complete market where arbitrage is possible, these inferior portfolios should not even exist. While monotonicity is an extremely logical concept, the practical implications are less clear.

SAMPLE PROBLEM

Question:

Show that standard deviation is not monotonic. First compute the sample standard deviation of Portfolio A and Portfolio B, given the following sets of returns. Note that the returns for Portfolio A are always 5% less than those of Portfolio B.

	1	2	3	4	5
A	2.00%	−5.00%	−3.00%	1.00%	5.00%
B	7.00%	0.00%	2.00%	6.00%	10.00%

Next prove that, in general, adding or subtracting a constant from a random variable leaves the standard deviation unchanged.

Answer:

We start by calculating the sum of the returns for both portfolios and dividing by 5 to get the mean for each portfolio. The mean for Portfolio A is 0% and the mean for Portfolio B is 5%. In the next two rows of the table, we subtract the corresponding mean from each data point to get the deviations. Notice that the deviations are the same for each portfolio. In the next two rows, we square these deviations and total them.

	1	2	3	4	5	sum	mean
A	2.00%	−5.00%	−3.00%	1.00%	5.00%	0.00%	0.00%
B	7.00%	0.00%	2.00%	6.00%	10.00%	25.00%	5.00%
$A - \mu_A$	2.00%	−5.00%	−3.00%	1.00%	5.00%		
$B - \mu_B$	2.00%	−5.00%	−3.00%	1.00%	5.00%		
$(A - \mu_A)^2$	0.04%	0.25%	0.09%	0.01%	0.25%	0.64%	
$(B - \mu_B)^2$	0.04%	0.25%	0.09%	0.01%	0.25%	0.64%	

To calculate the sample variance, we divide this sum of the squared deviations, 0.64%, by $(n - 1) = 4$, to get 0.16%. Finally, we take the square root of this value to get the standard deviation of 4.00%. As expected, the standard deviations of both portfolios are equal.

More generally, for a random variable, X, variance is defined as

$$\sigma_X^2 = E[(X - E[X])^2]$$

If we add a constant, c, to X, then we have

$$\sigma_{X+c}^2 = E[(X + c - E[X + c])^2]$$
$$= E[(X + c - c - E[X])^2]$$
$$= E[(X - E[X])^2]$$
$$= \sigma_X^2$$

If the variance is unaltered by the addition of a constant then it follows that the square root of the variance, standard deviation, is also unaltered.

Positive Homogeneity

Imagine that you double the size of all the positions in your portfolio. The returns in all scenarios will also be doubled, and you should consider the new portfolio to be twice as risky. More generally, if you multiply all outcomes by a constant, c, and the associated risk measure is c times as great, then the risk measure is said to display positive homogeneity.

If we increase the size of all of the positions in a portfolio by 10 times, then that portfolio will make or lose 10 times as much in all scenarios. It seems reasonable that a risk measure would judge the new portfolio to be 10 times as risky as the original.

Positive homogeneity also insures that no matter what units we measure the risk of a portfolio in, the measured risk is the same. Imagine if the exchange rate of the U.S. dollar (USD) to Japanese yen (JPY) were 100 to 1. Then, if a portfolio returns 1 USD this is the same as returning 100 JPY, if a portfolio loses 10 USD it is the same as losing 1,000 JPY. If we measure the risk of a portfolio as 1 million USD based on USD returns, then we should measure the risk of the same portfolio as 100 million JPY when using JPY returns.

Both VaR and standard deviation display positive homogeneity. The proof for standard deviation is left as an exercise for the end of the chapter.

Translation Invariance

A portfolio composed solely of risk-free assets—cash or short-term Treasuries, for example—has, by definition, zero risk. Adding or subtracting risk-free assets to a portfolio should not alter the risk of that portfolio. A risk measure that is unaltered by the addition or subtraction of a risk-free asset is said to obey translation invariance. Both standard deviation and VaR are translation invariant.

Translation invariance is sometimes defined in a slightly different fashion, which can lead to some confusion. By far the most common way of defining risk is in terms of uncertainty about the *change* in the value of an asset. This is the approach we have used up until now, and the approach we will use throughout the rest of this book.

Another approach is to define risk in terms of the uncertainty about the future value of an asset. Pretend we have $100 and we invest it in a security that will either gain or lose $100 tomorrow. After tomorrow, we will either have $0 or $200. If we had added an additional $100 of cash to the initial portfolio, but still only invested $100 in the security, then our potential return distribution is unchanged, we will still either gain $100 or lose $100. By our standard definition, risk is unchanged. That said, the final distribution of our wealth has changed. Because we have an additional $100 of cash, our final distribution of wealth will be either $100 or $300. By the alternative definition of risk, adding cash to our portfolio has changed our risk. There is a certain logic to this alternative definition. If we are worried about going bankrupt (i.e., ending up with $0), then the portfolio with an additional $100 of cash seems less risky. If you define risk in this second way, then translation invariance means that adding $X of a risk-free asset to a portfolio reduces the risk of that portfolio by $X. Not only does this seem counterintuitive to many risk managers, but this new method of defining risk requires us to redefine VaR, standard deviation, and most other risk measures.

Even more unfortunate, Artzner et al. decided to use this second approach in their paper on coherent risk measures. Even they struggled with this alternative definition. Earlier drafts of the paper used the standard approach. We will use the standard approach for the remainder of this book, but it is worth knowing that this second approach exists.

Subadditivity

Subadditivity is basically a fancy way of saying that diversification is good, and a good risk measure should reflect that. Assume our risk measure is a function, f, that takes as its input a random variable representing an asset or portfolio of assets. Higher values of the risk measure are associated with greater risk. If we have two risky portfolios, X and Y, then f is said to be subadditive if

$$f(X + Y) \leq f(X) + f(Y) \tag{4.1}$$

In other words, the risk of the combined portfolio, $(X + Y)$, is less than or equal to the sum of the risks of the separate portfolios.

Variance and standard deviation are subadditive risk measures. VaR, does not always satisfy the requirement of subadditivity. The following example demonstrates a violation of subadditivity for VaR.

SAMPLE PROBLEM

Question:
Imagine a portfolio with two bonds, each with a 4% probability of defaulting. The bonds are currently worth $100 each. If a bond defaults, it is worth $0; if it does not, it is worth $105. Assume that default events are uncorrelated. What is the 95% VaR of each bond separately? What is the 95% VaR of the bond portfolio?

Answer:

For each bond separately, the 95% VaR is −$5. For an individual bond, in (over) 95% of scenarios, the bond increases in value by $5. In the combined portfolio, however, there are three possibilities, with the following probabilities:

P[x]	x
0.16%	−$200
7.68%	−$100
92.16%	$10

As we can see, there are no defaults in $92.16\% = (1 - 4\%)^2$ of the scenarios. In the other 7.84% of scenarios, the loss is greater than or equal to $100. The 95% VaR of the portfolio is therefore $100.

Because the VaR of the combined portfolio is greater than the sum of the VaRs of the separate portfolios, it seems to suggest that there is no diversification benefit. Even though the bonds are uncorrelated, it seems to indicate that holding a portfolio with $100 of each bond is riskier than holding $200 of just one of the bonds. Clearly this is not correct. For this portfolio, VaR is not subadditive.

When assets have payout functions that are discontinuous near the VaR critical level we are likely to have problems with subadditivity. However, if the payout functions of the assets in a portfolio are continuous, then VaR *will be* subadditive. In many settings this is not an onerous assumption. Reality is usually somewhere in between these two extremes, but—at least when we are dealing with large, diversified portfolios—reality tends to be closer to the continuous case. For these portfolios, subadditivity will likely be only a minor issue, if it is an issue at all.

EXPECTED SHORTFALL

One criticism of VaR is that it does not tell us anything about the tail of the distribution. Two portfolios could have the exact same 95% VaR but very different distributions beyond the 95% confidence level.

Beyond VaR, then, we may also want to know how big the loss will be when we have an exceedance event. Using the concept of conditional probability, we can define the expected value of a loss, given an exceedance, as

$$E[L|L \geq VaR_\gamma] = S \tag{4.2}$$

We refer to this conditional expected loss, S, as the expected shortfall. The use of the term expected shortfall is not universal. Many practitioners refer to this statistic as *conditional VaR* (cVaR). For the rest of this book, however, we will use the term *expected shortfall*.

If the expected profit of a fund can be described by a probability density function given by $f(x)$, and VaR is the VaR at the γ confidence level, we can find the expected shortfall as

$$S = -\frac{1}{1-\gamma} \int_{-\infty}^{VaR} xf(x)dx \tag{4.3}$$

As with VaR, risk managers tend to talk about expected shortfall in terms of losses. Just as VaR tends to be positive for reasonable confidence levels for most portfolios, expected shortfall, as we have defined it in Equation 4.3, will also tend to be positive. As with VaR, this convention is not universal, and risk managers should be careful to avoid ambiguity when quoting expected shortfall numbers.

Expected shortfall does answer an important question. What's more, it turns out to be subadditive, thereby avoiding one of the major criticisms of VaR. As our discussion on backtesting suggests, though, because it is concerned with the tail of the distribution, the reliability of our expected shortfall measure may be difficult to gauge.

In addition to being difficult to backtest, expected shortfall is very sensitive to the possibility of extremely unlikely but extremely large losses. In this respect, VaR and expected shortfall are analogous to the mean and median of a distribution. For example, pretend that you are trying to estimate the per capita net worth of people living in the greater Seattle area. You go door to door, asking everybody their net worth. Once you have all the data, you calculate that of the 1 million people in the area, the median net worth is $80,000 and the mean is $100,000. But wait! Bill Gates was out of town, and you forgot to include him in your sample. Now, including Bill Gates will hardly change the median, but it will have a huge impact on the mean. Assuming a net worth of approximately $90 billion, adding Bill Gates to the sample will increase the mean by approximately $90,000, almost doubling it. In a similar way, if we are calculating the one-day 95% VaR and expected shortfall of a portfolio, the difference between including or excluding a 0.10% probability of losing all of our money will not impact the one-day 95% VaR, but will likely have a very meaningful impact on the expected shortfall.

As risk managers, we want to know as much about the tail of the distribution as possible. Expected shortfall tells us something about the tail, but it is potentially unstable and difficult to backtest. VaR does not tell us anything about the shape of the tail, but it is more robust to outliers. As risk managers, it is important to understand these tradeoffs.

SAMPLE PROBLEM

Question:

In a previous example, the probability density function (PDF) of Triangle Asset Management's daily profits could be described by the following piecewise function:

$$p = \frac{1}{10} + \frac{1}{100}\pi \quad \text{for} -10 \leq \pi \leq 0$$

$$p = \frac{1}{10} - \frac{1}{100}\pi \quad \text{for } 0 \leq \pi \leq 10$$

The PDF is also shown in Figure 4.1. We calculated Triangle's one-day 95% VaR as a loss of $(10 - \sqrt{10}) = 6.84$. For the same confidence level and time horizon, what is the expected shortfall?

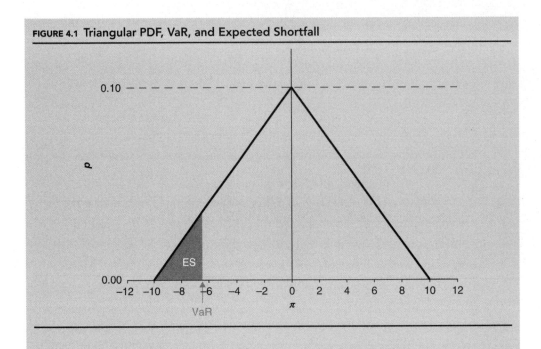

FIGURE 4.1 Triangular PDF, VaR, and Expected Shortfall

Answer:

Because the VaR occurs in the region where $\pi < 0$, we need to utilize only the first half of the function. Using Equation 4.3, we have

$$S = -\frac{1}{0.05} \int_{-10}^{VaR} \pi p\, d\pi$$

$$= -20 \int_{-10}^{VaR} \pi \left(\frac{1}{10} + \frac{1}{100}\pi \right) d\pi$$

$$= \left[-\pi^2 - \frac{1}{15}\pi^3 \right]_{-10}^{VaR}$$

$$= 10 - \frac{2}{3}\sqrt{10}$$

$$= 7.89$$

Thus, the expected shortfall is a loss of 7.89. Intuitively this should seem reasonable. The expected shortfall must be greater than the VaR, 6.84, but less than the maximum loss of 10. Because extreme events are less likely for this PDF (the height of the PDF decreases away from the center), it also makes sense that the expected shortfall is closer to the VaR than it is to the maximum loss.

All of the methods that we have explored up until now for calculating VaR (i.e., delta-normal, historical simulation, Monte Carlo, and Cornish-Fisher) can be used to calculate expected shortfall. Because expected shortfall is so closely related to VaR, the two are often calculated at the same time, using the same underlying model. As we will see in the next section, while this is often the case, sometimes we will use a different model when examining the tail of the distribution.

EXTREME VALUE THEORY

Imagine that your firm owns a security, and that you are asked to predict what the worst daily return for the security will be over the next 20 days. One way you could do this is to gather historical returns for the security, divide the historical data into non-overlapping 20-day periods, and collect the worst return from each period into a new series. For example, if you had 2,000 historical daily returns, then there would be 100 20-day periods, each with a worst day. You could then use this worst-day series to make a prediction for what the worst day will be over the next 20 days. You could even use the distribution of worst days to construct a confidence interval. For example, if the 10th worst day in our 100 worst-day series is −5.80%, you could say that there is a 10% chance that the worst day over the next 20 days will be less than or equal to −5.80%. This is the basic idea behind extreme value theory (EVT), that extreme values (minimums and maximums) have distributions that can be used to make predictions about future events.

There are two basic approaches to sampling historical data for EVT. The approach outlined above, where we divide the historical data into periods of equal length and determine the worst return in each period, is known as the block-maxima approach. Another approach, known as the peaks-over-threshold (POT) approach, is similar, but only makes use of returns that exceed a certain threshold. The POT approach has some nice technical features, which has made it more popular in recent years, but the block-maxima approach is easier to understand. For this reason, we will focus primarily on the block-maxima approach.

Figure 4.2 shows the distribution of minimum daily returns generated in two Monte Carlo simulations. In each case, 40,000 returns were generated and divided into 20-day periods, producing 2,000 minimum returns. In the first simulation, the daily returns were generated by a normal distribution with a mean of 0.00% and a standard deviation of 1.00%. In the second simulation, daily returns were generated using a fat-tailed Student's t-distribution, with the same mean and standard deviation. The median of both distributions is very similar, close to −1.80%, but, as we might expect, the fat-tailed t-distribution generates more extreme minimums. For example, the normal distribution generated only one minimum less than −4.00%, while the t-distribution generated 82.

FIGURE 4.2 Distributions of Extreme Values

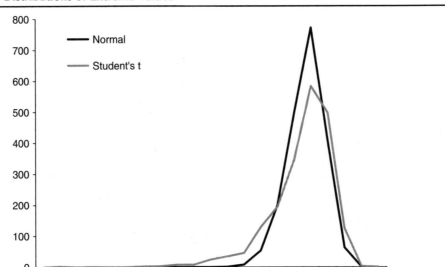

While the two distributions in Figure 4.2 are not exactly the same, they are similar in some ways. One of the most powerful results of EVT has to do with the shape of the distribution of extreme values for a random variable. Provided certain conditions are met, the distribution of extreme values will always follow one of three continuous distributions, either the Fréchet, Gumbel, or Weibull distribution. These three distributions can be considered special cases of a more general distribution, the generalized extreme value distribution. That the distribution of extreme values will follow one of these three distributions is true for most parametric distributions. One note of caution: This result will *not* be true if the distribution of returns is changing over time. The distribution of returns for many financial variables is far from constant, making this an important consideration when using EVT.

Table 4.1 shows the formulas for the probability density function (PDF) and cumulative distribution function (CDF) for each of the three EVT distributions, as well as for the generalized Pareto distribution, which we will come to shortly. Here, s is a scale parameter, k is generally referred to as a shape parameter, and m is a location parameter. The location parameter, m, is often assumed to be zero.

Figures 4.3, 4.4, and 4.5 show examples of the probability density function for each distribution. As specified here these are distributions for maximums, and m is the minimum for the distributions. If we want to model the distribution of minimums, we can either alter the formulas for the distributions, or simply reverse the signs of all of our data. The later approach is consistent with how we defined VaR and expected shortfall, working with losses instead of returns. This is the approach we will adopt for the remainder of this chapter.

TABLE 4.1 Functions and Restrictions of EVT Distributions and the Generalized Pareto Distribution

	PDF	CDF	Restrictions
Fréchet	$\dfrac{k}{s}\left(\dfrac{x-m}{s}\right)^{-1-k} e^{-\left(\frac{x-m}{s}\right)^{-k}}$	$e^{-\left(\frac{x-m}{s}\right)^{-k}}$	$k>0$ $s>0$
Gumbel	$\dfrac{1}{s}e^{-\left(\frac{x-m}{s}\right)-e^{-\left(\frac{x-m}{s}\right)}}$	$e^{-e^{-\left(\frac{x-m}{s}\right)}}$	$s>0$
Weibull	$-\dfrac{k}{s}\left(\dfrac{x-m}{s}\right)^{-1-k} e^{-\left(\frac{x-m}{s}\right)^{-k}}$	$-e^{-\left(\frac{x-m}{s}\right)^{-k}}$	$k<0$ $s>0$
Generalized Pareto	$\dfrac{1}{s}\left(1+\dfrac{k(x-m)}{s}\right)^{-1-1/k}$	$1-\left(1+\dfrac{k(x-m)}{s}\right)^{-1/k}$	$s>0$ $1+kx/s>0$

FIGURE 4.3 Fréchet Probability Density Functions

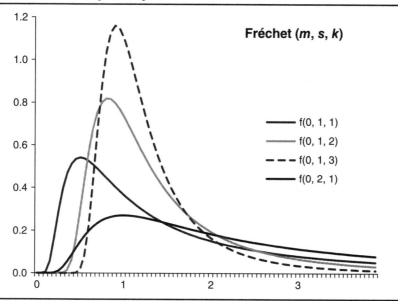

If the underlying data-generating process is fat-tailed, then the distribution of the maximums will follow a Fréchet distribution. This makes the Fréchet distribution a popular choice in many financial risk management applications.

How do we determine which distribution to use and the values of the parameters? For block-maxima data, the most straightforward method is maximum likelihood estimation. (For a review of maximum likelihood estimation see Appendix A.) As an example, in Figure 4.6, 40,000 returns were generated using a Student's t-distribution with a mean of 0.00% and a standard deviation of 1.00%. These were divided into 2,000 non-overlapping 20-day periods, just as in the previous example. The actual distribution in the figure shows

FIGURE 4.4 Gumbel Probability Density Functions

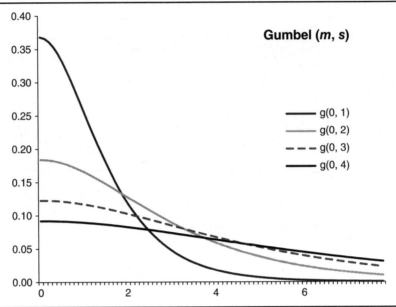

FIGURE 4.5 Weibull Probability Density Functions

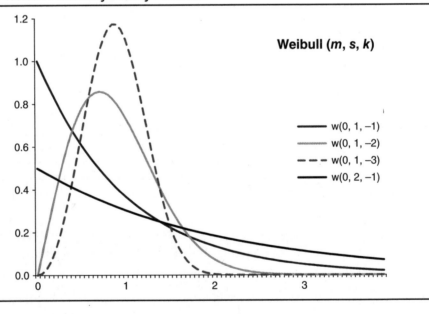

the distribution of the 2,000 minimum points, with their signs reversed. (The distribution looks less smooth than in the previous figure because finer buckets were used.) On top of the actual distribution, we show the best-fitting Fréchet and Weibull distributions. As expected, the Fréchet distribution provides the best fit overall.

FIGURE 4.6 Determining the EVT Distribution

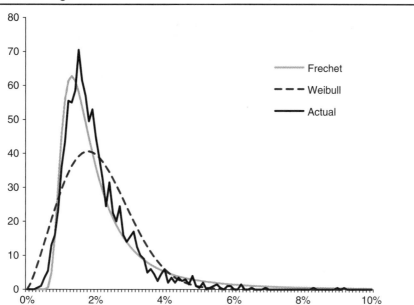

One problem with the block-maxima approach, as specified, is that all of the EVT distributions have a defined minimum. In Figure 4.6, both EVT distributions have a minimum of 0.00%, implying that there is no possibility of a maximum below 0.00% (or, reversing the sign, a minimum above 0.00%). This is a problem because the *t*-distribution has an infinite range. In theory, the minimum in any month could be positive. In practice, the probability is very low, but it can happen.

The POT approach avoids this problem at the outset by considering only the distribution of extremes beyond a certain threshold. This and some other technical features make the POT approach appealing. One drawback of the POT approach is that the parameters of the EVT distribution are usually determined using a relatively complex approach that relies on the fact that, under certain conditions, the EVT distributions will converge to a Generalized Pareto distribution.

SAMPLE PROBLEM

Question:

Based on the 2,000 maxima generated from the *t*-distribution, as described earlier, you have decided to model the maximum loss over the next 20 days using a Fréchet distribution with $m = 0.000$, $s = 0.015$, and $k = 2.368$. What is the probability that the maximum loss will be greater than 7.00%?

Answer:

We can use the CDF of the Fréchet distribution from Table 4.1 to solve this problem.

$$P[L > 0.07] = e^{-\left(\frac{x-m}{s}\right)^{-k}} = e^{-\left(\frac{0.07-0.00}{0.015}\right)^{-2.368}} = 0.9743$$

That is, given our distribution assumption, 97.43% of the distribution is less than 7.00%, meaning 2.57% of the distribution is greater or equal 7.00%. The probability that the maximum loss over the next 20 days will be greater than 7.00% is 2.57%.

Be careful how you interpret the EVT results. In the preceding example, there is a 2.57% chance that the maximum loss over the next 20 days will exceed 7%. It is tempting to believe that there is only a 2.57% chance that a loss in excess of 7% will occur tomorrow. This is not the case. EVT is giving us a conditional probability, $P[L > 7\%|$ max$]$, meaning the probability that the loss is greater than 7%, *given that* tomorrow is a maximum. This is not the same as the unconditional probability, $P[L > 7\%]$. These two concepts are related, though. Mathematically,

$$P[L > 7\%] = P[L > 7\%|\text{max}]P[\text{max}] + P[L > 7\%|\overline{\text{max}}]P[\overline{\text{max}}] \qquad (4.4)$$

where we have used $\overline{\text{max}}$ to denote L *not* being the maximum. In our current example we are using a 20-day window, so the probability that any given day is a maximum is simply 1/20. Using this and the EVT probability, we have

$$P[L > 7\%] = 2.57\%\frac{1}{20} + P[L > 7\%|\overline{\text{max}}]\frac{19}{20} \qquad (4.5)$$

The second conditional probability, $P[L > 7\%|\overline{\text{max}}]$, must be less than or equal to the first conditional probability. This makes Equation 4.5 a weighted average of 2.57% and something less than or equal to 2.57%, so we know the unconditional probability must be less than or equal to 2.57%,

$$P[L > 7\%] \leq 2.57\% \qquad (4.6)$$

If we didn't know anything about the underlying distribution, this is as far as we would be able to go.

A popular approach at this point is to assume a parametric distribution for the non-extreme events. This combined approach can be viewed as describing a mixture distribution. For example, we might use a normal distribution to model the non-extreme values and a Fréchet distribution to model the extreme values.

Continuing with our example, suppose we use a normal distribution and determine that the probability that L is greater than 7%, when L is *not* the maximum, is 0.05%. The unconditional probability would then be 0.17%,

$$P[L > 7\%] = 2.57\%\frac{1}{20} + 0.05\%\frac{19}{20} = 0.13\% + 0.04\% = 0.17\% \tag{4.7}$$

If the parametric distribution does a good job at modeling the nonextreme values and the EVT distribution does a good job at modeling the extreme values, then we may be able to accurately forecast this unconditional probability using this combination approach. This combined approach also allows us to use EVT to forecast VaR and expected shortfall, something we cannot do with EVT alone.

There is a certain logic to EVT. If we are primarily concerned with extreme events, then it makes sense for us to focus on the shape of the distribution of extreme events, rather than trying to approximate the distribution for all returns. But, in the past some proponents of EVT have gone a step further and claimed that this focus allows them to be very certain about extremely rare events. Once we have determined the parameters of our extreme value distribution, it is very easy to calculate the probability of losses at any confidence level. It is not uncommon to see EVT used as the basis of one-day 99.9% or even 99.99% VaR calculations, for example. Recall the discussion on VaR back-testing, though. Unless you have a lot of data and are sure that the data generating process is stable, you are unlikely to be able to make these kinds of claims. This is a fundamental limit in statistics. There is no way to get around it.

The remarkable thing about EVT is that we can determine the distribution of the minimum or maximum even if we don't know the distribution of the underlying data-generating process. It doesn't matter if the data-generating process is a normal distribution, a t-distribution, or some strange distribution that has no name. As long as certain requirements are met, the distribution of the maxima will follow one of the EVT distributions. Proponents of EVT see this as a great advantage, and it is a very remarkable result. But knowing the *type* of distribution is very different from knowing the distribution itself. It's as if we knew that the distribution of returns for a security followed a lognormal distribution, but didn't know the mean or standard deviation. If we know that extreme losses for a security follow a Fréchet distribution, but are highly uncertain about the parameters of the distribution, then we really don't know much.

EVT is potentially a very powerful tool but the math can be very complicated, and it is tempting to gloss over the assumptions, which are critical to a proper implementation. One requirement of EVT that is unlikely to be met in most financial settings is that the underlying data-generation process is constant over time. There are ways to work around this assumption, but this typically leads to more assumptions and more complication.

Though we did not mention it before, the EVT results are only strictly true in the limit, as the frequency of the extreme values approaches zero. In theory, the EVT distributions should describe the distribution of the maxima reasonably well as long as the frequency of the extreme values is sufficiently low. Unfortunately, defining "sufficiently low" is not easy, and EVT can perform poorly in practice for frequencies as low as 5%.

In the next chapter we will talk about stress testing, which is a very different approach to evaluating extreme financial scenarios.

END-OF-CHAPTER QUESTIONS

1. Prove that standard deviation displays positive homogeneity.

2. You are asked to evaluate the risk of a portfolio containing two securities. The first security has an expected shortfall of −$400 (a loss of $400). The second security has an expected shortfall of −$300. What is the minimum (worst-possible) expected shortfall of the portfolio?

3. In the previous chapter, we calculated the VaR for Box Asset Management, which has profits that are described by the following PDF:

$$p = \frac{1}{200} \quad \text{for} -100 \le \pi \le 100$$

What is the one-day 95% expected shortfall of Box Asset Management?

4. The PDF for daily profits at Euler Fund is given by the following equation:

$$f(\pi) = ce^{\pi} \quad -10\% \le \pi \le 10\%$$

where π is the profits and c is a constant. Calculate the one-day 95% expected shortfall for Euler Fund.

5. Which of the following distributions are associated with EVT:
    a) Poisson
    b) Weibull
    c) Fréchet
    d) Clayton
    e) Gumbel

6. ABC stock is currently trading at $100 and has a one-day 95% VaR of $4. What is the one-day 95% VaR of a portfolio that consists of $200 of cash and $800 of ABC?

7. You have created a Monte Carlo simulation to calculate the one-day, 99% VaR of a portfolio containing a large number of options. In your simulation, you generate 1,000 sample one-day returns. The following table contains the 12 worst losses from your simulation. (Here, losses are represented as positive numbers, so 16% is a loss of 16% or a profit of −16%.)

	Loss (%)
1	17%
2	14%
3	14%
4	13%
5	13%
6	12%
7	12%
8	12%
9	12%
10	11%
11	11%
12	11%

What is the one-day 99% VaR? What is the one-day 99% expected shortfall?

8. In the proceeding example, if instead of 17% and 14%, the two worst losses were 27% and 24%, what would the one-day 99% VaR and expected shortfall be? Losses 3 through 12 in the table remain the same.

9. The CEO of your firm wants to know what the worst possible monthly return could be over the coming year. You decide to use extreme value theory to answer this question. Specifically, you decide to use the block-maxima approach using the past eight years of data, as provided in the table below. What do you expect the worst (most negative) monthly return to be in the coming year?

		Year							
		1	**2**	**3**	**4**	**5**	**6**	**7**	**8**
Month	**1**	6%	4%	4%	12%	−1%	−1%	−3%	1%
	2	7%	1%	−3%	2%	−2%	1%	1%	4%
	3	2%	−1%	6%	5%	1%	2%	4%	5%
	4	2%	1%	−5%	-2%	−3%	8%	−4%	3%
	5	−4%	0%	−6%	-2%	−6%	−4%	8%	−10%
	6	1%	−1%	−5%	4%	6%	3%	−15%	6%
	7	−23%	1%	−2%	−14%	−2%	4%	−13%	−7%
	8	−5%	6%	−1%	−7%	−1%	0%	4%	−9%
	9	1%	0%	8%	−5%	9%	−4%	-6%	9%
	10	6%	1%	5%	−3%	0%	3%	7%	−3%
	11	−1%	−2%	0%	−6%	−4%	−4%	1%	−3%
	12	3%	2%	−3%	0%	4%	0%	5%	−3%

5

MARKET RISK: PORTFOLIOS AND CORRELATION

Up until this point, we have been considering the risk of a single security or portfolio in isolation. In this chapter we begin to look at how risk managers model the relationship between different securities.

COVARIANCE

Up until now we have mostly been looking at statistics that summarize one variable. In risk management, we often want to describe the relationship between two or more random variables. For example, is there a relationship between the returns of an equity and the returns of a market index?

Covariance is analogous to variance, but instead of looking at the deviation from the mean of one variable, we are going to look at the relationship between the deviations of two variables. More formally, for two random variables, X and Y, with means μ_X and μ_Y, respectively, we can define the covariance between them as

$$\text{Cov}[X, Y] = \sigma_{XY} = \text{E}[(X - \mu_X)(Y - \mu_Y)] \tag{5.1}$$

As you can see from the definition, variance is just a special case of covariance. Variance is the covariance of a variable with itself.

If X tends to be above μ_X when Y is above μ_Y (both deviations are positive) and X tends to be below μ_X when Y is below μ_Y (both deviations are negative), then the covariance will be positive (a positive number multiplied by a positive number is positive; likewise, for two negative numbers). If the opposite is true and the deviations tend to be of opposite sign, then the covariance will be negative. If the deviations have no discernible relationship, then the covariance will be zero.

We can rewrite Equation 5.1 as

$$\sigma_{XY} = E[XY] - \mu_X \mu_Y$$
$$= E[XY] - E[X]E[Y] \tag{5.2}$$

In the special case where the covariance between X and Y is zero, the expected value of XY is equal to the expected value of X multiplied by the expected value of Y, that is

$$\sigma_{XY} = 0 \Rightarrow E[XY] = E[X]E[Y] \tag{5.3}$$

If the covariance is anything other than zero, then the two sides of this equation cannot be equal.

In order to calculate the covariance between two random variables, X and Y, assuming the means of both variables are known, we can use the following formula:

$$\hat{\sigma}_{XY} = \frac{1}{n} \sum_{i=1}^{n} (x_i - \mu_X)(y_i - \mu_Y) \tag{5.4}$$

As with variance, if the means are unknown and must also be estimated, we replace n with $(n - 1)$, to get

$$\hat{\sigma}_{XY} = \frac{1}{n-1} \sum_{i=1}^{n} (x_i - \hat{\mu}_X)(y_i - \hat{\mu}_Y) \tag{5.5}$$

If we had replaced y_i in these formulas with x_i, calculating the covariance of X with itself, the resulting equations would be the same as the equations for calculating variance in Chapter 2.

CORRELATION

Closely related to the concept of covariance is correlation. To get the correlation of two variables, we simply divide their covariance by their respective standard deviations,

$$\rho_{XY} = \frac{\sigma_{XY}}{\sigma_X \sigma_Y} \tag{5.6}$$

Correlation has the nice property that it varies between -1 and $+1$. If two variables have a correlation of $+1$, then we say they are perfectly correlated. If the ratio of one variable to another is always the same and positive, then the two variables will be perfectly correlated.

If two variables are highly correlated, it is often the case that one variable *causes* the other variable, or that both variables share a common underlying driver. Be careful, as we will see in later chapters, it is very easy for two random variables with no causal link to be highly correlated. *Correlation does not prove causation.* Similarly, if two variables are uncorrelated, it does not necessarily follow that they are unrelated. For example, a random variable that is symmetrical around zero and the square of that variable will have zero correlation.

SAMPLE PROBLEM

Question:

X is a random variable. X has an equal probability of being -1, 0, or $+1$. What is the correlation between X and Y if $Y = X^2$?

Answer:

We have

$$P[X = -1] = P[X = 0] = P[X = 1] = \frac{1}{3}$$

$$Y = X^2$$

First, we calculate the mean of both variables

$$E[X] = \frac{1}{3}(-1) + \frac{1}{3}(0) + \frac{1}{3}(1) = 0$$

$$E[Y] = \frac{1}{3}(-1^2) + \frac{1}{3}(0^2) + \frac{1}{3}(1^2) = \frac{2}{3}$$

The covariance can be found as

$$\sigma_{XY} = E[(X - \mu_X)(Y - \mu_Y)]$$

$$= \frac{1}{3}(-1 - 0)\left(1 - \frac{2}{3}\right) + \frac{1}{3}(0 - 0)\left(0 - \frac{2}{3}\right) + \frac{1}{3}(1 - 0)\left(1 - \frac{2}{3}\right)$$

$$= 0$$

Because the covariance is zero, the correlation is also zero. There is no need to calculate the variances or standard deviations.

In this case, even though X and Y are clearly related (Y is a function of X), the correlation between them is zero. Just because the correlation between two variables is zero, it does not mean they are unrelated.

PORTFOLIO VARIANCE AND HEDGING

If we have a portfolio of securities and we wish to determine the variance of that portfolio, all we need to know is the variance of the underlying securities and their respective correlations.

For example, if we have two securities with random returns X_A and X_B, with means μ_A and μ_B and standard deviations σ_A and σ_B, respectively, we can calculate the variance of X_A plus X_B as follows:

$$\sigma_{A+B}^2 = \sigma_A^2 + \sigma_B^2 + 2\rho_{AB}\sigma_A\sigma_B \tag{5.7}$$

where ρ_{AB} is the correlation between X_A and X_B. The proof of Equation 5.7 is left as an exercise at the end of the chapter. Notice that the last term can either increase or decrease the total variance. Both standard deviations must be positive; therefore, if the correlation is positive, the overall variance will be higher than if the correlation is negative.

Assume the variance of both securities is equal. Defining a new variable, σ, we have $\sigma_A^2 = \sigma_B^2 = \sigma^2$. Equation 5.7 then simplifies to

$$\sigma_{A+B}^2 = 2\sigma^2(1 + \rho_{AB}) \tag{5.8}$$

We know that correlation can vary between -1 and $+1$, so, substituting into our new equation, the portfolio variance must be bound by 0 and $4\sigma^2$. If we take the square root of both sides of the equation, we see that the standard deviation is bound by 0 and 2σ: Intuitively, this should make sense. If, on the one hand, we own one share of an equity with a standard deviation of \$10 and then purchase another share of the *same* equity, then the standard deviation of our two-share portfolio must be \$20. (Trivially, the correlation of a random variable with itself must be one, $\rho_{AB} = 1$.) On the other hand, if we own one share of this equity and then purchase another security that always generates the exact opposite return ($\rho_{AB} = -1$), the portfolio is perfectly balanced. The returns are always zero, which implies a standard deviation of zero.

In the special case where the correlation between the two securities is zero, we can further simplify our equation. Taking the square-root of Equation 5.8, the standard deviation is

$$\rho_{AB} = 0 \Rightarrow \sigma_{A+B} = \sigma\sqrt{2} \tag{5.9}$$

We can extend Equation 5.9 to any number of variables. Given a new random variable, Y, which is the sum of n random variables,

$$Y = \sum_{i=1}^{n} X_i \tag{5.10}$$

the variance of Y is

$$\sigma_Y^2 = \sum_{i=1}^{n}\sum_{j=1}^{n} \rho_{ij}\sigma_i\sigma_j \tag{5.11}$$

In the case where all of the X_i's are uncorrelated and all the standard deviations are equal to σ, Equation 5.11 simplifies to

$$\sigma_Y^2 = \sigma^2 n \tag{5.12}$$

Or, taking the square root of both sides,

$$\sigma_Y = \sigma\sqrt{n} \tag{5.13}$$

This is the famous square-root rule for the addition of uncorrelated random variables. In statistics we often come across collections of random variables that are independent and have the same statistical properties. We term these variables independent and identically distributed (i.i.d.). In risk management we might have a large portfolio of securities, which can be approximated as a collection of i.i.d. variables. This i.i.d. assumption also plays an important role in estimating the uncertainty inherent in statistics derived from sampling, and in the analysis of time series. In each of these situations, we make use of this square-root rule.

Assume Y is a linear combination of X_A and X_B, such that

$$Y = aX_A + bX_B \tag{5.14}$$

Remember that for any random variable, X, and a constant c, $\sigma_{cX} = c\sigma_X$. Using this fact and substituting into Equation 5.7, we have

$$\sigma_Y^2 = a^2\sigma_A^2 + b^2\sigma_B^2 + 2ab\rho_{AB}\sigma_A\sigma_B \tag{5.15}$$

Correlation is central to the problem of hedging. Using the same notation as before, imagine we have $1 of Security A, and we wish to hedge it with h of Security B (if h is positive, we are buying the security; if h is negative, we are shorting the security). We can refer to h as the hedge ratio. We introduce the random variable P for our hedged portfolio. We can easily compute the variance of the hedged portfolio using Equation 5.15. Given

$$P = X_A + hX_B \tag{5.16}$$

The variance of the hedged portfolio is

$$\sigma_P^2 = \sigma_A^2 + h^2\sigma_B^2 + 2h\rho_{AB}\sigma_A\sigma_B \tag{5.17}$$

As risk managers, we might be interested to know what hedge ratio would achieve the portfolio with the least variance. To find this minimum variance hedge ratio, we first take the derivative of our equation for the portfolio variance with respect to h,

$$\frac{\partial \sigma_P^2}{\partial h} = 2h\sigma_B^2 + 2\rho_{AB}\sigma_A\sigma_B \tag{5.18}$$

Setting this equal to zero, we have

$$h^* = -\rho_{AB}\frac{\sigma_A}{\sigma_B} \tag{5.19}$$

You can check that this is indeed a minimum by calculating the second derivative.

Substituting h^* back into our original equation, we see that the smallest variance we can achieve is

$$\min[\sigma_P^2] = \sigma_A^2(1 - \rho_{AB}^2) \tag{5.20}$$

At the extremes, where ρ_{AB} equals -1 or $+1$, we can reduce the portfolio standard deviation to zero by buying or selling the hedge security in proportion to the standard deviations, σ_A/σ_B. In between these two extremes, we will always be left with some positive portfolio variance. This risk that we cannot remove by hedging is referred to as *idiosyncratic risk*.

If the two securities in the portfolio are positively correlated, then selling $\$h$ of Security B will reduce the portfolio's volatility to the minimum possible level. Sell any less, and the portfolio will be underhedged. Sell any more, and the portfolio will be overhedged. In risk management it is possible to have too much of a good thing. A common mistake made by portfolio managers is to overhedge with a low-correlation instrument.

Notice that when the two securities are uncorrelated, when ρ_{AB} equals zero, the optimal hedge ratio is zero. You cannot hedge one security with another security if they are uncorrelated to each other. Adding an uncorrelated security to a portfolio will not decrease its variance.

This last statement is not an argument against diversification. It comes down to the difference between having a larger portfolio and having a portfolio that is the same size but more diversified. If your entire portfolio consists of $\$100$ invested in Security A and you *add* any amount of an uncorrelated Security B to the portfolio, the dollar standard deviation of the portfolio will increase. Alternatively, if Security A and Security B are uncorrelated and have the same standard deviation, then *replacing* some of Security A with Security B will decrease the dollar standard deviation of the portfolio. For example, $\$80$ of Security A plus $\$20$ of Security B will have a lower standard deviation than $\$100$ of Security A, but $\$100$ of Security A *plus* $\$20$ of Security B will have a higher standard deviation—again, assuming Security A and Security B are uncorrelated and have the same standard deviation.

LINEAR REGRESSION (UNIVARIATE)

One of the most popular models in statistics is the linear regression model. Given two constants, α and β, and a random error term, ε, in its simplest form the model posits a relationship between two variables, X and Y, where

$$Y = \alpha + \beta X + \varepsilon \tag{5.21}$$

As specified, X is known as the regressor, or independent variable. Similarly, Y is known as the regressand, or dependent variable. As *dependent* implies, traditionally we think of X

FIGURE 5.1 Linear Regression Example

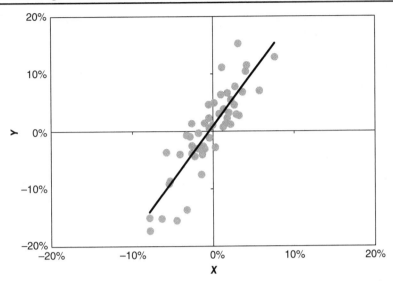

as *causing* Y. This relationship is not necessary and, in practice, especially in finance, this cause-and-effect relationship is either ambiguous or entirely absent. In finance, it is often the case that both X and Y are being driven by a common underlying factor.

The linear-regression relationship is often represented graphically as a plot of Y against X, as shown in Figure 5.1. The solid line in the chart represents the deterministic portion of the linear regression equation, $Y = \alpha + \beta X$. For any particular point, the distance above or below the line is the error for that point, ε.

Because there is only one regressor in Equation 5.21, this model is often referred to as a univariate regression. Mainly, this is to differentiate it from the multivariate model, with more than one regressor, which we will explore later in this chapter. While everybody agrees that a model with two or more regressors is multivariate, not everybody agrees that a model with one regressor is univariate. Even though the univariate model has one regressor, X, it has two variables, X and Y, which leads some people to refer to Equation 5.21 as a bivariate model. The former convention seems to be more common within financial risk management. From here on, we will refer to Equation 5.21 as a univariate model.

In Equation 5.21, α and β are constants. In the univariate model, α is typically referred to as the intercept, and β is often referred to as the slope. β is referred to as the slope because it measures the slope of the solid line when Y is plotted against X. By taking the derivative of Y with respect to X, we can see that β measures this change in Y with respect to X, or slope:

$$\frac{dY}{dX} = \beta \tag{5.22}$$

The final term in Equation 5.21, ε, represents a random error, or residual. The error term allows us to specify a relationship between X and Y even when that relationship is not exact. In effect, the model is incomplete; it is an approximation. Changes in X may drive changes in Y, but there are other variables, which we are not modeling, that also impact Y. These unmodeled variables cause X and Y to deviate from a purely deterministic relationship. That deviation is captured by ε, our residual.

In risk management, this division of the world into two parts, a part that can be explained by the model and a part that cannot, is a common dichotomy. We refer to risk that can be explained by our model as systematic risk, and to the part that cannot be explained by the model as idiosyncratic risk. In our regression model, Y is divided into a systematic component, $\alpha + \beta X$, and an idiosyncratic component, ε.

$$Y = \underbrace{\alpha + \beta X}_{\text{systematic}} + \underbrace{\varepsilon}_{\text{idiosyncratic}} \qquad (5.23)$$

Which component of the overall risk is more important? It depends on what our objective is. As we will see, portfolio managers who wish to hedge certain risks in their portfolios are basically trying to reduce or eliminate systematic risk. Portfolio managers who try to mimic the returns of an index, on the other hand, can be viewed as trying to minimize idiosyncratic risk.

Ordinary Least Squares

The univariate regression model is conceptually simple. In order to uniquely determine the parameters in the model, though, we need to make some assumption about our variables. While relatively simple, these assumptions allow us to derive some very powerful statistical results.

By far the most popular linear regression model is ordinary least squares (OLS). If you have seen a regression before—unless you were told otherwise—it was almost certainly an OLS regression. Because it is so popular, we often refer to OLS regression analysis simply as regression analysis, but there are other types.

The objective of OLS is to explain as much of the variation in Y as possible, based on the constants α and β. This is equivalent to minimizing the role of ε, the error term. More specifically, OLS attempts to minimize the sum of the squared error terms; hence the "least squares."

OLS makes several assumptions about the form of the regression model, which can be summarized as follows:

A1: The relationship between the regressor and the regressand is linear.

A2: $E[\varepsilon|X] = 0$

A3: $Var[\varepsilon \,|\, X] = \sigma^2$

A4: $Cov[\varepsilon_i, \varepsilon_j] = 0$ for all $i \neq j$

A5: $\varepsilon_i \sim N(0, \sigma^2)$ for all i

A6: The regressor is nonstochastic.

We examine each assumption in turn.

The first assumption A1 really just reiterates what Equation 5.21 implies, that we are assuming a linear relationship between X and Y. This assumption is not nearly as restrictive as it sounds. Suppose we suspect that default rates are related to interest rates in the following way,

$$D = \alpha + \beta R^{3/4} + \varepsilon \tag{5.24}$$

Because of the exponent on R, the relationship between D and R is clearly nonlinear. Still, the relationship between D and $R^{3/4}$ *is* linear. Though not necessary, it is perfectly legitimate to substitute X, where $X = R^{3/4}$, into the equation to make this explicit.

As specified, the model implies that the linear relationship should be true for *all* values of D and R. In practice, we often only require that the relationship is linear within a given range. In this example, we don't have to assume that the model is true for negative interest rates or rates over 500%. As long as we can restrict ourselves to a range within which the relationship is linear, this is not a problem. What could be a problem is if the relationship takes one form over most of the range, but changes for extreme but plausible values. In our example, maybe interest rates tend to vary between 0% and 5%; there is a linear relationship between D and $R^{3/4}$ in this range, but beyond 5% the relationship becomes highly nonlinear. As risk managers, these extreme but plausible outcomes are what we are most interested in. We will return to this topic later in the chapter when we discuss stress testing.

Assumption A2 states that for any realization of X, the expected value of ε is zero. From a very practical standpoint, this assumption resolves any ambiguity between α and ε. Imagine ε could be modeled as

$$\varepsilon = \alpha' + \varepsilon' \tag{5.25}$$

where α' is a nonzero constant and ε' is mean zero. By substituting this equation into Equation 5.21, we get

$$Y = (\alpha + \alpha') + \beta X + \varepsilon' \qquad (5.26)$$

In practice, there is no way to differentiate between α and α', and it is the combined term, $(\alpha + \alpha')$, that is our constant.

Using assumption A2 and taking the expectation of both sides of Equation 5.21, we arrive at our first result for the OLS model, namely

$$E[Y|X] = \alpha + \beta X \qquad (5.27)$$

Given X, the expected value of Y is fully determined by α and β. In other words, the model provides a very simple linear and unbiased estimator of Y.

Assumption A2 also implies that the error term is independent of X. We can express this as

$$\mathrm{Cov}[X, \varepsilon] = 0 \qquad (5.28)$$

This result will prove useful in deriving other properties of the OLS model.

Assumption A3 states that the variance of the error term is constant. This property of constant variance is known as homoscedasticity, in contrast to heteroscedasticity, where the variance changes (as in the GARCH model in Chapter 2). This assumption means that the variance of the error term does not change over time or depending on the level of the regressor. In finance, many models that appear to be linear often violate this assumption. For example, some interest rate models have a linear form, but specify an error term that varies in relation to the level of interest rates.

Assumption A4 states that the error terms for various data points should be uncorrelated with each other. As we will also see in the next chapter, this assumption is often violated in time-series models, where today's error is correlated with the previous day's error. Assumptions A3 and A4 are often combined. A random variable that has constant variance and is uncorrelated with itself is termed *spherical*. OLS assumes spherical errors.

Combining assumptions A2 and A3 allows us to derive a very useful relationship, which is widely used in finance. Given X and Y in Equation 5.21, we have

$$\beta = \frac{\mathrm{Cov}[X, Y]}{\sigma_X^2} = \rho_{XY} \frac{\sigma_Y}{\sigma_X} \qquad (5.29)$$

where σ_X and σ_Y are the standard deviation of X and Y, respectively, and ρ_{XY} is the correlation between the two. The proof is left as an exercise at the end of the chapter.

One of the most popular uses of regression analysis in finance is to regress stock returns against market index returns. As specified in Equation 5.21, index returns are represented by X, and stock returns by Y. This regression is so popular that we frequently speak of a stock's beta, which is simply β from the regression equation. While there are other ways to calculate a stock's beta, the functional form given in Equation 5.29 is extremely popular. This is because it relates two values, σ_X and σ_Y, with which traders and risk managers are often familiar, to two other terms, ρ_{XY} and β, for which market participants usually have some intuition.

OPTIMAL HEDGING REVISITED

Earlier in the chapter, we determined that the optimal hedge ratio for two assets, A and B, was given by

$$h^* = -\rho_{AB}\frac{\sigma_A}{\sigma_B}$$

where σ_A is the standard deviation of the returns of asset A, σ_B is the standard deviation of the returns of asset B, and ρ_{AB} is the correlation between the returns of A and B.

Although we didn't know it at the time, our optimal hedge ratio is simply the negative of our slope from the following regression:

$$r_A = \alpha + \beta r_B + \varepsilon$$
$$h^* = -\beta$$

(5.30)

In other words, in order to minimize the variance of the portfolio's returns, r_A, we need to short β units of asset B. This completely negates the βr_B term in the portfolio, leaving us with a constant, α, and the idiosyncratic residual, ε, which cannot be hedged,

$$r_A - \beta r_B = \alpha + \varepsilon$$

This is the minimum variance portfolio.

As an example, pretend we are monitoring a portfolio with \$100 million worth of assets, and the portfolio manager wishes to hedge the portfolio's exposure to fluctuations in the price of oil. We perform an OLS analysis and obtain the following regression equation, where r_P is the portfolio's percentage return, and r_{oil} is the return associated with the price of oil:

$$r_P = 0.01 + 0.43 r_{oil} + \varepsilon$$

This tells us that for every unit of the portfolio, the optimal hedge would be to short 0.43 units of oil. For the entire \$100 million portfolio, the hedge would be −\$43 million of oil.

Assumption A5 states that the error terms in the model should be normally distributed. Many of the results of the OLS model are true, regardless of this assumption. This assumption is most useful when it comes to defining confidence levels for the model parameters.

Finally, assumption A6 assumes that the regressor is nonstochastic, or nonrandom. In science, the regressor is often carefully controlled by an experimenter. A researcher might vary the amount of a drug given to mice, to determine the impact of the drug on their weight. One mouse gets one unit of the drug each day, the next gets two, the next three, and so on. Afterward, the regressand, the weight of each mouse, is measured. Ignoring measurement errors, the amount of the drug given to the mice is nonstochastic. The experiment could be replicated, with another researcher providing the exact same dosages as in the initial experiment. Unfortunately, the ability to carefully control the independent variable and repeat experiments is rare in finance. More often than not, all of the variables of interest are random. Take, for example, the regression of stock returns on index returns. As the model is specified, we are basically stating that the index's returns *cause* the stock's returns. In reality, both the index's returns and the stock's returns are random, determined by a number of factors, some of which they might have in common. At some point, the discussion around assumption A6 tends to become deeply philosophical. From a practical standpoint, most of the results of OLS hold true, regardless of assumption A6. In many cases the conclusion needs to be modified only slightly.

Estimating the Parameters

Now that we understand the assumptions behind the model, how do we go about determining the constants, α and β? For OLS, we need to find the combination of constants that minimizes the squared errors. In other words, given a sample of regressands, $y_1, y_2, \ldots, y_n$, and a set of corresponding regressors, $x_1, x_2, \ldots, x_3$, we want to minimize the sum

$$\text{RSS} = \sum_{i=1}^{n} \varepsilon_i^2 = \sum_{i=1}^{n} (y_i - \alpha - \beta x_i)^2 \tag{5.31}$$

where RSS is the commonly used acronym for the residual sum of squares. (*Sum of squared residuals* would probably be a more accurate description, but RSS is the convention.) In order to minimize this sum, we first take its derivative with respect to α and β separately. We set the derivatives to zero and solve the resulting simultaneous equations. The result is the equations for the OLS parameters,

$$\alpha = \mu_Y - \beta \mu_X$$

$$\beta = \frac{\sum_{i=1}^{n} x_i y_i - n \mu_Y \mu_X}{\sum_{i=1}^{n} x_i^2 - n \mu_X^2} \tag{5.32}$$

where μ_X and μ_Y are the sample mean of X and Y, respectively. The proof is left for an exercise at the end of the chapter.

Evaluating the Regression

Unlike a controlled laboratory experiment, the real world is a very noisy and complicated place. In finance it is rare that a simple univariate regression model is going to completely explain a large data set. In many cases, the data are so noisy that we must ask ourselves if the model is explaining anything at all. Even when a relationship appears to exist, we are likely to want some quantitative measure of just how strong that relationship is.

Probably the most popular statistic for describing linear regressions is the coefficient of determination, commonly known as R-squared, or just R^2. R^2 is often described as the goodness of fit of the linear regression. At one end of the spectrum, when R^2 equals one, the regression model completely explains the data; all the residuals are zero, and the residual sum of squares is zero. At the other end of the spectrum, when R^2 equals zero, the model does not explain any variation in the observed data. In other words, Y does not vary with X, and β is zero.

To calculate the coefficient of determination, we need to define two additional terms: the total sum of squares (TSS) and the explained sum of squares (ESS). They are defined as

$$\text{TSS} = \sum_{i=1}^{n} (y_i - \mu_Y)^2$$

$$\text{ESS} = \sum_{i=1}^{n} (\widehat{y}_i - \mu_Y)^2 = \sum_{i=1}^{n} (\alpha + \beta x_i - \mu_Y)^2$$

(5.33)

Here, $\widehat{y}_i$ is the expected value of Y, given x_i. As before, μ_Y is the sample mean of Y.

These two sums are related to the previously encountered residual sum of squares, as

$$\text{TSS} = \text{ESS} + \text{RSS} \tag{5.34}$$

In other words, the total variation in our regressand, TSS, can be broken down into two components: ESS, which is the part the model can explain, and RSS, which is the part the model cannot. These sums can be used to compute R^2:

$$R^2 = \frac{\text{ESS}}{\text{TSS}} = 1 - \frac{\text{RSS}}{\text{TSS}} \tag{5.35}$$

As promised, when RSS is zero (i.e., there are no residual errors), R^2 is one. Looked at another way, when ESS is zero (when RSS is equal to TSS), R^2 is also zero. It turns out that for the univariate linear regression model, R^2 is also equal to the correlation between X

and Y, squared. If X and Y are perfectly correlated ($\rho_{xy} = 1$) or perfectly negatively correlated ($\rho_{xy} = -1$), then R^2 will equal one.

Estimates of the regression parameters are just like any parameter estimates, and subject to hypothesis testing. In regression analysis, the most common null hypothesis is that the slope parameter, β, is zero. If β is zero, then the regression model does not explain any variation in the regressand.

In finance, we often want to know if α is significantly different from zero, but for different reasons. In modern finance, *alpha* has become synonymous with the ability of a portfolio manager to generate excess returns. This is because, in a regression equation that models the returns of a portfolio manager, after we remove all the randomness, ε, and the influence of the explanatory variable, X, if α is still positive, then it suggests that the portfolio manager is producing positive excess returns, something that should be very difficult in efficient markets. Of course, it's not just enough that α is positive; we require that the α be positive *and* statistically significant.

In order to test the significance of the regression parameters, we first need to calculate the variance of α and β, which we can obtain from the following formulas:

$$\hat{\sigma}_\alpha^2 = \frac{\sum_{i=1}^n x_i^2}{n \sum_{i=1}^n (x_i - \mu_X)^2} \hat{\sigma}_\varepsilon^2$$

$$\hat{\sigma}_\beta^2 = \frac{\hat{\sigma}_\varepsilon^2}{\sum_{i=1}^n (x_i - \mu_X)^2} \qquad (5.36)$$

$$\hat{\sigma}_\varepsilon^2 = \frac{\sum_{i=1}^n \varepsilon_i^2}{n - 2}$$

The last formula gives the variance of the error term, ε, which is simply the RSS divided by the degrees of freedom for the regression. Using the equations for the variance of our estimators, we can then form an appropriate t-statistic. For example, for β we would have

$$\frac{\hat{\beta} - \beta}{\hat{\sigma}_\beta} \sim t_{n-2} \qquad (5.37)$$

Here, we are comparing our estimated value of beta from the regression analysis, $\hat{\beta}$, to the ideal or hypothetical value of beta from our null hypothesis, β. The most common null hypothesis when testing regression parameters is that the parameters are equal to zero. More often than not, we do not care if the parameters are significantly greater than or less than zero; we just care that they are significantly different. Because of this, rather than using the standard t-statistics, as in Equation 5.37, some practitioners report the absolute value of the t-statistic. Some software packages also follow this convention.

SAMPLE PROBLEM

Question:

As a risk manager and expert on statistics, you are asked to evaluate the performance of a long/short equity portfolio manager. You are given a data set containing 10 years of monthly returns. You regress the log returns of the portfolio manager against the log returns of a market index.

$$r_{portfolio\_manager} = \alpha + \beta r_{market} + \varepsilon$$

Assume both series are normally distributed and homoscedastic. From this analysis, you obtain the following regression results:

	Constant	Beta
Value	1.13%	20.39%
Standard deviation	0.48%	9.71%
R^2	8.11%	

What can we say about the performance of the portfolio manager?

Answer:

The R^2 for the regression is low. Only 8.11% of the variation in the portfolio manager's returns can be explained by the constant, beta, and variation in the market returns. The rest is idiosyncratic risk, which is unexplained by the model.

That said, both the constant and the beta are statistically significant (i.e., they are statistically different from zero). We can get the t-statistic by dividing the value of the coefficient by its standard deviation. For the constant, we have:

$$\frac{\hat{\alpha} - \alpha}{\hat{\sigma}_\alpha} = \frac{1.13\% - 0\%}{0.48\%} = 2.36$$

Similarly, for beta we have a t-statistic of 2.10. Using a statistical package, we calculate the corresponding probability associated with each t-statistic. This should be a two-tailed test with 118 degrees of freedom (10 years × 12 months per year − 2 parameters). We can reject the hypothesis that the constant and slope are zero at the 2% level and the 4% level, respectively. In other words, there seems to be a significant market component to the fund manager's return, but the manager also appears to be generating statistically significant excess returns.

In the preceding example, both regression parameters were statistically significant, even though the R^2 was fairly modest. This result is surprising for some people who are new to finance. Many of us first encounter regression analysis in the sciences. In a scientific experiment where conditions can be precisely controlled, it is not unusual to see R^2 above

90%. In finance, more often than not, our models can only explain a small part of the variation in the dependent variable, the error term dominates, and R^2 is much lower. That β can be statistically significant even with a low R^2 may seem surprising, but in finance this is often the case.

LINEAR REGRESSION (MULTIVARIATE)

Univariate regression models are extremely common in finance and risk management, but sometimes we require a slightly more complicated model. In these cases, we might use a multivariate regression model. The basic idea is the same, but instead of one regressand and one regressor, we have one regressand and multiple regressors. Our basic equation will look something like

$$Y = \beta_1 + \beta_2 X_2 + \beta_3 X_3 + \ldots + \beta_n X_n \tag{5.38}$$

Notice that rather than denoting the first constant with α, we chose to go with β_1. This is the more common convention in multivariate regression. To make the equation even more regular, we can assume that there is an X_1, which, unlike the other X's, is constant and always equal to one. This convention allows us to easily express a set of observations in matrix form. For t observations and n regressands, we can write

$$\begin{bmatrix} y_1 \\ y_2 \\ \vdots \\ y_t \end{bmatrix} = \begin{bmatrix} x_{11} & x_{12} & \cdots & x_{1n} \\ x_{21} & x_{22} & \cdots & x_{2n} \\ \vdots & \vdots & \ddots & \vdots \\ x_{t1} & x_{t2} & \cdots & x_{tn} \end{bmatrix} \begin{bmatrix} \beta_1 \\ \beta_2 \\ \vdots \\ \beta_n \end{bmatrix} + \begin{bmatrix} \varepsilon_1 \\ \varepsilon_2 \\ \vdots \\ \varepsilon_t \end{bmatrix} \tag{5.39}$$

where the first column of the **X** matrix—$x_{11}, x_{21}, \ldots, x_{t1}$—is understood to consist entirely of ones. The entire equation can be written more succinctly as

$$\mathbf{Y} = \mathbf{X}\boldsymbol{\beta} + \boldsymbol{\varepsilon} \tag{5.40}$$

where, we have used bold letters to denote matrices.

Multicollinearity

In order to determine the parameters of the multivariate regression, we again turn to our OLS assumptions. In the multivariate case, the assumptions are the same as before, but with one addition. In the multivariate case, we require that all of the independent variables be linearly independent of each other. We say that the independent variables must lack multicollinearity:

A7: The independent variables have no multicollinearity.

To say that the independent variables lack multicollinearity means that it is impossible to express one of the independent variables as a linear combination of the others.

This additional assumption is required to remove ambiguity. To see why this is the case, imagine that we attempt a regression with two independent variables where the second independent variable, X_3, can be expressed as a linear function of the first independent variable, X_2, as follows,

$$Y = \beta_1 + \beta_2 X_2 + \beta_3 X_3 + \varepsilon_1$$
$$X_3 = \lambda_1 + \lambda_2 X_2 + \varepsilon_2$$

(5.41)

If we substitute the second line of Equation 5.41 into the first, we get

$$Y = (\beta_1 + \beta_3 \lambda_1) + (\beta_2 + \beta_3 \lambda_2)X_2 + (\beta_3 \varepsilon_2 + \varepsilon_1)$$
$$= \beta_4 + \beta_5 X_2 + \varepsilon_3$$

(5.42)

In the second line, we have simplified by introducing new constants and a new error term. We have replaced $(\beta_1 + \beta_3 \lambda_1)$ with β_4, replaced $(\beta_2 + \beta_3 \lambda_2)$ with β_5, and replaced $(\beta_3 \varepsilon_2 + \varepsilon_1)$ with ε_3. β_5 can be uniquely determined in a univariate regression, but there is an infinite number of combinations of β_2, β_3, and λ_2 that we could choose to equal β_5. If $\beta_5 = 10$, any of the following combinations would work:

$$\beta_2 = 10, \beta_3 = 0, \lambda_2 = 100,$$
$$\beta_2 = 0, \beta_3 = 10, \lambda_2 = 1,$$
$$\beta_2 = 500, \beta_3 = -49, \lambda_2 = 10,$$

(5.43)

In other words, β_2 and β_3 are ambiguous in the initial equation. This ambiguity is why we want to avoid multicollinearity.

Even in the presence of multicollinearity, the regression model still works in a sense. In the preceding example, even though β_2 and β_3 are ambiguous, any combination where $(\beta_2 + \beta_3 \lambda_2)$ equals β_5 will produce the same value of Y for a given set of X's. If our only objective is to predict Y, then the regression model still works. The problem is that the value of the parameters will be unstable. A slightly different data set can cause wild swings in the value of the parameter estimates, and may even flip the signs of the parameters. A variable that we expect to be positively correlated with the regressand may end up with a large negative beta. This makes interpreting the model difficult. Parameter instability is often a sign of multicollinearity.

There is no well-accepted procedure for dealing with multicollinearity. Often, the easiest course of action is simply to eliminate a variable from the regression. While easy, this is not always satisfactory.

Another possibility is to transform the variables, to create uncorrelated variables out of linear combinations of the existing variables. In the previous example, even though X_3 is correlated with X_2, $X_3 - \lambda_2 X_2$ is uncorrelated with X_2.

$$X_3 - \lambda_2 X_2 = \lambda_1 + \varepsilon_3$$
$$\text{Cov}[X_2, X_3 - \lambda_2 X_2] = \text{Cov}[X_2, \lambda_1 + \varepsilon_3] = \text{Cov}[X_2, \varepsilon_3] = 0$$

(5.44)

One potential problem with this approach is that a particular linear combination of variables may be difficult to interpret. If we are lucky, a linear combination of variables will have a simple economic interpretation. For example, if X_2 and X_3 are two equity indexes, then their difference might correspond to a familiar spread. Similarly, if the two variables are interest rates, their difference might bear some relation to the shape of the yield curve. Other linear combinations might be difficult to interpret, and if the relationship is not readily identifiable, then it may be more likely to be unstable or spurious.

Global financial markets are becoming increasingly integrated. More now than ever before, multicollinearity is a problem that risk managers need to be aware of.

Estimating the Parameters

Assuming our variables meet all of the OLS assumptions, how do we go about estimating the parameters of our multivariate model? The math is a bit more complicated, but the process is the same as in the univariate case. Using our regression equation, we calculate the residual sum of squares and seek to minimize its value through the choice of our parameters. The result is our OLS estimator for $\boldsymbol{\beta}$, $\hat{\boldsymbol{\beta}}$, such that

$$\hat{\boldsymbol{\beta}} = (\mathbf{X}'\mathbf{X})^{-1}\mathbf{X}'\mathbf{Y}$$

(5.45)

Where we had two parameters in the univariate case, now we have a vector of n parameters, which define our regression equation.

Given the OLS assumptions, $\hat{\boldsymbol{\beta}}$ is the best linear unbiased estimator of $\boldsymbol{\beta}$. (Technically, for this result, we don't require assumption A6, that the regressors are nonstochastic.) It is the "best" in the sense that it minimizes the residual sum of squares. This result is known as the Gauss-Markov theorem.

Evaluating the Regression

Just as with the univariate model, once we have calculated the parameters of our multivariate model, we need to be able to evaluate how well the model explains the data.

We can use the same process that we used in the univariate case to calculate R^2 for the multivariate regression. All of the necessary sums, RSS, ESS, and TSS, can be calculated without further complication. As in the univariate case, in the multivariate model, R^2 varies between zero and one and indicates how much of the dependent variable is being explained by the model. One problem in the multivariate setting is that R^2 tends to increase as we add independent variables to our regression. In fact, adding variables to a regression can never decrease the R^2. At worst, R^2 stays the same. This might seem to suggest that adding variables to a regression is always a good thing, even if they have little or no explanatory power. In practice, however, we often prefer simpler models, models with fewer variables. This principle is known *parsimony*. If we do prefer simpler models, then there should be some penalty for adding variables to a regression. An attempt to quantify this preference is the adjusted R^2, which is often denoted by $\overline{R}^2$, and defined as

$$\overline{R}^2 = 1 - (1 - R^2)\frac{t-1}{t-n} \tag{5.46}$$

where t is the number of sample points and n is the number of regressors, including the constant term. While there is clearly a penalty for adding independent variables and increasing n, one odd thing about $\overline{R}^2$ is that the value can turn negative in certain situations.

Just as with the univariate model, we can calculate the variance of the error term. Given t data points and n regressors, the variance of the error term is

$$\hat{\sigma}_\varepsilon^2 = \frac{\sum_{i=1}^{t} \varepsilon_i^2}{t-n} \tag{5.47}$$

The variance of the ith estimator is then:

$$\hat{\sigma}_i^2 = \hat{\sigma}_\varepsilon^2 [(\mathbf{X'X})^{-1}]_{i,i} \tag{5.48}$$

where the final term on the right-hand side is the ith diagonal element of the matrix $(\mathbf{X'X})^{-1}$. We can then use this to form an appropriate t-statistic, with $(t - n)$ degrees of freedom:

$$\frac{\hat{\beta}_i - \beta_i}{\hat{\sigma}_i} \sim t_{t-n} \tag{5.49}$$

Instead of just testing one parameter, we can actually test the significance of all of the parameters, excluding the constant, using what is known as an F-test. The F-statistic can be calculated using R^2,

$$\frac{R^2/(n-1)}{(1-R^2)/(t-n)} \sim F_{n-1,t-n} \tag{5.50}$$

As the name implies, the F-statistic follows an F-distribution with $(n-1)$ and $(t-n)$ degrees of freedom. If the R^2 is zero, the F-statistic will be zero as well.

Table 5.1 shows 5% and 10% critical values for the F-distribution for various values of n and t, where the appropriate degrees of freedom are $(n-1)$ and $(t-n)$. For a univariate regression, $n = 2$, with a large number of data points, a good rule of thumb is that values over 4.00 will be significant at the 5% level.

TABLE 5.1 *F*-Distribution Critical Values

n	*t*	5%	10%
2	20	4.41	3.01
2	50	4.04	2.81
2	100	3.94	2.76
2	1,000	3.85	2.71
4	20	3.24	2.46
4	50	2.81	2.21
4	100	2.70	2.14
4	1,000	2.61	2.09

STRESS TESTING

In risk management, stress testing assesses the likely impact of an extreme but plausible scenario on a portfolio. There is no universally accepted method for performing stress tests. One popular approach, which we consider here, is based on regression analysis.

The first step in stress testing is defining a scenario. Scenarios can be either ad hoc or based on a historical episode. An ad hoc scenario might assume that equity markets decline 20% or that interest rates jump 3%, for example. A historical scenario might examine the Russian debt crisis of 1998 or the Asian currency crisis of 1997. Black Monday, the equity market crash of 1987, is probably one of the most popular scenarios for historical stress tests. For both the ad hoc and the historical approaches, we want to quantify our scenario by specifying the returns of a few key instruments, or factors. For the 3% jump in interest rates, we might specify that 10-year U.S. Treasury rates increase 1%, BBB credit spreads increase 2%, and the Standard & Poor's (S&P) 500 index decreases 10%. In the Black Monday scenario, we might choose to focus on the change in the Dow Jones Industrial Average, the price of gold, and the London Interbank Offered Rate (LIBOR). We should be careful that the instruments defining our scenario are not highly correlated in order to avoid issues with multicollinearity.

The second step, is to determine how all other underlying financial instruments react, given our scenario. In order to do this, we construct multivariate regressions. We regress the returns of each underlying financial instrument against the returns of the instruments that define our scenario. What might seem strange is that, even in the case of the historical scenarios, we typically use recent returns in our regression. In the case of the historical scenarios, why don't we just use the actual returns from that period? The reason we use current returns and not returns from the historical episode is partly practical. Consider Black Monday, 1987. Credit default swaps didn't exist in 1987. The euro, the world's second largest currency, didn't exist. Many of today's largest companies, including Google (IPO in 2004) and ExxonMobil (Exxon and Mobil did not merge until 1999), didn't exist. If our current portfolio holds any of these securities and we tried to use actual returns from the stress period, we would have no data to use for those securities. Even if we did have historical returns for all of the securities in our portfolio, would we want to use them? The world has changed significantly over the past 30 years. Companies and relationships between companies are likely to be very different now than they were 30 years ago. In most cases, it makes more sense to base our stress test on current market data.

So why do we choose a specific historical episode in the first place for some of our scenarios? It's not because we expect that event to repeat exactly, in every detail, but because we expect something similar could happen again. As Mark Twain was supposed to have said, "History does not repeat itself, but it often rhymes."

In the last step, after we have defined the scenario and generated the returns for all of the underlying financial instruments, we price any options or other derivatives. This last step is important. While using delta approximations might have been acceptable for calculating VaR statistics at one point in time, it should never have been acceptable for stress testing. By definition, stress testing involves extreme events, so approximations that work for small returns could easily lead to a significant underestimation of risk.

As an example of how a stress test might work in practice, let's imagine a scenario that we'll call Simple Oil Crisis. In this scenario, crude oil prices increase 20% and the Standard & Poor's 500 index (SPX) decreases by 10%. Imagine that our portfolio consists solely of $100 worth of shares in ExxonMobil (XOM). To see how it reacts, we would construct the following regression:

$$R_{xom} = \beta_1 + \beta_2 R_{oil} + \beta_3 R_{spx} + \varepsilon \tag{5.51}$$

using daily returns from the past year. We'll assume that R_{oil} and R_{spx} are uncorrelated, so there are no issues with multicollinearity. Assume that the ordinary least squares (OLS) regression produces the following equation describing ExxonMobil's returns:

$$R_{xom} = 0.0000 + 0.0899 R_{oil} + 0.7727 R_{spx} + \varepsilon \tag{5.52}$$

Based on this equation, we expect ExxonMobil to return −5.93% in our stress scenario,

$$E[R_{xom}|stress] = 0.0000 + 0.0899 \times 0.20 + 0.7727 \times (-0.10)$$

$$= -0.0593 \tag{5.53}$$

Given our starting value of $100, we would expect to lose $5.93 in this scenario. To evaluate the expected return of a portfolio with multiple securities, we could proceed stepwise, evaluating each security in turn and adding up the gains or losses. Alternatively, we could calculate the backcast dollar return series for the entire portfolio and use this series in our regression analysis to calculate the expected portfolio return directly.

The OLS model assumes that the linear relationship between the regressand and regressors is true over the entire range being considered. This assumption could be problematic if the relationship takes one form over most of the range, but changes for extreme but plausible values. In other words, if the relationship between securities for small moves and for big moves is very different, then our regression analysis might lead us astray. One possible remedy for this problem is to place more weight on extreme returns using a weighted least squares regression (WLS). This approach may help, but it won't entirely eliminate the problem. In the end, there will always be considerable uncertainty around extreme events.

At the start of this section we stated that stress scenarios describe extreme but plausible scenarios. Traditionally the precise probability of a stress scenario occurring is not specified. As we have seen before, assigning a probability to an extremely rare event is not generally recommended, so this is a logical procedure to follow. Still, this leaves wide open what we mean when we say a stress scenario is plausible. That the stress scenario should be extreme is also wide open to interpretation. The benefit of stress testing is that it is extremely simple and transparent. The clear downside is that developing stress scenarios is typically more art than science.

DELTA-NORMAL MODEL

In Chapter 3, we introduced the delta-normal model for one security. The delta-normal model assumes that the log returns for all underlying securities are normally distributed, and that the returns of any derivatives can be approximated based on their delta-adjusted exposure. When applied to portfolios, the delta-normal model assumes that the relationship between all underlying securities can be explained in terms of correlation or covariance. Starting with Equation 5.11 and using our definitions of covariance and variance, we can show that for a portfolio of n securities, each with weight w_i, for $i = 1, 2, \dots, n$, the portfolio variance is

$$\sigma_p^2 = \sum_i^n \sum_j^n w_i w_j \sigma_{ij} \qquad (5.54)$$

Here, σ_{ij} is the covariance between securities i and j. When i and j are equal, the covariance term is the covariance of the security with itself, which, by definition, is the variance of the security. You should verify that for $n = 2$, Equation 5.54 is equivalent to Equation 5.15.

It is often easier to write Equation 5.54 in matrix form. Given an $n \times 1$ vector of weights, **w**, and an $n \times n$ covariance matrix, $\mathbf{\Sigma}$, the portfolio variance is

$$\sigma_p^2 = \mathbf{w}'\mathbf{\Sigma}\mathbf{w} \qquad (5.55)$$

To estimate the VaR for a portfolio of securities using the delta-normal model, we simply calculate the standard deviation using Equation 5.54 or Equation 5.55, and multiply by the appropriate number of standard deviations to get the desired confidence level. To get the standard deviation, all we need is the covariances of all the underlying securities (the entries in Σ), and the corresponding exposures or delta-adjusted exposures for each security (the entries in $\mathbf{w}$).

As was the case for one security, the delta-normal model for portfolios has the advantage of being simple to understand and very easy to compute. Even with multiple securities, this is still a model that can be implemented in a spreadsheet.

We already discussed some disadvantages to the delta-normal model when modeling one security. In addition to those disadvantages, there are now two additional problems. The first is that the number of nontrivial entries in the covariance matrix grows rapidly as the size of the matrix increases. For n securities, there are $n(n + 1)/2$ nontrivial covariances to calculate. (The covariance matrix is symmetric, so half of the non-diagonal elements are duplicates.) For example, for $n = 2$, there are just three unique values: the variance of each security and the covariance between them. For 100 securities, though, there are 5,050 unique values to calculate. Calculating 5,050 covariances is not difficult from a computational standpoint. The problem is that we will rarely have enough data to estimate this many parameters accurately. If we had 250 returns each for 100 securities, we would have approximately five data points per nontrivial entry in the covariance matrix.

The second problem is that correlation only describes the average relationship between two random variables. If the degree of association between two financial variables is higher when returns are negative and lower when returns are positive, this can have a significant impact on risk. Unfortunately, correlation cannot help us detect this kind of asymmetry. In the next chapter, we will explore methods that can directly model this type of behavior.

The problem of large covariance matrices and the shortcomings of covariance as a description of the relationship between two random variables are not unique to the delta-normal model. These are potential issues for any model based on a covariance matrix. As was the case with one security, the shortcomings of the delta-normal model are more obvious because the model is so simple. As mentioned before, the delta-model is no longer widely used in practice.

CHOLESKY DECOMPOSITION AND MONTE CARLO SIMULATIONS

In risk management, it is often useful to generate simulations in which we can specify the covariance between different variables. Imagine that we wanted to create a Monte Carlo simulation of a portfolio containing N stocks. The variance of the portfolio will be a function of the variance of each of the stocks, the position sizes, and the covariances between the stocks.

Imagine that we have n random variables, X_1, X_2, ..., X_n, representing the returns of different stocks. In order to describe the relationships between each of the variables, we could form an $n \times n$ covariance matrix, where each element, σ_{ij}, corresponds to the covariance between the ith and jth random variables:

$$\Sigma = \begin{bmatrix} \sigma_{11} & \sigma_{12} & \cdots & \sigma_{1n} \\ \sigma_{21} & \sigma_{22} & \cdots & \sigma_{2n} \\ \vdots & \vdots & \ddots & \vdots \\ \sigma_{n1} & \sigma_{n2} & \cdots & \sigma_{nn} \end{bmatrix} \tag{5.56}$$

Each of the elements along the main diagonal represents the covariance of a random variable with itself, which is simply that variable's variance. For the off-diagonal elements, because $\sigma_{ij} = \sigma_{ji}$, the covariance matrix is necessarily symmetrical.

If the covariance matrix satisfies certain minimum requirements, we can decompose the covariance matrix, rewriting it in terms of a lower triangular matrix, $\mathbf{L}$, and its transpose, $\mathbf{L}'$, which is an upper triangular matrix,

$$\Sigma = \mathbf{L}\mathbf{L}' \tag{5.57}$$

This is what is known as a Cholesky decomposition.

It turns out that if we take the matrix $\mathbf{L}$ from our Cholesky decomposition and multiply it by a vector of i.i.d. standard normal variables, we will obtain a new vector of normal variables that satisfy the original covariance matrix, Σ. To see why this is the case, designate an $n \times 1$ vector of i.i.d. standard normal variables as $\mathbf{\Phi}$, and the resulting product as $\mathbf{C}$, so that

$$\mathbf{L}\mathbf{\Phi} = \mathbf{C} \tag{5.58}$$

As with any matrix product, we can write any element of $\mathbf{C}$ as

$$c_r = \sum_{k=1}^{n} l_{rk}\varphi_k \tag{5.59}$$

We can see that the c_r's are normally distributed random variables, because each is a linear combination of other normal variables. Furthermore, it is easy to see that the expected value of each c_i is zero:

$$\mathrm{E}[c_r] = \mathrm{E}\left[\sum_{k=1}^{n} l_{rk}\varphi_k\right] = \sum_{k=1}^{n} l_{rk}\mathrm{E}[\varphi_k] = \sum_{k=1}^{n} l_{rk} \times 0 = 0 \tag{5.60}$$

For the last step, we were able to set $E[\varphi_k]$ equal to zero, since the mean of any standard normal variable is zero by definition.

Now that we have the means of each of the c_r's, we can easily calculate the covariance between any two elements:

$$\mathrm{Cov}[c_i, c_j] = E[c_i c_j] + E[c_i]E[c_i]$$

$$= E[c_i c_j]$$

$$= E\left[\sum_{k=1}^{n} l_{ik}\varphi_k \sum_{k=1}^{n} l_{jk}\varphi_k \right] \qquad (5.61)$$

$$= E\left[\sum_{k=1}^{n} l_{jk}l_{ik}\varphi_k^2 + \sum_{k=1}^{n}\sum_{m\neq k} l_{jk}l_{im}\varphi_k\varphi_m \right]$$

$$= \sum_{k=1}^{n} l_{jk}l_{ik}E[\varphi_k^2] + \sum_{k=1}^{n}\sum_{m\neq k} l_{jk}l_{im}E[\varphi_k\varphi_m]$$

The mean of a standard normal variable is 0, and the variance is 1, so it must be the case that $E[\varphi_k^2] = 1$. Similarly, because the standard normal variables in $\boldsymbol{\Phi}$ are uncorrelated, it must be the case that $E[\varphi_k\varphi_m] = 0$ when $m \neq k$; therefore,

$$\mathrm{Cov}[c_i, c_j] = \sum_{k=1}^{n} l_{jk}l_{ik} \times 1 + \sum_{k=1}^{n}\sum_{m\neq k} l_{jk}l_{im} \times 0$$

$$= \sum_{k=1}^{n} l_{jk}l_{ik} \qquad (5.62)$$

$$= \sigma_{ik}$$

The last line follows from our initial decomposition of $\boldsymbol{\Sigma}$ into $\mathbf{LL}'$.

Given $\boldsymbol{\Sigma}$, how do we go about getting $\mathbf{L}$ and $\mathbf{L}'$ in the first place, though? Many statistical packages will perform a Cholesky decomposition, and, in practice, that might be the best solution. That said, there is a simple algorithm that can be used to perform the decomposition. Given our covariance matrix $\boldsymbol{\Sigma}$, with entries σ_{ij}, we can calculate entries in $\mathbf{L}$, l_{ij}, proceeding row by row, from left to right, using the following set of equations,

$$l_{ii} = \sqrt{ \sigma_{ii} - \sum_{m=1}^{i-1} l_{i,m}^2 }$$

$$l_{ij} = \frac{1}{l_{jj}} \left(\sigma_{ij} - \sum_{m=1}^{j-1} l_{im}l_{jm} \right) \quad \forall i > j$$

$$l_{ij} = 0 \quad \forall i < j \qquad (5.63)$$

SAMPLE PROBLEM

Question:

For the following covariance matrix, Σ, develop a set of equations that converts three uncorrelated normal variables into three correlated normal variables:

$$\Sigma = \begin{bmatrix} 16 & 8 & 12 \\ 8 & 29 & 26 \\ 12 & 26 & 61 \end{bmatrix}$$

Answer:

We can use our Cholesky algorithm to calculate the entries of a lower triangular matrix, **L**:

$$l_{11} = \sqrt{16} = 4$$

$$l_{21} = \frac{1}{4}(8) = 2$$

$$l_{22} = \sqrt{29 - 2^2} = 5$$

$$l_{31} = \frac{1}{4}(12) = 3$$

$$l_{32} = \frac{1}{5}(26 - 3 \times 2) = 4$$

$$l_{33} = \sqrt{61 - 3^2 - 4^2} = 6$$

Next, place the entries in a matrix,

$$L = \begin{bmatrix} 4 & 0 & 0 \\ 2 & 5 & 0 \\ 3 & 4 & 6 \end{bmatrix}$$

You should verify that $LL' = \Sigma$.

Given a vector of three uncorrelated standard normal variables, Φ, and using Equation 8.37,

$$L\Phi = C$$

we can create a vector of correlated random variables, **C**. The elements of **C** are

$$c_1 = 4\varphi_1$$

$$c_2 = 2\varphi_1 + 5\varphi_2$$

$$c_3 = 3\varphi_1 + 4\varphi_2 + 6\varphi_3$$

END-OF-CHAPTER QUESTIONS

1. You are asked to evaluate the risk of a portfolio that is long $100 of AAPL and short $100 of XOM. The standard deviation of returns for AAPL is 40%. The standard deviation of returns for XOM is 30%. The correlation between the two is 37.5%. What is the standard deviation of the portfolio? What is the standard deviation of each position separately?

2. In addition to the information in the previous question, assume that the correlation of AAPL to the S&P 500 is 50% and that the correlation of XOM to the S&P 500 is 80%. The standard deviation of the S&P 500 is 20%. How much S&P 500 would you need to buy or sell in order to minimize the variance of the portfolio?

3. Based on your analysis of Company ABC's stock returns, r_{ABC}, you develop the following OLS regression model:

$$r_{ABC} = 0.01 + 1.25r_A + 0.34r_B + \varepsilon$$

    where r_A and r_B are two uncorrelated indexes, and ε is a mean-zero disturbance term. If $r_A = 10\%$ and $r_B = 50\%$, what is the expected value of r_{ABC}?

4. Calculate the population covariance and correlation of the following series:

Series #1	21%	53%	83%	19%
Series #2	20%	32%	80%	40%

5. Given two random variables, X_A and X_B, with corresponding means μ_A and μ_B and standard deviations σ_A and σ_B, prove that the variance of X_A plus X_B is

$$\sigma_{A+B}^2 = \sigma_A^2 + \sigma_B^2 + 2\rho_{AB}\sigma_A\sigma_B$$

6. You perform a regression analysis of a hedge fund's returns against an industry benchmark. You have 50 data points. The total sum of squares (TSS) is 13.50%. The residual sum of squares (RSS) is 10.80%. What is the R^2?

7. In the previous question, what is the critical value for the F-test? Is the F-statistic significant at the 95% confidence level?

8. Prove Equation 5.29. That is, given the standard univariate regression

    $$Y = \alpha + \beta X + \varepsilon$$

    prove that

    $$\beta = \frac{\text{Cov}[X, Y]}{\sigma_X^2} = \rho_{XY} \frac{\sigma_Y}{\sigma_X}$$

    where σ_X and σ_Y are the standard deviations of X and Y, respectively, and ρ_{XY} is the correlation between the two. Hint: Start by calculating the covariance between X and Y.

9. Calculate the Cholesky decomposition for the following covariance matrix:

    $$\Sigma = \begin{bmatrix} 4 & 14 & 16 \\ 14 & 50 & 58 \\ 16 & 58 & 132 \end{bmatrix}$$

10. The following regression equation describes the daily returns of stock XYZ, r_{XYZ}, in terms of an index return, r_{index}, and a mean-zero disturbance term, ε:

    $$r_{XYZ} = \alpha + \beta r_{index} + \varepsilon$$

    where α and β are constants, ε is mean zero with a standard deviation of 1.0%, α is 0.01%, and β is 1.20. If the index return on a given day is 5%, what is the expected return of XYZ?

11. In addition to the assumption in the previous question, assume r_{index} has a mean of 0.05% and a standard deviation of 1.5%. What is the expected value of r_{XYZ}? What is the standard deviation of r_{XYZ}?

12. Using all the information from the previous two questions, determine the correlation between the index returns and the returns of XYZ.

6

MARKET RISK: BEYOND CORRELATION

In this chapter we explore other methods for describing the relationship between random variables. We start with two interesting but rarely used statistics, coskewness and cokurtosis, before moving on to multivariate distributions and copulas.

COSKEWNESS AND COKURTOSIS

Just as we generalized the concept of mean and variance to moments and central moments, we can generalize the concept of covariance to cross-central moments. The third and fourth standardized cross-central moments are referred to as coskewness and cokurtosis, respectively. Though used less frequently, higher-order cross moments can be very important in risk management.

As an example of how higher-order cross moments can impact risk assessment, take the series of returns shown in Table 6.1 for four fund managers, A, B, C, and D.

In this admittedly contrived setup, each manager has produced exactly the same set of returns; only the order in which the returns were produced is different. It follows that the mean, standard deviation, skew, and kurtosis of the returns are exactly the same for each manager. In this example it is also the case that the covariance between managers A and B is the same as the covariance between managers C and D.

If we combine A and B in an equally weighted portfolio and combine C and D in a separate equally weighted portfolio, we get the returns shown in Table 6.2.

TABLE 6.1 **Fund Returns**

Time	A	B	C	D
1	0.0%	−3.8%	−15.3%	−15.3%
2	−3.8%	−15.3%	−7.2%	−7.2%
3	−15.3%	3.8%	0.0%	−3.8%
4	−7.2%	−7.2%	−3.8%	15.3%
5	3.8%	0.0%	3.8%	0.0%
6	7.2%	7.2%	7.2%	7.2%
7	15.3%	15.3%	15.3%	3.8%

TABLE 6.2 **Combined Fund Returns**

Time	A + B	C + D
1	−1.9%	−15.3%
2	−9.5%	−7.2%
3	−5.8%	−1.9%
4	−7.2%	5.8%
5	1.9%	1.9%
6	7.2%	7.2%
7	15.3%	9.5%

The two portfolios have the same mean and standard deviation, but the skews of the portfolios are different. Whereas the worst return for A + B is −9.5%, the worst return for C + D is −15.3%. As a risk manager, knowing that the worst outcome for portfolio C + D is more than 1.6 times as bad as the worst outcome for A + B could be very important.

It is very important to note that there is no way for us to differentiate between A + B and C + D, based solely on the standard deviation, variance, covariance, or correlation of the original four funds. That is, there is no way for us to differentiate between the two combined portfolios based solely on the information contained in a covariance matrix. Even though they have very different risk profiles, a risk model based only on a covariance matrix would not be able to differentiate between these two portfolios. Worryingly, many financial models are based in part or entirely on covariance matrices. As risk managers, we need to be on the lookout for these types of models, and to be aware of their limitations.

So how did two portfolios whose constituents seemed so similar end up being so different? One way to understand what is happening is to graph the two sets of returns for each portfolio against each other, as shown in Figures 6.1 and 6.2.

The two graphs share a certain symmetry, but are clearly different. In the first portfolio, A + B, the two managers' best positive returns occur during the same time period, but their worst negative returns occur in different periods. This causes the distribution of points to be skewed toward the top-right of the chart. The situation is reversed for managers C and D:

FIGURE 6.1 Funds A and B

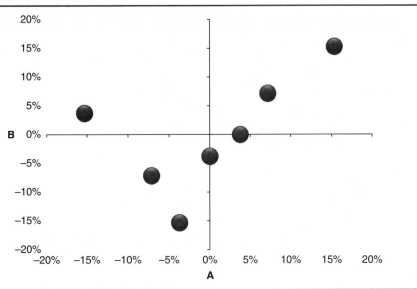

FIGURE 6.2 Funds C and D

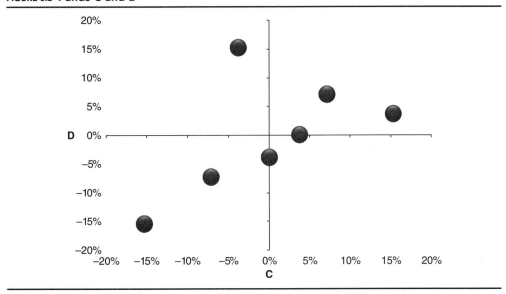

their worst negative returns occur in the same period, but their best positive returns occur in different periods. In the second chart, the points are skewed toward the bottom-left of the chart.

The reason the charts look different, and the reason the returns of the two portfolios are different, is because the coskewness between the managers in each of the portfolios is different. For two random variables, there are actually two nontrivial coskewness statistics. For example, for managers A and B, we have

$$S_{AAB} = \frac{E[(A - \mu_A)^2(B - \mu_B)]}{\sigma_A^2 \sigma_B}$$

$$S_{ABB} = \frac{E[(A - \mu_A)(B - \mu_B)^2]}{\sigma_A \sigma_B^2} \tag{6.1}$$

The complete set of sample coskewness statistics for the sets of managers is shown in Table 6.3.

TABLE 6.3 Sample Coskewness

	A + B	C + D
S_{XXY}	0.99	−0.58
S_{XYY}	0.58	−0.99

Both coskewness values for A and B are positive, whereas they are both negative for C and D. Just as with skewness, negative values of coskewness tend to be associated with greater risk.

Just as we defined coskewness, we can define cokurtosis. For two random variables, X and Y, there are three nontrivial cokurtosis statistics,

$$K_{XXXY} = \frac{E[(X - \mu_X)^3(Y - \mu_Y)]}{\sigma_X^3 \sigma_Y}$$

$$K_{XXYY} = \frac{E[(X - \mu_X)^2(Y - \mu_Y)^2]}{\sigma_X^2 \sigma_Y^2}$$

$$K_{XYYY} = \frac{E[(X - \mu_X)(Y - \mu_Y)^3]}{\sigma_X \sigma_Y^3} \tag{6.2}$$

In general, for n random variables, the number of nontrivial cross-central moments of order m is

$$k(m, n) = \frac{(m + n - 1)!}{m!(n - 1)!} - n \tag{6.3}$$

In this case, nontrivial means that we have excluded the cross moments that involve only one variable (e.g., our standard skewness and kurtosis). To include the nontrivial moments, we would simply add n to the preceding result. For coskewness, Equation 6.3 simplifies to

$$k(3, n) = \frac{(n + 2)(n + 1)n}{6} - n \tag{6.4}$$

Despite their obvious relevance to risk management, many standard risk models do not explicitly define coskewness or cokurtosis. One reason that many models avoid these higher-order cross moments is practical. As the number of variables increases, the number

TABLE 6.4 **Number of Nontrivial Cross Moments**

n	Covariance	Coskewness	Cokurtosis
2	1	2	3
5	10	30	65
10	45	210	705
20	190	1,520	8,835
30	435	4,930	40,890
100	4,950	171,600	4,421,175

of nontrivial cross moments increases rapidly. With 10 variables there are 30 coskewness parameters and 65 cokurtosis parameters. With 100 variables, these numbers increase to 171,600 and over 4 million, respectively. Table 6.4 compares the number of nontrivial cross moments for a variety of sample sizes. In most cases there is simply not enough data to calculate all of these higher-order cross moments.

Risk models with time-varying volatility (e.g., GARCH; see Chapter 2) or time-varying correlation can display a wide range of behaviors with very few free parameters. Copulas, which we will discuss in the next section, can also be used to describe complex interactions between variables that go beyond covariances, and have become popular in risk management in recent years. All of these approaches capture the essence of coskewness and cokurtosis, but in a more tractable framework. As a risk manager, it is important to differentiate between these models—which address the higher-order cross moments indirectly—and models that simply omit these risk factors altogether.

MULTIVARIATE DISTRIBUTIONS

A multivariate distribution or joint distribution is a distribution involving two or more variables. We begin our exploration of multivariate distributions by examining discrete distributions, before moving on to continuous distributions.

Discrete Distributions

A probability matrix is an example of a discrete multivariate distribution. The probability matrix in Table 6.5 lists various probabilities for the performance of the equity and bonds of a company. This is a discrete joint distribution with two random variables, one for the performance of the equity and one for the performance of the bonds. A joint distribution with two random variables can also be referred to as a bivariate distribution. In Table 6.5, there are six distinct joint probabilities. For example, the joint probability of both equity

TABLE 6.5 Probability Matrix

		Equity	
		Outperform	Underperform
Bonds	Upgrade	15%	5%
	No Change	30%	25%
	Downgrade	5%	20%

outperforming *and* bonds being downgraded is 5%. As is required of any distribution, the sum of all the probabilities is equal to 100%.

We can easily create a joint distribution for any number of random variables, though displaying the results in a simple probability matrix becomes more difficult with more than two variables. No matter how many variables there are, the basic idea is the same: To define a discrete distribution, we assign a probability to every possible joint outcome, and the sum of those probabilities must add up to 100%.

As another example, pretend we are interested in three mutual funds, Fund A, Fund B, and Fund C. Furthermore, assume we are interested only in the probability of the funds generating returns that are under or over a particular benchmark. With three funds and two possible outcomes for each fund, there is a total of eight distinct outcomes, each with an associated joint probability. We could list them in a table as in Table 6.6.

Rather than increasing the number of variables, we could increase the number of possible outcomes for each variable. In Table 6.7 we have the joint distribution for two bonds, each of which can have one of eight possible letter ratings at the end of the year. This gives us a total of 64 possible outcomes.

In theory, we could create a matrix of any size. As the number of possible outcomes approaches infinity, the discrete multivariate distribution converges to a continuous multivariate distribution, or continuous joint distribution.

TABLE 6.6 Joint Probabilities Table

Fund A	Fund B	Fund C	Probability
Under	Under	Under	1%
Under	Under	Over	2%
Under	Over	Under	8%
Under	Over	Over	22%
Over	Under	Under	35%
Over	Under	Over	22%
Over	Over	Under	8%
Over	Over	Over	2%
			100%

TABLE 6.7 Joint Distribution Matrix

		Bond #1							
		AAA	**AA**	**A**	**BBB**	**BB**	**B**	**C**	**D**
Bond #2	**AAA**	0.0%	0.2%	0.2%	0.4%	0.2%	0.1%	0.0%	0.0%
	AA	0.1%	0.6%	1.8%	2.9%	1.8%	0.4%	0.2%	0.1%
	A	0.2%	1.8%	5.3%	8.3%	5.3%	1.5%	0.3%	0.2%
	BBB	0.3%	2.9%	8.3%	13.0%	8.3%	2.6%	0.4%	0.0%
	BB	0.2%	1.8%	5.0%	8.0%	5.3%	1.8%	0.1%	0.1%
	B	0.1%	0.5%	1.8%	2.6%	1.3%	0.6%	0.1%	0.0%
	C	0.1%	0.1%	0.3%	0.6%	0.5%	0.3%	0.0%	0.0%
	D	0.0%	0.1%	0.2%	0.4%	0.2%	0.2%	0.0%	0.0%

Continuous Distributions

Just as with a single random variable, we can define a continuous joint distribution using a probability density function (PDF). For example, if we have two random variables, X and Y, we could define the joint PDF, $f(x,y)$, such that the probability of finding X between x_1 and x_2 and at the same time finding Y between y_1 and y_2 is given by

$$P[x_1 \leq X \leq x_2, y_1 \leq Y \leq y_2] = \int_{x_1}^{x_2} \int_{y_1}^{y_2} f(x,y)dxdy \qquad (6.5)$$

where $x_1 < x_2$ and $y_1 < y_2$. As with any distribution, some event has to occur, and if we integrate over all possible values of X and Y, the total must be

$$\int_x \int_y f(x,y)dxdy = 1 \qquad (6.6)$$

For a joint distribution, we can also define a cumulative distribution function (CDF), $F(x,y)$,

$$F(x,y) = P[X \leq x, Y \leq y] = \int_{-\infty}^{x} \int_{-\infty}^{y} f(t,u)dtdu \qquad (6.7)$$

To go from a joint cumulative distribution to a joint probability density function, we simply take the partial derivative with respect to all the underlying variables. For our bivariate distribution, we have

$$f(x,y) = \frac{\partial^2 F(x,y)}{\partial x \partial y} \qquad (6.8)$$

The right-hand side of Equation 6.8 is the second-order cross partial derivative of $F(x,y)$.

SAMPLE PROBLEM

Question:

Imagine we have two bonds, whose value can vary between $0 and $100. Assume the joint distribution function for the value of the bonds is a joint uniform distribution, such that $f(x,y)$ equals c, a constant, for all values of X and Y between $0 and $100, and is zero everywhere else. That is:

$$f(x, y) = c \quad \forall \, 0 \le X \le 100, 0 \le Y \le 100$$

Find c.

Answer:

Integrating over all possible values, it must be the case that

$$\int_0^{100} \int_0^{100} c\,dx\,dy = 1$$

Solving, we have

$$\int_0^{100} \int_0^{100} c\,dx\,dy = c[xy]_{x=0,y=0}^{x=100,y=100} = c(100 \times 100 - 0 \times 0) = 10{,}000c$$

$$10{,}000c = 1$$

$$c = 1/10{,}000$$

We can define joint probability density functions and joint cumulative distribution functions for any number of variables. For example, with n variables, $X_1, X_2, \ldots, X_n$, the joint cumulative distribution, $F(x_1, x_2, \ldots, x_n)$, in terms of the probability density function, $f(x_1, x_2, \ldots, x_n)$, would be

$$F(x_1, x_2, \ldots, x_n) = P[X_1 \le x_1, X_2 \le x_2, \ldots, X_n \le x_n]$$

$$= \int_{-\infty}^{x_1} \int_{-\infty}^{x_2} \int_{-\infty}^{x_3} f(y_1, y_2, \ldots, y_n)\,dy_1\,dy_2 \ldots dy_n \qquad (6.9)$$

Visualization

Just as we can graph the probability density function for one variable in two dimensions, we can graph the probability density function for a joint distribution of two variables in three dimensions. Figure 6.3 shows the probability density function from the previous sample problem. Here, the value of the density function corresponds to the distance along the z-axis, or the height of the distribution. As we might expect, the joint PDF resembles a box, whose volume is equal to one.

FIGURE 6.3 Joint Uniform Probability Density Function

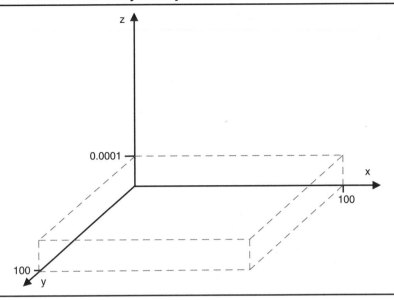

Figure 6.4 shows a multivariate normal distribution. In this case it is a joint standard normal distribution, where both variables, X and Y, are standard normal variables.

Three-dimensional graphs look nice, but the perspective can hide details. An alternative way to visualize a joint distribution of two variables is by using a contour graph. In a contour

FIGURE 6.4 Bivariate Standard Normal PDF

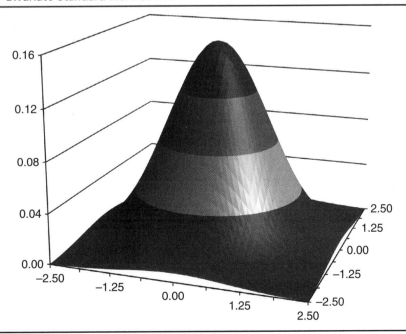

FIGURE 6.5 Bivariate Standard Normal PDF Contour Graph

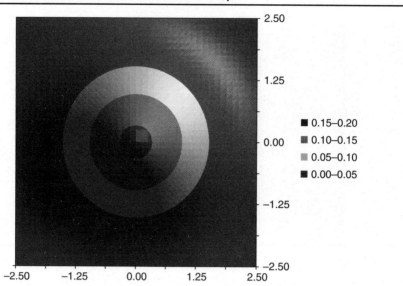

graph it is as if we are looking at the three-dimensional graph from directly overhead. Figure 6.5 is a contour graph corresponding to the joint normal PDF in Figure 6.4. Different shades of gray represent different values for the density function. The borders between different regions are called isolines or isoquants, because all of the points on one isoquant have the same value.

Beyond two variables, visualization becomes more difficult. Even when more variables are involved, starting with the two-variable case can be convenient for purposes of exposition or for gaining intuition.

Correlation

Up until this point, we have not said anything about correlation. How would we recognize correlation in a joint distribution? One way would be to examine the contour graph of the distribution. Notice in Figure 6.3 how the distribution is symmetrical across both axes. This tells us that, for a given value of X, positive values and negative values of Y are equally likely, and vice versa. Because X and Y are both mean zero, we could also say that positive and negative deviations of Y are equally likely for a given value of X, and vice versa. This suggests that X and Y are uncorrelated.

Now look at Figure 6.6. Rather than forming concentric circles around the origin, the contour lines in this chart form ellipses. This graph is symmetrical, but not about the

FIGURE 6.6 Joint Standard Normal Distribution with Positive Correlation

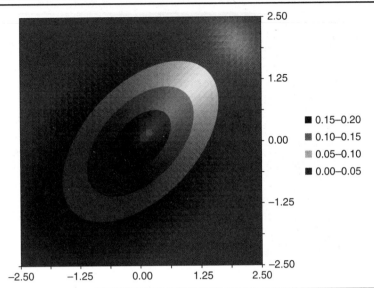

x- and y-axes. As it turns out, this graph is also based on the PDF of a joint standard normal distribution. The only difference between this joint distribution and the previous joint distribution is the correlation between X and Y.

In Figure 6.6 we can see from the contour graph that X is more likely to be positive when Y is positive (the density function is higher), and X is more likely to be negative when Y is negative. In other words, X and Y are positively correlated.

If X and Y were negatively correlated, the contour graph would be oriented in the opposite way. Figure 6.7 shows a contour graph of the PDF of two negatively correlated standard normal variables.

Marginal Distributions

Given a joint distribution, we can easily recover the distribution for each of the underlying random variables. In this context the individual univariate distributions are known as marginal distributions.

We illustrate this first with discrete distributions. The probability matrix from the beginning of the chapter is reproduced here as Table 6.8 with the addition of subtotals for the rows and columns. These subtotals form the marginal distributions.

By adding up the columns of the matrix, we see that there is a 50% chance that the equity outperforms the market and a 50% chance that the equity underperforms the market.

FIGURE 6.7 Joint Standard Normal Distribution with Negative Correlation

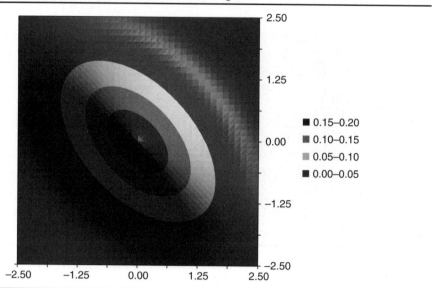

- 0.15–0.20
- 0.10–0.15
- 0.05–0.10
- 0.00–0.05

This is the marginal distribution of the equity. Likewise, the marginal distribution of the bonds has three possible states, whose probabilities can be found by summing across each row. The probability of an upgrade is 20%, the probability of no change is 55%, and the probability of a downgrade is 25%. The marginal distributions are proper distributions in and of themselves. In both cases, the probabilities of the marginal distributions sum to one.

We can summarize this process for obtaining marginal distributions mathematically. For a discrete joint distribution of two random variables, X and Y, with a joint probability density function, $f(x,y)$, the marginal probability density function of X, $f_x(x)$, can be found as follows:

$$f_x(x) = \sum_y f(x, y) \tag{6.10}$$

In other words, to get the value of the marginal PDF of X for a given value of X, x, we simply sum over all values of Y, with X set equal to x. To get the marginal distribution of Y, we simply reverse variables, summing over all possible values of X for a given value of Y.

TABLE 6.8 Probability Matrix with Subtotals

		Equity		
		Outperform	Underperform	
Bonds	Upgrade	15%	5%	**20%**
	No Change	30%	25%	**55%**
	Downgrade	5%	20%	**25%**
		50%	**50%**	

For a continuous joint distribution, the analogous process involves integrating over all possible values of the other variable. For a continuous joint distribution of two random variables, X and Y, with a joint probability density function, $f(x,y)$, the marginal probability density function of X, $f_x(x)$, can be found as follows:

$$f_x(x) = \int_y f(x,y)dy \tag{6.11}$$

As before, we can reverse the variables to obtain the marginal distribution for Y.

There is an important link between the marginal distributions and independence. If two random variables, X and Y, are independent, then the joint PDF will be equal to the product of the marginal PDFs. The reverse is also true: If the joint PDF is equal to the product of the marginal PDFs, then X and Y are independent, as shown.

$$f(x,y) = f_x(x)f_y(y) \Longleftrightarrow X \text{ and } Y \text{ are independent} \tag{6.12}$$

If two random variables are independent, then the product of their cumulative distribution functions is also equal to the CDF of their joint distribution.

Another way that we can test for independence is to look at the joint and marginal probabilities. In general, if two random variables A and B are independent, then $P[A \text{ and } B] = P[A] \times P[B]$. In Table 6.8, the probability of equity outperforming is 50% and the probability of bonds outperforming is 20%. If equity and bonds were independent, then the probability of both equity and bonds outperforming would be 50% × 20% = 10%. According to the table, however, the joint probability is 15%. From this, we can conclude that equity and bonds are not independent.

SAMPLE PROBLEM

Question:

Given the following joint probability density function, prove that X and Y are independent.

$$f(x,y) = c \,\forall\, 0 \le X \le 100, \, 0 \le Y \le 100$$

where c is equal to 1/10,000.

Answer:

We start by calculating the marginal distribution of X,

$$f_x(x) = \int_y f(x,y)dy$$

$$= \int_0^{100} cdy$$

$$= c[y]_0^{100}$$

$$= c(100 - 0)$$

$$= 100c$$

$$= 1/100$$

Because $f(x,y)$ only involves a constant, it is not surprising that we get the same answer for the marginal distribution of Y.

$$f_y(y) = \int_x f(x, y)dx = \int_0^{100} cdx = c[x]_0^{100} = c(100 - 0) = 100c = 1/100$$

Putting the two together, we can see that the product of the marginal distributions is equal to the joint distribution.

$$f(x, y) = \frac{1}{10,000} = \frac{1}{100}\frac{1}{100} = f_x(x)f_y(y)$$

Because the joint PDF is equal to the product of the marginal PDFs, it follows that X and Y must be independent.

COPULAS

In this section we introduce the concept of the copula. In statistics, copulas are used to model various types of multivariate distributions.

What Is a Copula?

In the previous section we showed three graphs of joint normal distributions: one where the two variables were uncorrelated, one where the two variables were positively correlated, and one where the two variables were negatively correlated. So, what about Figure 6.8?

It might seem surprising at first, but it turns out that Figure 6.8 is also a joint normal distribution. Unlike the previous three examples where the contour lines were all ellipses (circles being special types of ellipses), this new chart has more of a teardrop shape. In this new graph, it also appears that extreme negative-negative results are more likely than extreme positive-positive results.

The graph in Figure 6.8 was produced using a special function known as a copula. In everyday parlance, a copula is simply something that joins or couples. In statistics, a copula is a function used to combine two or more cumulative distribution functions in order to produce one joint cumulative distribution function.

FIGURE 6.8 Bivariate Standard Normal PDF with Clayton Copula

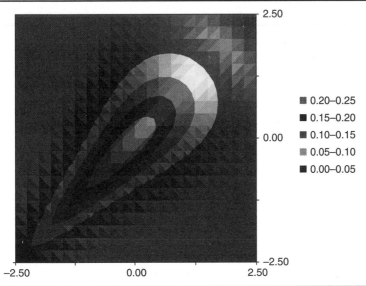

In many fields, when it comes to joint distributions, ellipses are all that you will see. In finance, assuming a joint distribution is elliptical when in fact it is not can lead to a serious underestimation of risk. Earlier, we saw how coskewness and cokurtosis could impact the risk of a portfolio. Though we did not recognize it as such at the time, the sample distributions with extreme coskewness were nonelliptical. Copulas provide us with a method for producing and describing nonelliptical joint distributions.

There is an infinite number of ways in which two distributions can be related to each other, but statisticians have found it useful to describe a few prototypical patterns. Examples include the Gaussian, t, Gumbel, Frank, and Clayton copulas. The last three copulas—the Gumbel, Frank, and Clayton copulas—are members of a class of copulas known as the Archimedean copulas. Each of these named copulas has a characteristic way of distorting the relationship between two variables. Figure 6.8 is an example of a joint distribution based on the Clayton copula. The Clayton copula exhibits greater dependence in the negative tail than in the positive tail, a not-uncommon feature of financial returns, making it a popular choice in risk management. Appendix B contains a brief summary of several popular copulas.

A copula only defines a relationship between univariate distributions. The underlying distributions themselves can be any shape or size. For instance, we can talk about a normal Gumbel copula, meaning the marginal distributions are all normal, and we can talk about a lognormal Gumbel copula, meaning the marginal distributions are lognormal. We can even talk about a normal-lognormal Gumbel copula, meaning one of the marginal distributions is normal and one is lognormal.

Mechanically, copulas take as their inputs two or more cumulative distributions and output a joint cumulative distribution. The advantage of working with cumulative distributions is that the range is always the same. No matter what the distribution is, the output of a cumulative distribution always ranges from 0% to 100%.

We typically represent cumulative distributions with capital letters, for example $F(x)$. In order to make the formulas more readable, when describing copulas we often use lowercase letters instead. For example, given two cumulative distributions, u and v, and a constant, α, we can write Frank's copula as

$$C(u, v) = \frac{1}{\alpha} \ln\left[1 + \frac{(e^{\alpha u} - 1)(e^{\alpha v} - 1)}{e^{\alpha} - 1}\right] \qquad (6.13)$$

As used in Equation 6.13, α determines the shape of the joint cumulative distribution, $C(u,v)$. In the case of Frank's copula, it is fairly easy to see that when both u and v are 100%, $C(u,v)$ is also 100%. In other words, if an outcome for the first variable is certain, and another outcome is certain for the second variable, then the chance of both outcomes occurring is also certain. It's slightly more difficult to see, but in the limit, as both u and v go to zero, $C(u,v)$ also goes to zero.

SAMPLE PROBLEM

Question:

Assume we have two standard uniform random variables, X and Y, whose joint distribution is defined by Frank's copula. What is the formula for the cumulative distribution of the two variables? What is the formula for the probability density function for $\alpha = 1$?

Answer:

If X is a standard uniform variable, then its cumulative distribution function is defined as

$$F(x) = \begin{cases} 0 & \forall\, 0 > x > 1 \\ x & \forall\, 0 \leq x \leq 1 \end{cases}$$

Y is defined similarly. Using Equation 6.13, and setting $F(x)$ equal to u and $F(Y)$ equal to v, for values of X and Y less than 0 or greater than 1, we have

$$F(x, y) = \frac{1}{\alpha} \ln\left[1 + \frac{(e^{\alpha 0} - 1)(e^{\alpha 0} - 1)}{e^\alpha - 1}\right]$$

$$= \frac{1}{\alpha} \ln\left[1 + \frac{(1 - 1)(1 - 1)}{e^\alpha - 1}\right]$$

$$= \frac{1}{\alpha} \ln[1]$$

$$= 0$$

For values of X and Y between 0 and 1, we have

$$F(x, y) = \frac{1}{\alpha} \ln\left[1 + \frac{(e^{\alpha x} - 1)(e^{\alpha y} - 1)}{e^\alpha - 1}\right]$$

For $\alpha = 1$, this simplifies to

$$F(x, y) = \ln\left[1 + \frac{(e^x - 1)(e^y - 1)}{e - 1}\right]$$

$$= \ln(e^{x+y} - e^x - e^y + e) - \ln(e - 1)$$

We can quickly check that for $x = y = 0$, we have $F(x,y) = 0$; and for $x = y = 1$, we have $F(x,y) = 1$.

FIGURE 6.9 Frank's Joint Standard Uniform PDF, $\alpha = 1$

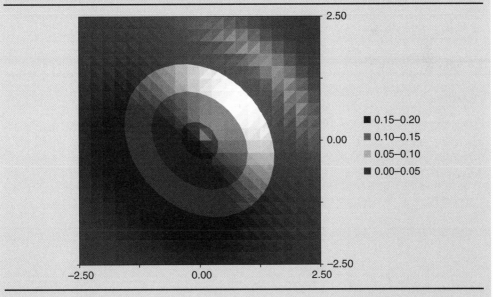

To get the probability density function, we need to calculate the second partial derivative with respect to x and then y:

$$f(x, y) = \frac{\partial^2 F(x, y)}{\partial x \partial y} = \frac{\partial}{\partial y}\left[\frac{e^{x+y} - e^x}{(e^{x+y} - e^x - e^y + e)}\right]$$

$$= \frac{e^{x+y}}{(e^{x+y} - e^x - e^y + e)} - \frac{(e^{x+y} - e^y)(e^{x+y} - e^x)}{(e^{x+y} - e^x - e^y + e)^2}$$

$$= \frac{e^{x+y}(e - 1)}{(e^{x+y} - e^x - e^y + e)^2}$$

The joint distribution is shown in Figure 6.9.

In the preceding sample problem, in order to calculate the joint PDF we first calculated the joint CDF. There is another way we could have proceeded. Assume we have two cumulative distributions, $u = F(x)$ and $v = F(y)$; then, making use of the chain rule, we have

$$f(x, y) = \frac{\partial^2 C(u, v)}{\partial x \partial y} = \frac{\partial^2 C(u, v)}{\partial u \partial v}\frac{\partial u}{\partial x}\frac{\partial v}{\partial y} = c(u, v)f(x)f(y) \tag{6.14}$$

Here we have denoted the second cross partial derivative of $C(u,v)$ by $c(u,v)$; $c(u,v)$ is often referred to as the density function of the copula. Because $c(u,v)$ depends on only the copula and not the marginal distributions, we can calculate $c(u,v)$ once and then apply it to many different problems. Appendix B contains the density functions for a number of copulas.

SAMPLE PROBLEM

Question:

Calculate the density function for Frank's copula when $\alpha = 1$. Use the results to calculate the joint probability density function for two standard uniform variables.

Answer:

We start by rearranging our formulas for Frank's copula,

$$C(u, v) = \frac{1}{\alpha}\ln\left[1 + \frac{(e^{\alpha u} - 1)(e^{\alpha v} - 1)}{e^{\alpha} - 1}\right]$$

$$= \frac{1}{\alpha}\ln(e^{\alpha} + e^{\alpha(u+v)} - e^{\alpha u} - e^{\alpha v}) - \frac{1}{\alpha}\ln(e^{\alpha} - 1)$$

Next, we calculate the density function for Frank's copula by taking the partial derivative with respect to u and v. The order is not important. We can take the derivative with respect to u and then v, or v and then u.

$$c(u,v) = \frac{\partial^2 C(u,v)}{\partial u \partial v}$$

$$= \frac{\partial}{\partial u}\left[\frac{1}{\alpha}\frac{\alpha e^{\alpha(u+v)} - \alpha e^{\alpha v}}{(e^\alpha + e^{\alpha(u+v)} - e^{\alpha u} - e^{\alpha v})}\right]$$

$$= \frac{\partial}{\partial u}\left[\frac{e^{\alpha(u+v)} - e^{\alpha v}}{(e^\alpha + e^{\alpha(u+v)} - e^{\alpha u} - e^{\alpha v})}\right]$$

$$= \frac{\alpha e^{\alpha(u+v)}}{(e^\alpha + e^{\alpha(u+v)} - e^{\alpha u} - e^{\alpha v})} - \frac{(e^{\alpha(u+v)} - e^{\alpha v})(\alpha e^{\alpha(u+v)} - \alpha e^{\alpha u})}{(e^\alpha + e^{\alpha(u+v)} - e^{\alpha u} - e^{\alpha v})^2}$$

$$= \frac{\alpha e^{\alpha(u+v)}(e^\alpha - 1)}{(e^\alpha + e^{\alpha(u+v)} - e^{\alpha u} - e^{\alpha v})^2} \qquad (6.15)$$

As in the previous sample problem, we use two standard uniform variables, X and Y, where the CDFs between 0 and 1 are x and y, respectively. Substituting x and y for u and v, respectively, and setting $\alpha = 1$, we have

$$c(x,y) = \frac{e^{(x+y)}(e - 1)}{(e + e^{(x+y)} - e^x - e^y)^2}$$

Finally, to get the joint PDF, using Equation 6.14, we multiply the density function by the PDFs for X and Y, $f(x)$ and $f(y)$, respectively. Because both variables are standard uniform random variables, their PDFs are equal to 1.

$$f(x,y) = c(u,v)f(x)f(y) = c(u,v) = \frac{e^{(x+y)}(e - 1)}{(e + e^{(x+y)} - e^x - e^y)^2}$$

To check the result, we note that the final equation matches the result from the previous sample problem.

Graphing Copulas

Figure 6.10 shows the joint PDF for a standard normal Frank's copula. As you can see from the exhibit, Frank's copula displays symmetrical tail dependence. How do we actually go about creating one of these graphs? One of the easiest ways is to use Equation 6.15. For any point on the graph, (x, y), we first calculate values for both the PDF and the CDF of X and Y. We use the CDFs to calculate the copula density function, and then multiply this value by the value of the PDFs to determine the value of the joint distribution at that point.

For example, suppose that we want to graph the joint PDF of a Frank's copula for two standard normal variables with $\alpha = 2$. To determine the height of the graph at $(x, y) = (0, 0)$, we start by calculating the cumulative distribution for both variables. At 0, the

FIGURE 6.10 Bivariate Standard Normal PDF with Frank's Copula, $\alpha = 2$

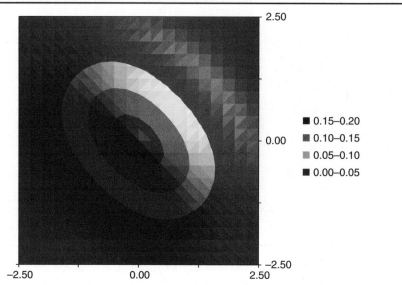

cumulative distribution for a standard normal variable is equal to 0.50. We can calculate this in Excel by using the NORM.S.DIST function with the cumulative option set to true. Plugging 0.50 into the copula's density function, Equation 6.15, for both x and y gives us a value of 1.08. Next, we multiply this by the value of the standard normal PDF for both x and y, which for 0 is 0.40. You can get this in Excel by using the NORM.S.DIST function, with the cumulative option set to false. Our final answer for the height of the distribution is then 0.17.

$$
\begin{aligned}
f(x,y) &= c(u,v)f(x)f(y) \\[2mm]
&= \frac{\alpha e^{\alpha(u+v)}(e^{\alpha}-1)}{(e^{\alpha}+e^{\alpha(u+v)}-e^{\alpha u}-e^{\alpha v})^2}f(x)f(y) \\[2mm]
&= \frac{2e^{2(0.5+0.5)}(e^{0.5}-1)}{(e^2+e^{2(0.5+0.5)}-e^{2\cdot0.5}-e^{2\cdot0.5})^2} \times 0.40 \times 0.40 \\[2mm]
&= 1.08 \times 0.40 \times 0.40 \\[2mm]
&= 0.17
\end{aligned}
\tag{6.16}
$$

To complete the graph, we would continue to calculate values of the PDF for various combinations of X and Y. Figure 6.10 was drawn using 441 evenly spaced (x, y) pairs.

Because Equation 6.14 allows us to separate the copula density function and the marginal distributions, it is relatively easy to go from a normal-normal Frank's distribution to, say, a uniform-uniform Frank's distribution. To do so, we simply change the PDF and CDF functions from normal to uniform.

An Excel spreadsheet with several examples is available online.

Using Copulas in Simulations

In this section, we demonstrate how copulas can be used in Monte Carlo simulations. Our example uses two random variables, but the same basic methodology can be extended to any number of variables.

In order to use copulas in a Monte Carlo simulation, we need to calculate the inverse marginal CDFs for the copula. To determine the marginal CDFs of a copula, we take the first derivative of the copula function with respect to one of the underlying distributions. For two cumulative distributions u and v, the marginal CDFs would be

$$C_1 = \frac{\partial C}{\partial u} = \int c(u, v)dv$$

$$C_2 = \frac{\partial C}{\partial v} = \int c(u, v)du \tag{6.17}$$

For example, for Frank's copula the marginal CDF for u would be

$$C_1 = \frac{\partial C}{\partial u} = \frac{(e^{-\alpha u} - 1)(e^{-\alpha v} - 1) + (e^{-\alpha v} - 1)}{(e^{-\alpha u} - 1)(e^{-\alpha v} - 1) + (e^{-\alpha} - 1)} \tag{6.18}$$

C_1 is a proper CDF, and varies between 0% and 100%. To determine the inverse of C_1, we solve for v.

$$v = -\frac{1}{\alpha} \ln\left[1 + \frac{C_1(e^{-\alpha} - 1)}{1 + (e^{-\alpha u} - 1)(1 - C_1)}\right] \tag{6.19}$$

Each iteration in the Monte Carlo simulation then involves three steps:

1. Generate two independent random draws from a standard uniform distribution. These are the values for u and C_1.
2. Use the inverse CDF of the copula to determine v. This is the essential step. Depending on the copula, different values of v will be more or less likely, given u.
3. Calculate values for x and y, using inverse cumulative distribution functions for the underlying distributions. For example, if the underlying distributions are normal, use the inverse normal CDF to calculate x and y based on u and v.

The easiest way to understand this process is to see it in action. We provide a brief example here. There is also an Excel example available online.

SAMPLE PROBLEM

Question:

Assume we are using the Frank's copula in a Monte Carlo simulation, with $\alpha = 3$. The underlying distributions of u and v are both standard normal distributions. For any given value of u and the marginal CDF, we want to determine the corresponding value of v. If our random number generator produces $u = 0.20$ and $C_1 = 0.50$, what are the values of our underlying random variables X and Y?

Answer:

First, we determine v using Equation 6.18.

$$v = -\frac{1}{3} \ln\left[1 + \frac{0.50(e^{-3} - 1)}{1 + (e^{-3 \cdot 0.20} - 1)(1 - 0.50)}\right] = 0.32$$

Notice that u, v, and C_1 are all between 0% and 100%. We then use an inverse standard normal function, NORM.S.INV in Excel, to calculate x and y from u and v. We get: $x = -0.84$ and $y = -0.48$. Notice that even though C_1 was 0.50, right in the center of its distribution, y is negative. This is because x is negative, and negative-negative pairs are more likely with Frank's copula.

Parameterization of Copulas

Given a copula, we know how to calculate values for that copula, but how do we know which copula to use in the first place? The answer is a mixture of art and science.

In picking which type of copula to use, there are quantitative methods we could use, such as maximum likelihood estimation, but in practice this choice is often based on the general characteristics of the data. If the data seem to exhibit increased correlation in crashes, then you should choose a copula that displays a higher probability in the negative-negative region such as the Clayton copula. Choosing a copula is often where the art comes into play.

Once we know which type of copula we are going to use, we need to determine the parameters of the copula. Take for example the Farlie-Gumbel-Morgenstern (FGM) copula, given by

$$C = uv[1 + \alpha(1 - u)(1 - v)] \tag{6.20}$$

As with most copulas, there is a single parameter, α, which needs to be determined, and this parameter is related to how closely the two underlying random variables are related to each other.

In statistics, the most popular method for measuring how closely two variables are related to each other is correlation. For two random variables, X and Y, with standard deviation σ_X and σ_Y, respectively, correlation is defined as

$$\rho_{XY} = \frac{E[(X - E[X])(Y - E[Y])]}{\sigma_X \sigma_Y} \tag{6.21}$$

To avoid any ambiguity, this standard correlation is often referred to as Pearson's correlation or linear correlation. While this measure is extremely popular, there are other ways to quantify the relationship between two variables. When working with copulas, two of these other measures, Kendall's tau and Spearman's rho, are often preferred. Rather than being based directly on the values of the variables, both Kendall's tau and Spearman's rho are based on the relative order or rank of the variables. We start by exploring Kendall's tau.

Two data sets are presented in Table 6.9. Both sets contain three points, A, B, and C. In Data Set #1, Y is always equal to five times X, and the Pearson's correlation between X and Y is 100%. We'll get to how you calculate it shortly, but it turns out that Kendall's tau is also equal to 100% for Data Set #1. Now look at Data Set #2. All of the values are the same as in Data Set #1, except for the Y value of point C, which has changed from 15 to 18. In Data Set #2 the correlation is less than 100%, but Kendall's tau is still 100%. This is because, even though the value of Y for point C has changed, the rank of Y for point C has not changed. The value of Y for point C is the highest for all the points in both data sets, and only the ranks of the variables are relevant for Kendall's tau.

Within both data sets, notice how if the X value of one point is greater than the X value of another point, then the Y value is also greater. Likewise, if the X value of one point is less than the X value of another point, then the Y value is also less. When the X and Y values of one point are both greater than or both less than the X and Y values of another point, we say that the two points are concordant. If two points are not concordant, we say they are discordant. More formally, for two distinct points i and j we have

$$\text{Concordance: } (X_i > X_j \text{ and } Y_i > Y_j) \text{ or } (X_i < X_j \text{ and } Y_i < Y_j)$$

$$\text{Disconcordance: } (X_i < X_j \text{ and } Y_i > Y_j) \text{ or } (X_i > X_j \text{ and } Y_i < Y_j) \tag{6.22}$$

TABLE 6.9 Comparing Two Data Sets

	Data Set #1					Data Set #2			
	X	Y	Rank[X]	Rank[Y]		X	Y	Rank[X]	Rank[Y]
A	1	5	3	3	A	1	5	3	3
B	2	10	2	2	B	2	10	2	2
C	3	15	1	1	C	3	18	1	1

Kendall's tau is defined as the probability of concordance minus the probability of discordance.

$$\tau = P[\text{concordance}] - P[\text{discordance}] \tag{6.23}$$

If P[concordance] is 100%, then P[discordance] must be 0%. Similarly, if P[discordance] is 100%, P[concordance] must be 0%. Because of this, like our standard correlation measure, Kendall's tau must vary between -100% and $+100\%$.

To measure Kendall's tau in a given data set, we simply need to compare every possible pair of points and count how many are concordant and how many are discordant. In a data set with n points, the number of unique combinations of two points is

$$\binom{n}{2} = \frac{n!}{(n-2)!2!} = \frac{1}{2}n(n-1) \tag{6.24}$$

For example, in Table 6.9 each data set has three points, A, B, and C, and there are three possible combinations of two points: A and B, A and C, and B and C. For a given data set, then, Kendall's tau is

$$\tau = \frac{\#\text{ of concordant pairs} - \#\text{ of discordant pairs}}{\binom{n}{2}} \tag{6.25}$$

A potentially interesting feature of Kendall's tau is that it is less sensitive to outliers than Pearson's correlation. In Table 6.9, as long as the Y value of point C is greater than 10, all of the points will be concordant, and Kendall's tau will be unchanged. Point C could be 11 or 11,000. In this way, measures of dependence based on rank are analogous to the median when measuring averages.

SAMPLE PROBLEM

Question:

Given the following data set, calculate Kendall's tau:

	X	Y
A	76	6
B	89	51
C	63	56
D	50	1

Answer:

In this data set there are four data points, giving us six possible pairings: $\frac{1}{2} \times 4 \times 3$ = 6. The pair of A and B is concordant; 89 is greater than 76, and 51 is greater than 6. We determine each pair in turn:

Pair	Concordant = +1, Discordant = −1
A, B	+1
A, C	−1
A, D	+1
B, C	−1
B, D	+1
C, D	+1

In all, there are four concordant pairs and two discordant pairs, giving us our final answer of

$$\tau = \frac{4-2}{6} = \frac{1}{3} = 33\%$$

Kendall's tau is 33%.

As the number of points grows, the number of unique pairings increases rapidly. For 100 points there are 4,950 unique pairings. For large data sets, you will need to use a computer to calculate Kendall's tau.

We have not said anything yet about how to approach ties—that is, if $x_i = x_j$ or $y_i = y_j$. There is no universally agreed upon approach. The simplest solution is to ignore ties, but there are more complex methods. These different methods are sometimes referred to as tau-a, tau-b, or similar names.

Besides being robust to outliers, measures of dependence based on rank are invariant under strictly increasing transformations. This is a fancy way of saying that we can stretch and twist our data set in certain ways, and, as long as we don't change the relative order of the points, Kendall's tau will not change. As an example, take a look at Figure 6.11, in which we have graphed two data sets. In both cases the relationship between the Y values and the X values is deterministic. In the first series, represented by dots, $y' = 4x$. In the second series, represented by $\times$'s, $y^* = \sin(2\pi x)$. The second series can be viewed as a transformation of the first, $y^* = \sin(0.5\pi y')$ for all values of X. Importantly, while we have moved the points, we have not changed the concordance. In both series, a higher value of X implies a higher value of Y. Because of this, Kendall's tau for both series is 100%.

In Figure 6.11, even though both relationships are deterministic, Pearson's correlation is 100% only for the first series, not for the second. In general, if the relationship between two

FIGURE 6.11 **Example of Transformed Data**

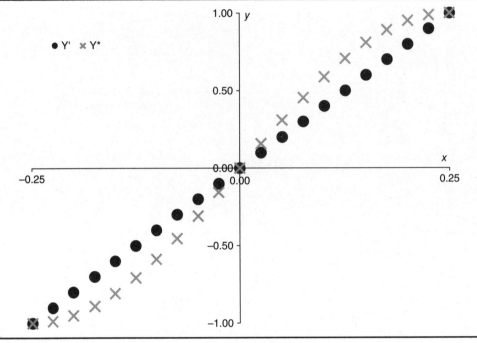

variables can be described by a deterministic linear equation, then the correlation will be ±100%. If the correlation is deterministic but nonlinear, this will not be the case. This is why we describe Pearson's correlation as being a linear measure of association.

As it turns out, for many copulas, changing the marginal distribution—say from a uniform distribution to a normal distribution—will transform the data in a similar way to Figure 6.11. Changing the marginal distribution will change the shape of the data, but not the relative order. For a given type of copula, then, Kendall's tau is often a function of the copula's parameter, α, and does not depend on the type of marginal distributions that are being used. For example, for the FGM copula, Equation 6.20, Kendall's tau is equal to $2\alpha/9$. This leads to a simple method for setting the parameter of the copula. First calculate Kendall's tau, and then set the shape parameter based on the appropriate formula for that copula as it relates Kendall's tau and the shape parameter.

Given an equation for a copula, $C(u,v)$ and its density function $c(u,v)$, Kendall's tau can be determined as follows:

$$\tau = 4\mathrm{E}[C(u, v)] - 1$$

$$= 4 \int_0^1 \int_0^1 C(u, v)c(u, v)dudv - 1 \tag{6.26}$$

Formulas for copulas and their density functions are not always compact. Using Equation 6.26 to calculate Kendall's tau can be tedious, but once you've gone through the calculation you can use the result again and again. Appendix B includes formulas defining Kendall's tau for several copulas.

SAMPLE PROBLEM

Question:

Using Equation 6.26, prove that Kendall's tau for the FGM distribution is equal to $2\alpha/9$. What would alpha be for a data set where Kendall's tau was equal to 10%?

Answer:

The FGM copula is defined by:

$$C = uv[1 + \alpha(1 - u)(1 - v)]$$

$$= uv + \alpha(v - v^2)(u - u^2)$$

We first determine the density function, c, as follows:

$$\frac{\partial C}{\partial u} = v + \alpha(v - v^2)(1 - 2u)$$

$$c = \frac{\partial^2 C}{\partial u \partial v} = 1 + \alpha(1 - 2v)(1 - 2u)$$

To determine Kendall's tau, we need to integrate the product of the copula and the density function. There are a number of ways we could do this. It looks complicated, but simply by multiplying and rearranging terms we get

$$Cc = uv[1 + \alpha(1 - u)(1 - v)][1 + \alpha(1 - 2u)(1 - 2v)]$$

$$= [v + \alpha v(2 - 3v)]u + \alpha v(5v - 3)u^2 + \alpha^2 v(1 - 3v + 2v^2)(u - 3u^2 - 2u^3)$$

To get Kendall's tau, we need to integrate with respect to u and v. Starting with u, we have

$$\int_0^1 Ccdu = \left[\frac{1}{2}(v + \alpha v(2 - 3v))u^2 + \frac{1}{3}\alpha v(5v - 3)u^3 \right.$$

$$\left. + \alpha^2 v(1 - 3v + 2v^2)\left(\frac{1}{2}u^2 - u^3 - \frac{1}{2}u^4\right)\right]_0^1$$

$$= \left[\frac{1}{2}(v + \alpha v(2 - 3v)) + \frac{1}{3}\alpha v(5v - 3)\right.$$

$$\left. + \alpha^2 v(1 - 3v + 2v^2)\left(\frac{1}{2} - 1 - \frac{1}{2}\right)\right] - [0 + 0 + 0]$$

$$= \left(\frac{1}{2} - \alpha^2\right)v + \left(\frac{1}{6}\alpha + 3\alpha^2\right)v^2 - 2\alpha^2 v^3$$

Using this result, we can calculate the following double integral:

$$\int_0^1 \int_0^1 Ccdudv = \int_0^1 \left(\left(\frac{1}{2} - \alpha^2 \right) v + \left(\frac{1}{6}\alpha + 3\alpha^2 \right) v^2 - 2\alpha^2 v^3 \right) dv$$

$$= \left[\frac{1}{2} \left(\frac{1}{2} - \alpha^2 \right) v^2 + \frac{1}{3} \left(\frac{1}{6}\alpha + 3\alpha^2 \right) v^3 - \frac{1}{2}\alpha^2 v^4 \right]_0^1$$

$$= \frac{1}{4} + \frac{1}{18}\alpha$$

We then use this to calculate Kendall's tau,

$$\tau = 4 \int_0^1 \int_0^1 Ccdudv - 1 = 4 \left(\frac{1}{4} + \frac{1}{18}\alpha \right) - 1 = \frac{2}{9}\alpha$$

As expected, Kendall's tau for the FGM copula is equal to $2\alpha/9$.
We can rearrange this result to express α in terms of Kendall's tau,

$$\alpha = \frac{9}{2}\tau$$

If τ is equal to 10%, then $\alpha = 0.45$,

$$\alpha = \frac{9}{2}\frac{1}{10} = \frac{4.5}{10} = 0.45$$

The preceding process of choosing a copula and then determining the parameter of the copula based on Kendall's tau is extremely flexible. As we mentioned at the beginning of the section, there is another measure of dependence based on rank, Spearman's rho. Both Kendall's tau and Spearman's rho range between −1 and +1, and their values are often very similar. To calculate Spearman's rho from sample data, we simply calculate our standard correlation measure using the ranks of the data. We can also calculate Spearman's rho from a copula function as

$$\rho_S = 12 \int_0^1 \int_0^1 C(u, v)dudv - 3 \tag{6.27}$$

In many situations, we can use either Kendall's tau or Spearman's rho. Both are valid. The choice often comes down to familiarity and to which is easier to calculate. For some copulas there is no discrete solution for Spearman's rho. That said, when such a solution does exist, it is often easier to calculate Spearman's rho.

INDEPENDENT AND IDENTICALLY DISTRIBUTED RANDOM VARIABLES

In finance we often assume that draws of a random variable are independent and identically distributed (i.i.d.). For example, we might assume that the daily returns of a stock are i.i.d. We have already come across examples of i.i.d. random variables in Chapters 2 and 5.

Given a set of i.i.d. random variables, we often want to know how the distribution of the sum or mean of the variables is related to the distribution of the individual variables. The famous square-root rule, which we came across in Chapter 5, is a perfect example. It states that the standard deviation of an i.i.d. variable increases with the square root of time. If we assume that the returns of a stock are i.i.d., then the standard deviation of annual returns will be approximately 16 times the standard deviation of daily returns (there are approximately 256 business days in a year, and $\sqrt{256} = 16$).

If draws from a random variable are i.i.d. then the covariance, coskewness, and cokurtosis between two different draws should be zero. Using our definitions of covariance, coskewness, and cokurtosis, we can easily calculate the variance, standard deviation, skewness, and kurtosis of the sum or mean of a set of i.i.d. variables.

For a set of i.i.d. draws from a random variable, $x_1, x_2, \ldots, x_n$, we define the sum, S, and mean, μ, as

$$S = \sum_{i=1}^{n} x_i$$

$$\mu = \frac{1}{n} S \tag{6.28}$$

Denoting the variance, standard deviation, third central moment, fourth central moment, skewness and kurtosis of x by $f(x)$, we define two constants, a and b, such that

$$S = af(x)$$

$$\mu = bf(x) \tag{6.29}$$

Table 6.10 provides values for a and b for each statistic. The second row contains the familiar square-root rule for standard deviation.

The last row tells us that the kurtosis of both the sum and mean of n i.i.d. variables is $1/n$ times the kurtosis of the individual i.i.d. variables. Interestingly, while the standard deviation and variance of the sum of n i.i.d. variable is greater than the standard deviation or variance of the individual random variables, respectively, the skewness and kurtosis are smaller. It is easy to understand why this is the case by noting that the value of a is n for all central moments.

TABLE 6.10 Scaling Factors for i.i.d Random Variables

	a	b
Variance	n	$1/n$
Std. Dev.	$\sqrt{n}$	$1/\sqrt{n}$
m_3	n	$1/n^2$
m_4	n	$1/n^3$
Skewness	$1/\sqrt{n}$	$1/\sqrt{n}$
Ex. Kurtosis	$1/n$	$1/n$

By being familiar with the formulas in Table 6.10 you can often get a sense of whether or not financial variables are independent of each other. For example, consider the Russell 2000 stock index, which is a weighted average of 2,000 small-cap U.S. stocks. Even if the return distribution for each stock in the index was highly skewed, we would expect the distribution of the index to have very little skew if the stocks were independent (by table 6.10, the skewness of the index should be roughly $1/\sqrt{2,000} \approx 1/45$ the mean skewness of the individual stocks). In fact, the daily returns of the Russell 2000 exhibit significant negative skewness, as do the returns of most major stock indexes. This is possible because most stocks are influenced by a host of shared risk factors, and far from being independent of each other. In particular, stocks are significantly more likely to have large negative returns together, than they are to have large positive returns at the same time.

END-OF-CHAPTER QUESTIONS

1. Given the following annual return series for Fund A and Fund B, determine the coskewness, S_{AAB}.

Year	1	2	3	4	5
Fund A	−3%	−1%	0%	1%	3%
Fund B	−3%	0%	3%	1%	−1%

2. We will discuss bond defaults in greater detail in Chapter 8. In general, bond defaults tend to be correlated, but under certain circumstances, you may be able to assume that defaults are independent. For example, assume that your firm is considering investing in two bonds. The bonds were issued by different companies, in different industries, and in different countries. The probability of one of these bonds defaulting is independent of the other. Each bond has a 10% probability of defaulting.

What is the probability that both bonds default? That both bonds do not default? That one bond defaults? Construct a probability matrix.

3. You are evaluating the risk of two binary call options. The options have the same expiration date, but different underlying stocks. The following probability matrix gives the probabilities that either option expires in the money (ITM) or out of the money (OTM).

		Option A	
		ITM	**OTM**
Option B	**ITM**	40%	10%
	OTM	20%	30%

What is the probability that Option A ends up in the money? What is the probability that Option B ends up in the money? What is the probability that both options end up in the money? Are the two options independent?

4. Given the following joint probability density function, determine if X and Y are independent.

$$f(x,y) = \begin{cases} 0 & -2 > X > 2, -2 > Y > 2 \\ c(8 - x^2 - y^2) & -2 \leq X \leq 2, -2 \leq Y \leq 2 \end{cases}$$

where c is equal to 3/256.

5. Look at the two contour plots in Figure 6.12. For each plot, are the two variables positively or negatively correlated? Is the joint distribution elliptical or nonelliptical?

FIGURE 6.12 **Contour Plots for Question #4**

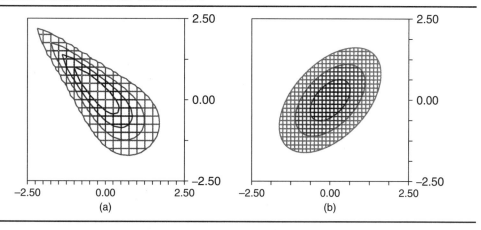

6. Calculate Kendall's tau and Spearman's rho for the following data set.

	X	Y
A	70%	5%
B	40%	35%
C	20%	10%

7. Calculate Kendall's tau for the independent copula, $C(u, v)$, given by

$$C(u, v) = uv$$

8. Calculate Spearman's rho for the FGM copula, Equation 6.20, in terms of α.

9. You have created a Monte Carlo simulation to model the risk of a stock index over 10,000 days. All of the daily log returns have a mean, standard deviation, skewness, and excess kurtosis of 0.10%, 1.00%, −1.60, and 5.12, respectively. If the daily log returns are also independent of each other, what should the mean, standard deviation, skewness, and excess kurtosis of the annual log returns be? Assume 256 business days per year.

7

MARKET RISK: RISK ATTRIBUTION

In this chapter, we introduce the concept of risk attribution, which describes how various positions and groups of positions contribute to the overall risk of a portfolio. Risk attribution can be useful for summarizing the contents of a portfolio, and for managing the risk in a portfolio. We also discuss the related concept of diversification. More specifically we discuss how to quantify diversification.

FACTOR ANALYSIS

In risk management, factor analysis is a form of risk attribution, which attempts to identify and measure common sources of risk within large, complex portfolios.[1] These underlying sources of risk are known as factors. Factors can include equity market risk, sector risk, region risk, country risk, interest-rate risk, inflation risk, or style risk (large-cap versus small-cap, value versus growth, momentum, etc.). Factor analysis is most popular for equity portfolios, but can be applied to any asset class or strategy.

In a large, complex portfolio, it is sometimes far from obvious how much exposure a portfolio has to a given factor. Depending on a portfolio manager's objectives, it may be desirable to minimize certain factor exposures or to keep the amount of risk from certain

---

[1] In statistics, factor analysis can also refer to a specific method of data analysis, similar to principal component analysis (PCA). What we are exploring in this section might be more formally referred to as risk-factor analysis. Risk-factor analysis is a much more general concept, which might utilize statistical-factor analysis, regression analysis, PCA, or any number of statistical methods.

TABLE 7.1 Geographic Exposures

	Market Value
Asia	
China	$359
Japan	$3,349
Europe	
Germany	–$823
Ireland	$500
North America	
United States	$4,865
Mexico	$2,393
Total	**$10,643**

factors within a given range. It typically falls to risk management to ensure that the factor exposures are maintained at acceptable levels.

The classic approach to factor analysis can best be described as risk taxonomy. For each type of factor, each security is associated with one and only one factor. If we were trying to measure country exposures, each security would be assigned to a specific country—France, South Korea, the United States, and so on. If we were trying to measure sector exposures, each security would similarly be assigned to an industry, such as technology, manufacturing, or retail. After we had categorized all of the securities, we would simply add up the exposures of the various securities to get our portfolio-level exposures. Table 7.1 shows how a portfolio's exposure to different regions and countries could be broken down.

In this portfolio, which has a total value of $10,643, there is $359 of exposure to China and a net –$323 of exposure to Europe. A limitation of the classic approach is that it is binary. A security is an investment in either China or Germany; it is either in utilities or in agriculture. It can't be one-third in Russia and two-thirds in Poland, or just 42% in value stocks. This creates a problem in the real world. What do you do with a company that is headquartered in France, has all of its manufacturing capacity in China, sells its products in North America, and has listed shares on the London Stock Exchange? Is a company that sells consumer electronics a technology company or a retailer?

These kinds of obvious questions led to the development of various statistical approaches to factor analysis. One very popular approach is to associate each factor with an index, and then to use that index in a regression analysis to measure a portfolio's exposure to that factor. For example, if we want to measure a portfolio's exposure to Japan, we would run a regression of our portfolio's returns against the returns of a Japanese equity index, using a calculation like

$$R_{\text{portfolio}} = \alpha + \beta R_{\text{index}} + \varepsilon \tag{7.1}$$

The Japanese index could be a publicly available index, such as the Nikkei 225 Index, or it could be an index of our own construction based on a basket of Japanese securities. The return series for our portfolio should reflect what the returns of the current portfolio would have been, given the current holdings of the portfolio. This type of return series is often referred to as a what-if or backcast return series. This is as opposed to the actual return series, which would be impacted by the changing composition of the portfolio over time. Of course, this analysis assumes that both return series obey all the ordinary least squares (OLS) assumptions.

In Equation 7.1, β represents our factor exposure. The exposure will be in the same units as the portfolio returns. If the portfolio returns are in U.S. dollars, the exposure will be in U.S. dollars, too. From this equation, we would already be able to predict that if the index return were −10%, then the impact on the portfolio's return would be −0.10β. Being able to summarize the risk of a large, complex portfolio in such simple terms is what makes regression-based factor analysis so powerful.

Another nice thing about factor analysis is that the factor exposures can be added across portfolios. If Portfolio A has $100 of exposure to technology, and Portfolio B has $200 of exposure to the same factor, then a combined portfolio, Portfolio A + B, would have $300 of exposure to technology. This result can be verified by simply adding together the regression equations of Portfolio A and Portfolio B:

$$R_A = \alpha_A + \beta_A R_{index} + \varepsilon_A$$

$$R_B = \alpha_B + \beta_B R_{index} + \varepsilon_B \tag{7.2}$$

$$R_{A+B} = (\alpha_A + \alpha_B) + (\beta_A + \beta_B)R_{index} + (\varepsilon_A + \varepsilon_B)$$

Because factor exposures are additive, this makes hedging a factor exposure relatively simple. If we have $300 of exposure to technology, and assuming the technology index is tradable, we can hedge this factor by shorting $300 of the technology index; $300 minus $300 leaves us with $0 of factor exposure.

Table 7.2 shows a sample exposure breakdown for an unspecified factor. Notice how the factor exposures are not necessarily proportional to the market values or even of the same sign. Even though there is not a fixed relationship between market value and factor exposure

TABLE 7.2 Adding Factor Exposures across Portfolios

	Market Value	Factor Exposure
Portfolio A	$9,378	−$30,592
Portfolio B	$39,348	$45,829
Portfolio C	−$2,938	−$2,674
Total	$45,788	$12,563

across portfolios, the market values and the factor exposures can each be added up separately to arrive at their respective totals.

In addition to giving us the factor exposure, the factor analysis allows us to divide the risk of a portfolio into systematic and idiosyncratic components. In this case, systematic risk refers to the risk in a portfolio that can be attributed to a factor. The risk that is not systematic (i.e., the risk that cannot be attributed to a factor) is referred to as idiosyncratic risk. In an equity portfolio, this is often referred to as stock-specific risk. From our OLS assumptions, we know that R_{index} and ε are not correlated. Calculating the variance of $R_{portfolio}$ in Equation 7.1, we arrive at

$$\sigma^2_{portfolio} = \beta^2 \sigma^2_{index} + \sigma^2_{\varepsilon} \tag{7.3}$$

In other words, the variance of the portfolio can be broken into two components, $\beta^2 \sigma^2_{index}$, the systematic component, and σ^2_{ε}, the idiosyncratic component. As mentioned previously, depending on the objectives of the portfolio manager, we might consider more or less idiosyncratic variance desirable. If our objective is to replicate an index, we might want to minimize idiosyncratic risk. If our goal is to produce portfolio returns that are uncorrelated with the market, we would want to minimize the systematic risk in the portfolio.

In theory, there is no reason why we cannot extend our factor analysis using multivariate regression analysis. In practice, many of the factors we are interested in will be highly correlated (e.g., most equity indexes are highly correlated with each other). This leads naturally to the use of spreads between indexes for secondary factors in order to avoid multicollinearity. For example, if we are using a broad market index as a primary factor, then the spread between that index and a country factor might be an interesting secondary factor. As outlined in the section on multicollinearity in Chapter 5, we can use the residuals from the regression of our secondary index on the primary index to construct a return series that is uncorrelated with the primary series.

In theory, factors can be based on almost any kind of return series. The advantage of indexes based on publicly traded securities is that it makes hedging very straightforward. At the same time, there might be some risks that are not captured by any publicly traded index. Some risk managers have attempted to resolve this problem by using statistical techniques, such as principal component analysis (PCA) or cluster analysis, to develop more robust factors. Besides the fact that these factors might be difficult to hedge, they might also be unstable, and it might be difficult to associate these factors with any identifiable macroeconomic variable. Even using these statistical techniques, there is always the possibility that we have failed to identify a factor that is an important source of risk for our portfolio. Factor analysis is a very powerful tool, but it is not without its shortcomings.

INCREMENTAL VaR

A number of statistics have been developed to quantify the impact of a position or sub-portfolio on the total value at risk (VaR) of a portfolio. One such statistic is incremental VaR (iVaR). For a position with exposure w_i, we define the iVaR of the position as

$$\text{iVaR}_i = \frac{d(\text{VaR})}{dw_i} w_i \tag{7.4}$$

Here VaR is the total VaR of the portfolio. It is easier to get an intuition for iVaR if we rearrange Equation 7.4 as

$$d(\text{VaR}) = \frac{dw_i}{w_i} \text{iVaR}_i \tag{7.5}$$

The first term on the right-hand side of Equation 7.5, dw_i/w_i, can be thought of as the percentage change in the position size. If we have $200 of a security, and we add $2 to the position, then dw_i/w_i is $2/$200 = 1%. On the left-hand side of the equation, $d(\text{VaR})$ is just the change in the VaR of the portfolio. In other words, if we change the size of a position in our portfolio by 3%, then the VaR of the portfolio will change by the iVaR of that position multiplied by 3%. Equation 7.5 is really only valid for infinitely small changes in w_i, but for small changes it can be used as an approximation. Using iVaR in this way is similar to using delta to approximate the change in the value of an option.

SAMPLE PROBLEM

Question:

You have measured the VaR of a portfolio as $2.4 million. One of the positions in the portfolio, a hedge, has an iVaR of −$4 million. If you increase the size of the hedge by 5%, what will the VaR of the portfolio be, approximately?

Answer:

Notice that the iVaR of the position is negative. Unlike VaR, which is almost always positive, iVaR can be positive or negative. In this particular case, iVaR is negative, so small increases in the size of this position will actually reduce the portfolio's overall risk.

To estimate the portfolio's new VaR, we first compute the change in the total VaR using Equation 7.5:

$$d(\textit{VaR}) \approx 5\% \times (-\$4,000,000) = -\$200$$

Increasing the hedge by 5% will reduce the portfolio VaR by approximately $200,000, leaving the total VaR at approximately $2.2 million:

$$\$2,200,000 = \$2,400,000 - \$200,000$$

One nice property of iVaR is that the sum of the iVaRs in a portfolio are equal to the total VaR of the portfolio. This is not always the case with risk measures. For example, the sum of the VaR of the positions in a portfolio will be greater than or equal to the total VaR of the portfolio. Likewise, the sum of the standard deviations of the positions in a portfolio will be greater than or equal to the total standard deviation of the portfolio.

That iVaR is additive is true no matter how we calculate VaR, but it is easiest to prove for the parametric case, where we define our portfolio's VaR as a multiple, m, of the portfolio's standard deviation, σ_p. Without loss of generality, we can divide the portfolio into two positions: first, the position for which we are calculating the iVaR with size and standard deviation w_1 and σ_1, and second, the rest of the portfolio with size and standard deviation w_2 and σ_2. If the correlation between the two parts of the portfolio is ρ, we have

$$\text{VaR} = m\sigma_p = m(w_1^2\sigma_1^2 + w_2^2\sigma_2^2 + 2\rho w_1 w_2 \sigma_1 \sigma_2)^{1/2} \tag{7.6}$$

Taking the derivative with respect to w_1, we have

$$\frac{d(\text{VaR})}{dw_1} = \frac{m}{\sigma_p}(w_1\sigma_1^2 + \rho w_2 \sigma_1 \sigma_2) \tag{7.7}$$

We then multiply this result by the weight of the position to get

$$\text{iVaR}_1 = w_1\frac{d(\text{VaR})}{dw_1} = \frac{m}{\sigma_p}(w_1^2\sigma_1^2 + \rho w_1 w_2 \sigma_1 \sigma_2) \tag{7.8}$$

We could follow the same procedure for the rest of the portfolio to get

$$\text{iVaR}_2 = w_2\frac{d(\text{VaR})}{dw_2} = \frac{m}{\sigma_p}(w_2^2\sigma_2^2 + \rho w_1 w_2 \sigma_1 \sigma_2) \tag{7.9}$$

Adding together the iVaRs of both parts of the portfolios, we have

$$\begin{aligned}
\text{iVaR}_1 + \text{iVaR}_2 &= \frac{m}{\sigma_p}(w_1^2\sigma_2^2 + w_2^2\sigma_2^2 + 2\rho w_1 w_2 \sigma_1 \sigma_2) \\
&= \frac{m}{\sigma_p}\sigma_p^2 \\
&= m\sigma_p \\
&= \text{VaR}
\end{aligned} \tag{7.10}$$

This is as we expected: The sum of the iVaRs is equal to the total VaR of the portfolio.

SAMPLE PROBLEM

Question:

You are managing the risk for a portfolio with three strategies, A, B, and C. Strategy B has four positions. You had calculated the total VaR and iVaR for all of the positions and strategies, but some of the values were accidentally deleted. All of the iVaRs are relative to the total portfolio VaR of $1,400. This is what you have left:

	VaR	iVaR
Strategy A	$500	$400
Strategy B	$800	$700
Position 1	$200	$300
Position 2	$500	-$200
Position 3	$600	?
Position 4	$300	$100
Strategy C	$800	?
Total	$1,400	?

Fill in the missing values.

Answer:

Notice that all of the positions and all of the strategies have positive VaR values—they are all risky in isolation—but there are both positive and negative iVaRs. Further note that the sum of the VaRs of the strategies, $500 + $800 + $800 = $2,100, is significantly more than the total VaR, $1,400. The same is true for the four positions in Strategy B. The sum of their VaRs, $1,600, is more than the VaR of the strategy, $800.

To fill in the table, we can start at the bottom with the total iVaR. The total iVaR must be equal to the total VaR, $1,400. Next, we can figure out the iVaR of Strategy C. There are only three strategies, and the sum of their iVaRs must equal the total VaR of the portfolio. The iVaR of Strategy C is $1,400 − $400 − $700 = $300. Similarly, within Strategy B we are only missing the iVaR of Position 3. The iVaR of Position 3 is $700 − $300 − (−$200) − $100 = $500.

	VaR	iVaR
Strategy A	$500	$400
Strategy B	$800	$700
Position 1	$200	$300
Position 2	$500	-$200
Position 3	$600	$500
Position 4	$300	$100
Strategy C	$800	$300
Total	$1,400	$1,400

For the last part of the problem, where we calculated the iVaR of Position 3, why did we assume the iVaRs of the positions in Strategy B would add to $700, the iVaR of Strategy B, and not $800, the VaR of Strategy B? The reason is that the iVaRs are relative to the portfolio level, as specified in the question.

Another way to look at this: The division of the portfolio into three strategies is somewhat arbitrary. We could just as easily have viewed the portfolio as consisting of six positions: Strategy A, Strategy C, and the four positions in Strategy B. If that were the case, then the iVaR of these six positions would have to add up to $1,400. That is,

$$\text{iVaR}_A + \text{iVaR}_C + \text{iVaR}_1 + \text{iVaR}_2 + \text{iVaR}_3 + \text{iVaR}_4 = \$1,400$$

Rearranging

$$\text{iVaR}_1 + \text{iVaR}_2 + \text{iVaR}_3 + \text{iVaR}_4 = \$1,400 - \text{iVaR}_A - \text{iVaR}_C$$

Substituting in the iVaR of Strategy A and Strategy C gives us

$$\text{iVaR}_1 + \text{iVaR}_2 + \text{iVaR}_3 + \text{iVaR}_4 = \$1,400 - \$400 - \$300 = \$700$$

Using the same logic, if we divided Strategy A into two strategies, Strategy A1 and A2, we could be certain that the iVaRs of the two new strategies would add up to $400.

In this particular case, the iVaRs were calculated relative to the total portfolio VaR, but this need not be the case. For the four positions, we could have calculated a second set of iVaRs relative to the total VaR of Strategy B, $800. This new set of iVaRs would indicate how changes to any of the four positions would impact the VaR of Strategy B. This might be useful information for a manager who was only responsible for managing Strategy B.

In practice, as risk managers, we usually are most interested in the overall risk of the portfolio and how specific positions impact it. If that is the case, then we should calculate iVaR relative to the entire portfolio.

Before closing, we should note that the naming conventions for statistics that describe the contribution of positions to VaR is not universal. What we have used here is the convention used by a number or risk software providers, and is widely used in practice. Other authors use iVaR to describe the impact of completely adding or removing a position from a portfolio (what most practitioners refer to as marginal VaR).

DIVERSIFICATION

Diversification is a concept closely related to risk attribution. In a way, risk attribution asks how much risk is coming from each source, while diversification asks how many different sources of risk there are. Up until now, we have talked about diversification as a general concept. In this section we introduce some methods for quantifying diversification.

Diworsification

Diversification is the idea we can reduce our overall risk by dividing up our portfolio among different securities. What surprises many portfolio managers and risk managers is that it doesn't take very many securities to greatly reduce risk *if* the securities are not highly correlated with each other. However, adding lots of securities to a portfolio may not reduce risk nearly as much as we might expect, *if* the securities are highly correlated with each other.

Imagine we have a $100 to invest, and we wish to divide it equally among a number of securities. Furthermore, assume all of the securities have the same standard deviation, and all have the same correlation to each other. Figure 7.1 shows how varying the number of securities and correlation impacts the standard deviation of the portfolio. Here, you can see the ratio of the standard deviation of a portfolio with *n* securities, to a portfolio with only 1 security. If the securities are perfectly correlated with each other (correlation = 100%), then no matter how many securities we add to the portfolio, the standard deviation of the portfolio will be unchanged. If the correlation is less than 100%, increasing the number of securities will reduce the standard deviation of the portfolio, but most of the reduction happens early on. If the securities are 50% correlated, we get a significant reduction in standard deviation going from 1 to 10 securities, but going from 10 to 100 has only a minimal impact.

Kent Osband used the term *diworsification* (originally coined by Peter Lynch in a different context), to describe the behavior of portfolio managers who create portfolios with a large number of securities in hopes of significantly lowering the risk of their portfolio. Many equity mutual funds would seem to fit this description. The last securities added to these portfolios are likely to have below-average expected returns, and if the securities are

FIGURE 7.1 Diversification or Diworsification

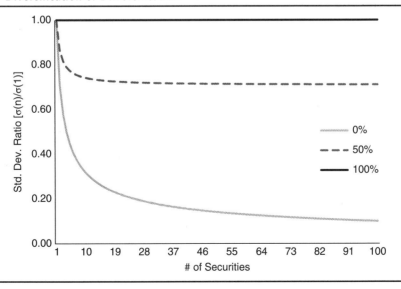

even moderately correlated with each other, then they are not going to reduce the standard deviation of the portfolio significantly. The additional securities don't really reduce risk and they make the expected return of the portfolio worse: diworsification.

To be fair, even if adding lots of securities does not lower standard deviation as much as we might expect, it might reduce other types of risk. If securities suffer large losses occasionally (e.g., defaults for bonds or blow-ups for equities) and these large losses are independent of each other, then having a large number of securities may make more sense. As we will see when we discuss behavioral finance, if investors are extremely risk averse, then going to extreme lengths to avoid these tail events, no matter how unlikely they are, could make even more sense.

Diversification Score

One way to measure diversification is to compare the standard deviation of the securities in a portfolio to the standard deviation of the portfolio itself. If the securities have low correlation to each other (i.e., if the portfolio is highly diversified), then the standard deviation of the portfolio could be low, even if the standard deviations of the securities in the portfolio are very high.

Given a portfolio with standard deviation σ_p and consisting of n securities, $i = 1, 2, \ldots n$, with corresponding standard deviations σ_i, we define the diversification score, h, as

$$h = 1 - \frac{\sigma_p}{\sum\limits_{i=1}^{n} \sigma_i} \tag{7.11}$$

The diversification score has the nice property that it varies between 0 and 1, with 0 being no diversification and 1 being total diversification. When the portfolio has no diversification, either because it is invested in only one security or because all of the securities are perfectly correlated, σ_p will equal the sum of the σ_i. This means the ratio on the right-hand side will be equal to 1 and h equal to 0. There could also be a situation where two or more securities perfectly cancel each other out. In this case, even though the individual securities have non-zero standard deviations, the portfolio standard deviation is zero, the ratio on the right-hand side would equal 0, and h would equal 1.

The diversification score is far from being a perfect measure of diversification. One shortcoming is that it is sensitive to how you group a portfolio. If one portfolio contains $100 million of an S&P 500 exchange-traded fund (ETF), and a second contains $100 million invested directly in the constituent stocks of the S&P 500, the second portfolio will have a higher diversification score, even though the risk profiles of the portfolios are exactly the same. The advantage of the diversification score is that it is easy to calculate and easy to understand.

It should be noted that the preceding definition for the diversification score is far from universal at this time. Similar ratios are widely used by practitioners, but some substitute VaR for standard deviation, don't subtract from 1, and/or invert the ratio.

Diversification Index

Meucci (2009) proposed measuring diversification using principal component analysis. More specifically, a portfolio with n securities will have n principal components. Of all of the principal components, the first explains the greatest amount of the variance in the portfolio, the second the second most, and so on. If we define p_i as the percentage of the variance explained by the ith principal component, then we can define the diversification index, N, as the entropy of the p_i.

$$N = e^{-\sum_{i=1}^{n} p_i \ln(p_i)} \text{ where } \sum_{i=1}^{n} p_i = 1 \qquad (7.12)$$

When the portfolio has no diversification, either because the portfolio has only one security, or all of the securities are perfectly correlated with the same underlying risk factor, then the first principal component will explain all of the variance in the portfolio and $N = 1$. At the other extreme, when the portfolio is maximally diversified, all of the principal components will explain an equal amount of the variance, and $N = n$.

Even though the formulation is rather complicated, this property of varying between 1 and n makes the diversification index somewhat intuitive. From our diworsification discussion, it is clear that some portfolio managers, when they invest in n securities, wrongly believe that they have n independent sources of risk, when in fact they have barely reduced their risk. In the worst-case scenario, even though they have n securities, they only have one source of risk and the diversification index is 1. Put another way, rather than counting securities, we should be counting how many independent sources of risk we have using our diversification index.

RISK-ADJUSTED PERFORMANCE

Risk and return are often said to be two sides of the same coin. Even though we often view them separately, risk and return are intimately related. Because risk and performance are linked and because the analysis of risk-adjusted performance can be mathematically challenging, risk managers are increasingly involved in performance analysis.

One of the most popular measures of risk-adjusted performance is the Sharpe ratio, first proposed by William Sharpe in 1966. For a security with expected return, R_i, and standard deviation, σ_i, given the risk-free rate, R_{rf}, the Sharpe ratio is

$$S_i = \frac{R_i - R_{rf}}{\sigma_i} = \frac{\mu_i}{\sigma_i} \qquad (7.13)$$

Here μ_i is the excess return of security i. The Sharpe ratio is immune to leverage. Assuming we can borrow and lend at the risk-free rate, we can increase and decrease the standard deviation of a portfolio and the ratio of $(R_i - R_{rf})$ to σ_i will remain the same.

If we assume that investors equate risk with standard deviation, then it makes sense that investors would want to maximize the Sharpe ratio of their portfolios. For a given level or risk, the portfolio with the higher Sharpe ratio will provide a higher expected return. Of course, investors may not be able to borrow at the risk-free rate, and financial risk is more than just the standard deviation of returns. Even so, Sharpe ratio maximization is a good first-order approximation to how rational investors should approach portfolio construction.

Assuming investors wish to maximize the Sharpe ratio of their portfolios, if you had to choose between putting all of your money in one of two portfolios, then you should choose the portfolio with the higher Sharpe ratio. Now assume that you already have a portfolio and you want to add one of two securities to your portfolio. Should you choose the security with the highest Sharpe ratio? Not necessarily. What we want to do is to choose the security that will maximize the Sharpe ratio of our new portfolio. In order to do this, we need to take into account not only the Sharpe ratio of the security, but how correlated it is with our existing portfolio. As a portfolio manager, you might be wise to choose a security with a slightly lower Sharpe ratio—if it has a much lower correlation with your existing portfolio—over a security with a higher Sharpe ratio that is highly correlated with your existing portfolio.

More precisely, if we wish to maximize the Sharpe ratio of our portfolio, at the margin we should choose the security with the highest incremental Sharpe, or iSharpe, where the incremental Sharpe ratio, S_i^*, is define as

$$S_i^* = S_i - \rho S_P \qquad (7.14)$$

Here, S_i is the Sharpe ratio of the security, S_p is the Sharpe ratio of the existing portfolio, and ρ is the correlation between their returns. Intuitively, if a security and a portfolio are perfectly correlated, then it will only make sense to add the security to the portfolio if the security has a higher Sharpe ratio than the existing portfolio. If the security has a lower Sharpe ratio, it might still make sense to add it if it provides enough diversification, if ρ is low enough. If S_i^* is negative, then adding the security to your portfolio will actually decrease the overall Sharpe ratio.

To see why, let's see what happens if we add a small amount, δ, of security i to a portfolio. The change in the Sharpe ratio will be

$$\Delta S_P = S_{P+\delta i} - S_P$$

$$= \frac{\mu_{P+\delta i}}{\sigma_{P+\delta i}} - \frac{\mu_P}{\sigma_P}$$

$$= \frac{\mu_P + \delta\mu_i}{\sqrt{\sigma_P^2 + \delta^2\sigma_i^2 + 2\delta\rho\sigma_P\sigma_i}} - \frac{\mu_P}{\sigma_P} \tag{7.15}$$

Without loss of generality, we can assume that $\sigma_P = \sigma_i$. Remember, if we can borrow at the risk-free rate, then we can always transform a security with one volatility into another security with a different volatility but the same Sharpe ratio. Looked at another way, rather than adding δ of the security, we could always add a small amount $\delta^* = \delta k$, where $k\sigma_i = \sigma_P$. Defining $\sigma_P = \sigma_i = \sigma$, then, Equation 7.15 simplifies to

$$\Delta S_P = \frac{\mu_P + \delta\mu_i}{\sigma\sqrt{1 + \delta^2 + 2\delta\rho}} - \frac{\mu_P}{\sigma} \tag{7.16}$$

We can approximate the square root in the denominator in Equation 7.16 using a first-order Taylor expansion. Expanding around $\delta = 0$,

$$(1 + \delta^2 + 2\delta\rho)^{\frac{1}{2}} \approx 1 + \delta\rho \tag{7.17}$$

Putting this back into Equation 7.16

$$\Delta S_P \approx \frac{\mu_P + \delta\mu_i}{\sigma(1 + \delta\rho)} - \frac{\mu_P}{\sigma}$$

$$\approx \frac{\mu_P + \delta\mu_i - \mu_P(1 + \delta\rho)}{\sigma(1 + \delta\rho)}$$

$$\approx \frac{\delta\mu_i - \mu_P\delta\rho}{\sigma(1 + \delta\rho)} \tag{7.18}$$

$$\approx \frac{\delta}{(1 + \delta\rho)}\left(\frac{\mu_i}{\sigma} - \rho\frac{\mu_P}{\sigma}\right)$$

$$\approx \frac{\delta}{(1 + \rho\delta)}S_i^*$$

Because $\rho \leq |1|$, when δ is small, $(1 + \rho\delta) \approx 1$, and

$$\Delta S_P \approx \delta S_i^* \tag{7.19}$$

As we set out to prove if S_i^* is positive, then adding a small amount of the new security will increase the Sharpe ratio of the portfolio. On the other hand, if S_i^* is negative, adding a small amount of the new security will lower the Sharpe ratio. Equation 7.19 also indicates that the greater S_i^*, the greater the change in the Sharpe of the portfolio.

CHOOSING STATISTICS

This was the last of six chapters on market risk. Among other topics, we have looked at standard deviation, VaR, expected shortfall, extreme value theory (EVT), correlation, coskewness, copulas, stress testing, incremental VaR and diversification. As we said at the beginning of Chapter 2, no single risk statistic is perfect. All have their strengths and weaknesses. Standard deviation is very easy to understand and to calculate, but does not take into account the shape of the distribution. Expected shortfall places more emphasis on extreme negative outcomes, but it requires us to make certain model assumptions and is difficult to back-test. Not all of these concepts are mutually exclusive. For example, we might be able to use copulas and EVT to improve our VaR forecast.

While there is not always one right answer, there is often a wrong answer. As our discussion of coskewness and copulas makes clear, if a joint distribution is not elliptical and we assume that it is, then we may severely underestimate risk. All of our models and statistics make certain assumptions. It is important that both the risk manager and portfolio manager understand the assumptions that underlie our models.

Modern financial markets are complex and move very quickly. The decision makers at large financial firms need to consider many variables when making decisions, often under considerable time pressure. Risk—even though it is a very important variable—will likely be only one of many variables that go into this decision-making process. As we mentioned in Chapter 1, an important task of risk managers is dimensionality reduction: taking very complicated financial portfolios and boiling them down to a few key risk statistics. This is not easy, but it is extremely important. Understanding the strengths and weaknesses of various risk statistics is the first step in deciding which statistics to calculate and how to report them.

END-OF-CHAPTER QUESTIONS

1. The total VaR of a portfolio is $10 million. The portfolio contains a position in XYZ worth $1 million, with an iVaR of $3 million. What would the approximate VaR of the portfolio be if the XYZ position was increased to $1.2 million?

2. You have been given the following VaR and iVaR statistics for a portfolio that contains three positions. What is the iVaR of Position B? Assume the iVaR and VaR are both one-day 95%, and have been calculated using the same methodology.

	VaR	**iVaR**
Position A	$500	$300
Position B	$400	?
Position C	$650	$800
Portfolio	$1,000	?

3. You have developed the following regression analysis to describe the returns to a portfolio, r_p, in terms of the returns to an index, r_{Index}, a mean-zero disturbance term, ε, and two constants, α and β:

$$r_p = \alpha + \beta r_{Index} + \varepsilon$$

Here, the systematic part of the portfolio return is $\alpha + \beta r_{Index}$, and the idiosyncratic part is ε. Prove that the attribution of risk to systematic and idiosyncratic parts is additive for variance. Is the same true for standard deviation?

4. A portfolio, with a standard deviation of $30 million contains three positions. The three positions, in turn, have standard deviations of $10 million, $20 million, and $30 million. What is the diversification score of the portfolio?

5. A portfolio contains three securities. You perform principal component analysis on the securities and find that the three principal components explain 60%, 30%, and 10% of the overall variance. What is the diversification index of the portfolio?

6. You are interested in creating a levered version of an ETF. The ETF has a Sharpe ratio of 0.80 and an annual return standard deviation of 20%. The risk-free rate is 2%. Assuming you can borrow at the risk-free rate, what would the Sharpe ratio and expected return be for a 3× levered version of the ETF? In other words, for each $1 invested, you plan to purchase $3 worth of the ETF.

7. A hedge fund is considering hiring two different portfolio managers, Alice and Bob. The fund's Sharpe ratio is currently believed to be 1.00. Based on historical data, you believe that Alice has a Sharpe ratio of 0.80 and is 30% correlated with the fund's existing portfolio. Bob has a Sharpe ratio of 1.10 and is 90% correlated with the existing portfolio. Calculate the incremental Sharpe ratio for both managers. Assuming these values are correct, at the margin, which manager would improve the fund's overall Sharpe ratio the most?

8

CREDIT RISK

Credit risk is the risk that one party in a financial transaction will fail to pay the other party in that transaction. Credit risk can arise in a number of different settings, from bonds and derivatives, to counterparty risk and settlement risk. Our quantitative analysis will focus on the default risk of bonds, but these same tools can be applied in many settings involving credit risk.

DEFAULT RISK AND PRICING

We begin with a brief review of bonds and basic fixed-income pricing. We first consider pricing without default, before moving on to pricing when default is possible.

Bond Pricing

Bonds can be issued by corporations and governments. Bonds issued by corporations are referred to as corporate bonds or simply corporates. Bonds issued by local governments are typically referred to as municipal bonds. Bonds issued by national governments are referred to as government or sovereign bonds. When referring to the risk of sovereign bonds defaulting we often talk of sovereign credit risk.

In each case, the bond issuer has promised to make future payments to the bondholders. If the issuer fails to make a payment, or makes only a partial payment, they are said to have defaulted. Some bonds are issued with covenants that restrict what the issuer can and cannot do. For example, a corporation might include a covenant stipulating that it will maintain a certain debt-to-equity ratio. If the issuer violates a covenant, it is also considered to be a default. While this type of technical default is of interest, in this chapter we will only consider the former type of default, where the issuer fails to make a payment in full.

In practice bonds can be very complicated instruments. They can be callable by the issuer, they can be convertible into common or preferred stock, or even have payments linked to other financial variables. Plain-vanilla bonds have only coupon and principal payments. The principal, also referred to as the face value or notional, is typically a round number—in the US, $100 and $1,000 are very popular—and is paid to the bondholder when the bond matures. Coupons are periodic payments that the bond issuer makes to the bondholders. They are typically a small percentage of the notional. Coupon payments can be fixed or floating. Floating rates are often tied to benchmark interest rates (e.g., LIBOR).

Assume that the discount rate, on an annual basis, at time t is R_t. If there is no probability of default, then the present value of the bond, V_0, that expires in T years, with notional, N, and annual coupon payments, c, is

$$V_0 = \sum_{t=1}^{T} \frac{c}{(1 + R_t)^t} + \frac{N}{(1 + R_T)^T} \tag{8.1}$$

If the coupon payments are certain (i.e., if there is no probability of default), then the appropriate discount rate will be equal to the risk-free rate.

SAMPLE PROBLEM

Question:

You are asked to determine the value of a two-year bond with a notional of $100 and a coupon rate of 5%. The one- and two-year risk-free rates are 3% and 4%, respectively. There is no probability of default. What is the price of the bond?

Answer:

The bond makes two coupon payments of $5 each (5% × $100 = $5). At the end of the second year, in addition to the coupon payment, the investor also receives the notional. The present value of the bond is $101.93:

$$V_0 = \frac{\$5}{(1 + 3\%)} + \frac{\$5}{(1 + 4\%)^2} + \frac{\$100}{(1 + 4\%)^2} = \$4.85 + \$4.62 + \$92.6 = \$101.93$$

We often refer to the notional of a bond as its face value. A bond that is worth more than its face value, as in this example, is said to be selling at a premium. A bond that is worth less than its face value is said to be selling at a discount. A bond worth exactly its face value is said to be selling at par.

Default and Recovery

Not all bonds include coupon payments. Bonds without coupon payments are known as zero-coupon bonds. Pretend we have a risk-free, zero-coupon bond with a notional of $100 that matures in one year, and that the one-year risk-free rate is 5%. The present value of this bond is $95.24:

$$V_t = \frac{\$100}{1.05} = \$95.24 \tag{8.2}$$

As long as the discount rate is positive, zero-coupon bonds will always sell at a discount.

Assume we are pricing the same zero-coupon bond as before, but now there is a 20% chance that the bond will default. Furthermore, assume that in the event of default that there is no payment and the bondholder receives nothing. For a risk-neutral investor, the present value of the bond is simply a weighted average of the two possible outcomes, the one where the bond defaults and the one where the bond does not default. In this particular case, the present value of the bond would be $76.19:

$$V_t = 20\%\frac{\$0}{1.05} + 80\%\frac{\$100}{1.05} = \$76.19 \tag{8.3}$$

When a bond defaults, it is possible that the bondholder will not receive anything, but, in practice, the bond holder usually receives some fraction of the anticipated payments. The loss, as a percentage of the anticipated value is known as the loss given default (LGD). Alternatively, the amount that is paid as a percentage of the anticipated value is known as the recovery rate. The LGD is simply one minus the recovery rate. If the recovery rate is 30%, then the LGD is 70%. In practice, after a bond defaults the determination of the ultimate recovery rate can be a long, drawn-out legal process and, in the case of sovereign debt, a political process as well. In practice, when we refer to LGD rates, rather than the ultimate loss, we are usually referring to how much the bond has lost on a mark-to-market basis immediately after default is announced. If a bond that should be worth $100 trades at $60 immediately after defaulting, then we would say that the LGD was 40%.

Using our zero-coupon bond from the previous example, assume that the recovery rate, rather than being 0%, is 40%. Now, in the event of default, the bondholder will receive 40% of the anticipated $100 principal payment, or $40. The present value is now $83.81:

$$V_t = 20\%\frac{\$40}{1.05} + 80\%\frac{\$100}{1.05} = \$83.81 \tag{8.4}$$

Risk-Neutral Default Estimates versus Actual Default Estimates

In the preceding analysis we used the risk-free rate to discount the bond's cash flows. This is known as risk-neutral pricing. Risk-neutral pricing is appropriate when investors are risk neutral, or when risk can be eliminated through diversification or hedging. We can use risk-neutral pricing to price options only because, in theory, we can eliminate the risk of movements in the underlying security through delta hedging. However, we almost always expect equities to earn more than the risk-free rate because, even though we can significantly reduce stock-specific risk by holding a large portfolio of stocks, we cannot completely eliminate market risk through diversification.

If bond defaults were truly independent of each other, then the default rate of a very large portfolio of bonds would always be very close to the expected default rate. Unfortunately, bond defaults are highly correlated. There are years when lots of bonds default and years when very few bonds default. The uncertainty of default losses cannot be entirely eliminated through diversification. Because of this, and because most investors are risk averse, investors require higher expected returns for riskier bonds. In other words, given an expected probability of default, risky bonds will sell at a lower price than we would expect based on risk-neutral pricing. Looked at another way, given the price of a bond, the expected default rate should be lower than what we would expect based on a risk-neutral valuation.

In addition to the fact that we cannot completely eliminate variation in default risk through diversification, risky bonds are often illiquid. This will also cause investors to require an even higher expected rate of return. This will tend to further reduce bond prices or decrease the actual rate of default relative to our risk-neutral model.

Yield

Even when bonds have the same maturity, different coupon rates and notionals can make it difficult to compare the value of bonds. Because of this, when comparing bonds, traders typically refer to the yield to maturity, or simply the yield, of the bond. The yield to maturity of a bond is simply the internal rate of return, assuming all payments are made. The yield to maturity is equal to the constant discount rate that solves the bond pricing equation, Equation 8.1. In other words, for a bond with notional, N, and annual coupons, c, and T years to maturity, the yield, Y, satisfies

$$V_0 = \sum_{t=1}^{T} \frac{c}{(1+Y)^t} + \frac{N}{(1+Y)^T} \qquad (8.5)$$

When coupon payments are involved, it is impossible to solve Equation 8.5 explicitly for Y, but most financial calculators and spreadsheets will be able to solve for Y using other methods. In the case where there are no coupons, the yield is simply

$$Y = \left(\frac{N}{V_o}\right)^{1/T} - 1 \qquad (8.6)$$

For a one-year zero-coupon bond, with probability of default D, and a loss given default L, the initial price is

$$V_0 = (1 - D)\frac{N}{(1 + R)} + D(1 - L)\frac{N}{(1 + R)} = (1 - DL)\frac{N}{(1 + R)} \qquad (8.7)$$

Substituting into Equation 8.6, we have

$$Y = \frac{R + DL}{1 - DL} \qquad (8.8)$$

Using Equation 8.8 it is easy to see that, for a zero-coupon bond, if the probability of default is zero or if the LGD is zero, then the yield will be equal to the discount rate, as we would expect.

As in our previous example, assume we have a one-year zero-coupon bond with a 20% probability of defaulting. The discount rate is 5%, and the recovery rate is 40%. The yield is then 19.32%:

$$Y = \frac{5\% + 20\% \times 60\%}{1 - 20\% \times 60\%} = 19.32\% \qquad (8.9)$$

Notice that the yield, 19.32%, is considerably higher than the discount rate of 5%. The yield is the return that an investor will get if everything works out and there is no default. All else being equal, a risky bond will need to offer a higher yield in order to compensate investors for bearing the additional risk of default.

DETERMINING THE PROBABILITY OF DEFAULT

How do we determine the probability of default for a given bond issuer? We could try to back out the default rate, based on observed market prices using an equation similar to Equation 8.7. But, as discussed, because investors are risk averse, this will only give us the risk-neutral implied default rate, not the actual default rate.

We could look at the historical default rate for a bond issuer, but for any particular bond issuer, defaults are likely to be rare. Many bond issuers have never defaulted. If we are going to forecast the probability of default for a given issuer, we cannot rely on the history of defaults for that issuer. We will need some other approach.

In this section we consider two basic approaches. First, the traditional approach, which relies on a mix of quantitative and qualitative data. Second, the quantitative approach, which is model-based and strictly quantitative.

Traditional Ratings Approach

The traditional approach to forecasting defaults is for rating agencies to assess the creditworthiness of an issuer. In assessing the creditworthiness of the issuer, the rating agency takes into account a number of factors. For corporations, the factors are likely to include financial ratios, such as debt-to-equity ratios and interest-coverage ratios. The factors could also include some qualitative assessments, such as the firm's business prospects, or, in the case of sovereigns, how fiscally responsible the government is likely to be. Ultimately, how the data are combined and how the final assessment is made is often highly subjective.

The three largest ratings agencies in the United States are Fitch, Moody's, and Standard & Poor's (S&P). All assign letter ratings to bonds. AAA is considered the highest rating and least likely to default. This is followed by AA, A, BBB, BB, B, and C. The precise labels vary by agency. All three agencies issue a number of more precise ratings, for example S&P's AA rating is further divided into AA+, AA, and AA− categories. Table 8.1 list the full set of ratings for all three agencies. In all cases, a rating of BBB or better is considered to be investment grade. A rating of BB or below, is considered to be non-investment grade, or speculative. These speculative bonds are commonly referred to as high-yield bonds or junk bonds.

To the extent that more highly rated issuers have been less likely to default than lower-rated issuers, the traditional approach seems to have worked historically. Table 8.2 shows the average five-year default rate for corporate bonds rated by Moody's from 1920 to 2011. As expected, AAA bonds have defaulted at a lower rate than AA bonds, which have defaulted at a lower rate than A bonds, and so on.

TABLE 8.1 Bond Ratings

Fitch	Moody's	S&P	
AAA	Aaa	AAA	Investment Grade
AA+	Aa1	AA+	
AA	Aa2	AA	
AA−	Aa3	AA−	
A+	A1	A+	
A	A2	A	
A−	A3	A−	
BBB+	Baa1	BBB+	
BBB	Baa2	BBB	
BBB−	Baa3	BBB−	
BB+	Ba1	BB+	Speculative
BB	Ba2	BB	
BB−	Ba3	BB−	
B+	B1	B+	
B	B2	B	
B−	B3	B−	
CCC	Caa1	CCC+	
	Caa2	CCC	
	Caa3	CCC−	
	Ca	CC	
		C	
DDD	C	D	Defaulted

TABLE 8.2 Five-Year Corporate Bond
Default Rate, 1920–2011.

	Default Rate
Aaa	0.16%
Aa	0.80%
A	1.31%
Baa	3.09%
Ba	9.81%
B	22.25%
Caa-C	41.72%

Source: Moody's Investors Service.

Over time default rates vary widely, overall and for individual letter ratings. Figure 8.1 shows the default rate for all corporate bonds between 1920 and 2011. The variation in default rates is driven largely by changes in the economic environment. As risk managers, if we were to base our forecast of default rates over the next year on long-run average default rates, our forecasts would be very inaccurate most of the time. Fortunately, some of the variation over time in default rates is predictable. The various rating agencies issue default forecasts on a regular basis. As with the ratings, these forecasts are based on both quantitative and qualitative inputs.

The disadvantage of the traditional approach to forecasting defaults is that it is labor intensive and lacks transparency. Because the traditional approach is labor intensive, ratings and default probabilities are updated infrequently. This can be especially disconcerting in rapidly

FIGURE 8.1 Corporate Bond Default Rate, All Issuers, 1920–2011.

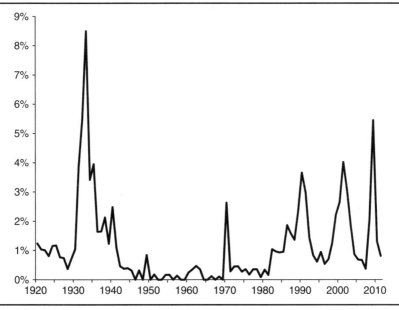

Source: Moody's Investors Service

evolving markets. The advantage of the traditional approach is that it is extremely flexible. Corporations and governments are extremely complex. By necessity, any quantitative model is likely to leave out a large amount of potentially relative information.

Transition Matrices

A ratings transition matrix provides the probability that a bond's rating will change or stay the same over a given time period, given its rating at the start of that period. Table 8.3 is a simple one-year ratings transition matrix. From this matrix, we can tell that an A-rated bond has a 90% probability of still being A-rated after one year, an 8% probability of migrating to a B rating, and a 2% probability of ending up with a C rating.

In our sample transition matrix, a B-rated bond has a 2% probability of defaulting over the course of one year. What about over two years? Your first guess might be that the probability is $4\% = 2\% + 2\%$, or that it is $3.96\% = 1 - (1 - 2\%)^2$. Both of these answers are wrong. To correctly calculate the probability of default over two years, we need to consider all of the possible paths that a B-rated bond could take to default. Over two years, there are four ways in which the bond could default:

1. It could migrate to A in the first year and then default.
2. It could remain at B during the first year and then default.
3. It could migrate to C and then default.
4. It could default the first year and stay defaulted.

We can easily calculate each of these probabilities. For example, the probability of migrating from B to C to D is just the probability of migrating from B to C, multiplied by the probability of migrating from C to D, or $8\% \times 15\% = 1.2\%$. The probability of the bond migrating from B to D over two years is just the sum of the probabilities of the four possible paths. The following set of equations shows this calculation with the final result, 4.80%.

$$P[B \rightarrow D] = P[B \rightarrow A \rightarrow D] + P[B \rightarrow B \rightarrow D] + P[B \rightarrow C \rightarrow D] + P[B \rightarrow D \rightarrow D]$$

$$= \quad x_{2,1}x_{1,4} \quad + \quad x_{2,2}x_{2,4} \quad + \quad x_{2,3}x_{3,4} \quad + x_{2,4}x_{4,4}$$

$$= \quad 10\% \times 0\% \quad + \quad 80\% \times 2\% \quad + \quad 8\% \times 15\% \quad + \quad 2\% \times 100\%$$

$$= 4.80\% \tag{8.10}$$

TABLE 8.3 **One-Year Ratings Transition Matrix**

1-Year		To a rating of:			
		A	**B**	**C**	**D**
From a rating of:	**A**	90%	8%	2%	0%
	B	10%	80%	8%	2%
	C	0%	25%	60%	15%
	D	0%	0%	0%	100%

TABLE 8.4 Five-Year Ratings Transition Matrix

5-Year		To a rating of:			
		A	B	C	D
From a rating of:	A	64.7%	24.8%	6.7%	3.7%
	B	28.1%	46.0%	12.1%	13.8%
	C	11.8%	35.0%	14.3%	39.0%
	D	0.0%	0.0%	0.0%	100.0%

In the second row of Equation 8.10, we have expressed the problem in terms of standard matrix notation, with $x_{2,1}$ indicating the element in the second row and first column of the ratings transition matrix. Notice that for the first element in each product, we are going across the second row of the transition matrix, and for the second element in each product we are going down the fourth column. This is exactly what we would do to get the element in the second row and fourth column if we were multiplying the transition matrix by itself. This is no coincidence. It turns out rather conveniently that we can calculate the complete two-year transition matrix by multiplying the one-year transition matrix by itself. If $\mathbf{T}_1$ is our one-year transition matrix, and $\mathbf{T}_2$ is our two-year transition matrix, then

$$\mathbf{T}_2 = \mathbf{T}_1 \mathbf{T}_1 = \mathbf{T}_1^2 \tag{8.11}$$

Interested readers should check this for themselves by calculating additional values for the two-year matrix.

What is even more convenient is that we can generalize this formula. To calculate the n-year transition matrix, we simply raise $\mathbf{T}_1$ to the nth power:

$$\mathbf{T}_n = \mathbf{T}_1^n \tag{8.12}$$

For example, starting with the one-year ratings transition matrix in Table 8.3, we could produce the five-year rating transition matrix in Table 8.4. In this example, an A-rated bond has a high probability of maintaining its rating and zero probability of defaulting over one year. Over five years, though, an A-rated bond has a much lower probability of staying at the same rating and a much higher probability of defaulting.

Quantitative Approach

Over time a number of practitioners and academics have tried to develop a more systematic, quantitative approach to predicting default. In this section we explore the widely used distance-to-default model, first proposed by Robert Merton in 1974.

What is a firm worth? One way to calculate the value of a firm would be to add up the value of all of its assets (e.g., its factories, intellectual property, the goodwill of its customers, etc.) and subtract any liabilities (e.g., money that the firm owes to suppliers, future pension or tax obligations, etc.). This is a perfectly legitimate way to proceed, but it poses a number of challenges, not least of which is valuing intangibles such as intellectual property and pension obligations. Another way to proceed would be to ask what value does the market place on the firm. For a firm that has issued both stocks and bonds the answer is simply the total value of its stock *plus* the value of its bonds. We refer to this total value as the enterprise value. As an equation, if we denote the enterprise value of the firm as V_E, and the value of the firm's stock as S, and the value of its bonds by B, we have

$$V_E = S + B \tag{8.13}$$

Note that the enterprise value of a firm is not the same as the firm's market capitalization, which is simply the value of the firm's stock.

To understand why the value of the firm is equal to the value of its stock plus its bonds—and what this has to do with default probabilities—imagine that we have just launched a firm. In order to raise funds, we sell $300 of equity and issue $200 worth of one-year bonds. For simplicity, pretend the bonds have no coupon, and are sold at par. At the end of the first day, we have $500 in cash from the sale of the equity and bonds. Now pretend that on day two we invest all of our new capital in a widget factory. In the first scenario, we'll imagine that the widgets sell well. At the end of the year, we have made $300 in profit and decide to sell the factory to another firm for $500, the same price we paid for it. At the end of the year, we have $800 in cash, a return of 60% on our initial $500. How did our investors do? Even though the firm was very successful, the bondholders still only get back their initial $200. The equity investors get the remaining $600, giving them a return of 100%. Using Equation 8.13, we can see that at the end of the year the firm's enterprise value is equal to the $800 in cash, our only asset, $V_E = \$800 = \$600 + \$200$.

Now pretend that instead of selling well, it turned out that nobody wanted to buy widgets. Rather than making a profit of $300, we lost $200 on sales. When we went to sell the factory, we were only able to get $400, $100 less than what we paid. At the end of the year, we have lost $300 ($200 on sales and $100 on the factory) and only have $200, just enough to pay back the bondholders. The equity holders would have lost everything, a return of −100%. That is pretty bad, but what if we had lost more than $300? In this case we would not be able to pay back the bondholders in full and we would be in default (the equity holders would still have a return of −100%).

These examples clearly illustrate the difference between debt and equity. The bondholders, as creditors to the firm, have only downside potential and no upside potential. The equity holders, as owners of the firm, reap all of the upside but they must always pay their creditors before they pay themselves. In the worst-case scenario, the equity holders end up with nothing. Merton's great insight was to realize that we can view the equity holders as having a call option on the value of the firm. Viewed this way, the value of the equity, S, at the end of the year is

$$S = \text{Max}(V_E - B, 0) \qquad (8.14)$$

In other words, the owning the stock of a firm is equivalent to owning a call option on the enterprise value of the firm, with a strike price equal to B, the value of the bonds. Because we can observe the price of the equity in the stock market, and we know B, we can use the Black-Scholes-Merton option pricing formula to back out the market-implied volatility of the enterprise value. If we know the current enterprise value, and we know the expected volatility of the enterprise value, then we can easily determine the probability of default, which is the probability that the enterprise value will fall below B. This scenario is illustrated in Figure 8.2, where the gap between V_E and B is labeled as Δ. Here, Δ is the amount that the enterprise value would need to decrease in order for the firm to go bankrupt. We refer to this amount as the distance to default. At expiry it is equal to the value of the firm's equity.

Rather than express the distance to default in dollar terms, what we really want to know is the probability of default. If we assume that the log returns of the enterprise value follow a normal distribution, then this is equivalent to asking how many standard deviations we are from default. Because we are using options pricing, we need to take into account the

FIGURE 8.2 The Merton Model of Default

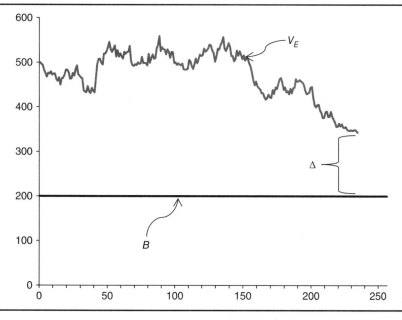

expected risk-neutral drift of the enterprise value, $(r - \sigma_V^2/2)T$, where r is the risk-free rate, σ_V is the implied volatility of the enterprise value, and T is the time to expiration. In order to default, the enterprise value must undergo a return of $\ln(1 - S/V_E) = \ln(B/V_E) = -\ln(V_E/B)$. Finally, the standard deviation of the returns over the remaining life of the option is $\sigma_V \sqrt{T}$. Putting it all together, the distance to default in standard deviations is

$$\Delta = \frac{-\ln\left(\frac{V_E}{B}\right) - \left(r - \frac{\sigma_V^2}{2}\right)T}{\sigma_V\sqrt{T}} = -d_2 \qquad (8.15)$$

Here we have introduced the variable $-d_2$, which is the common designation for this quantity in the Black-Scholes-Merton model. Finally, to convert this distance to default into a probability of default, we simply use the standard normal cumulative distribution function, $P[D] = N(-d_2)$.

SAMPLE PROBLEM

Question:

You are asked to calculate the probability of default over one year for a company with $100 of debt and a current market capitalization of $172. The implied volatility of the enterprise value is 40% and the risk-free rate is 8.00%.

Answer:

We first calculate the distance to default using Equation 8.15.

$$\Delta = \frac{-\ln\left(\frac{V}{B}\right) - \left(r - \frac{\sigma_V^2}{2}\right)T}{\sigma_V\sqrt{T}} = \frac{-\ln\left(\frac{\$172+\$100}{\$100}\right) - \left(8\% - \frac{40\%^2}{2}\right)1}{40\%\sqrt{1}}$$

$$\Delta = \frac{-\ln(2.72) - (8\% - 8\%)}{40\%} = \frac{-1.00}{40\%} = -2.50$$

The distance to default is −2.5 standard deviations. Using a spreadsheet or other application to find the corresponding probability from the normal cumulative distribution function, we have

$$P[D] = N(-2.5) = 0.62\%$$

0.62% is our final answer. According to Table 8.2, this is somewhere between the historical average default rates for AAA and AA bonds.

The preceding examples and sample problem all assume a relatively simple capital structure. In reality, firms often have very complicated capital structures, which can include short-term debt, bank loans, and bonds with different maturities and provisions. The Merton model can still be applied in these situations; it is just more complicated.

The Merton model has many advantages when compared to the traditional ratings approach. By observing equity prices, we can update default probabilities on a continuous basis. Because all of the inputs are market based, there are no subjective inputs and the results are free from human biases. This also makes it easy to automate the entire process of updating default probabilities. The default probabilities produced by the Merton approach can take on any value between 0% and 100%—unlike the traditional letter ratings, which are discrete—potentially allowing investors to better differentiate between various bonds. One disadvantage of the Merton approach is that it makes many simplifying assumptions—for example, that the log returns of the enterprise value are normally distributed. More sophisticated versions of the model can improve on the assumptions of the basic model, but there will always be simplifying assumptions. The more flexible ratings-based approach is not constrained in this way. Another problem with the Merton approach is that it cannot be easily extended to private firms or governments, both of which lack publicly traded equity, and represent a large share of the fixed-income market. Public firms with thinly traded equity may also be difficult to model using the Merton approach.

Which approach is better? In practice, asset managers with large fixed-income holdings often use both ratings and quantitative models. They are also likely to supplement public ratings and commercially available quantitative models with their own internal ratings and models. One of the best examples of how the two approaches are viewed in practice can be seen in the history of KMV. Prior to 2002, KMV was one of the leading firms offering software and ratings based on Merton-type quantitative models. KMV suggested that its approach was superior to the approach of the rating agencies, and the rating agencies shot right back, insisting that their approach was in fact superior. In 2002, one of those rating agencies, Moody's purchased KMV. Moody's now offers products and services combining both approaches.

PORTFOLIO CREDIT RISK

In this section we consider ways in which we can model credit risk at the portfolio level. The methods used to combine securities in a portfolio to assess credit risk are often very similar to those used to assess market risk. That said, there are some techniques which are unique to credit modeling, and even when the techniques are similar, there may be subtle differences that warrant careful attention.

Probability of *n* Defaults

If we have a portfolio of bonds, then it is natural to ask what the probability is that a given number of bonds will default. What is the probability of *n* defaults?

The simplest scenario to consider is a portfolio of identical bonds, with the same probability of default, where the actual event of default for any given bond is statically independent from the event of default any of the other bonds. In this scenario, the distribution of defaults follows a binomial distribution. Mathematically, this is very similar to how we modeled value at risk exceedances in Chapter 3.

A binomial distribution can be thought of as a collection of Bernoulli random variables. If we have two independent bonds and the probability of default for both is 10%, then there are three possible outcomes: no bond defaults, one bond defaults, or both bonds default. Labeling the number of defaults K,

$$P[K = 0] = (1 - 10\%)^2 = 81\%$$

$$P[K = 1] = 2 \times 10\% \times (1 - 10\%) = 18\%$$

$$P[K = 2] = 10\%^2 = 1\% \tag{8.16}$$

Notice that for $K = 1$ we have multiplied both the probability of a bond defaulting (10%) and the probability of a bond not defaulting $(1 - 10\%)$ by 2. This is because there are two ways in which exactly one bond can default: The first bond defaults and the second does not, or the second bond defaults and the first does not.

If we now have three bonds, still independent and with a 10% chance of defaulting, then,

$$P[K = 0] = (1 - 10\%)^3 = 72.9\%$$

$$P[K = 1] = 3 \times 10\% \times (1 - 10\%)^2 = 24.3\%$$

$$P[K = 2] = 3 \times 10\%^2 \times (1 - 10\%) = 2.7\%$$

$$P[K = 3] = 10\%^3 = 0.1\% \tag{8.17}$$

Notice that there are three ways in which we can get exactly one default and three ways in which we can get exactly two defaults.

We can extend this logic to any number of bonds. If we have n bonds, the number of ways in which k of those bonds can default is given by the number of combinations,

$$\binom{n}{k} = \frac{n!}{k!(n-k)!} \tag{8.18}$$

Similarly, if the probability of one bond defaulting is p, then the probability of any *particular* k bonds defaulting is simply $p^k(1 - p)^{n-k}$. Putting these two together, we can calculate the probability of any k bonds defaulting as

$$P[K = k] = \binom{n}{k} p^k(1 - p)^{n-k} \tag{8.19}$$

Equation 8.19 is the probability density function (PDF) for the binomial distribution. You should check that this equation produces the same result as our examples with two and three bonds. While the general proof is somewhat complicated, it is not difficult to prove that the probabilities sum to one for $n = 2$ or $n = 3$, no matter what value p takes. It is a common mistake when calculating these probabilities to leave out the combinatorial term.

For the formulation in Equation 8.19, the mean of random variable K is equal to np. So, for a bond portfolio with 40 bonds, each with a 20% chance of defaulting, we would expect eight bonds ($8 = 20 \times 0.40$) to default on average. The variance of a binomial distribution is $np(1 - p)$.

SAMPLE PROBLEM

Question:

Assume we have four bonds, each with a 10% probability of defaulting over the next year. The event of default for any given bond is independent of the other bonds defaulting. What is the probability that zero, one, two, three, or all of the bonds default? What is the mean number of defaults? The standard deviation?

Answer:

We can calculate the probability of each possible outcome as follows:

# of Defaults	$\binom{n}{k}$	$p^k(1 - p)^{n-k}$	Probability
0	1	65.61%	65.61%
1	4	7.29%	29.16%
2	6	0.81%	4.86%
3	4	0.09%	0.36%
4	1	0.01%	0.01%
			100.00%

We can calculate the mean number of defaults two ways. The first is to use our formula for the mean,

$$\mu = np = 4 \times 10\% = 0.40$$

On average there are 0.40 defaults. The other way we could arrive at this result is to use the probabilities from the table. We get

$$\mu = \sum_{i=0}^{4} p_i x_i$$

$$= 65.61\% \times 0 + 29.16\% \times 1 + 4.86\% \times 2 + 0.36\% \times 3 + 0.01\% \times 4 = 0.40$$

This is consistent with our earlier result.

To calculate the standard deviation, we also have two choices. Using our formula for variance, we have

$$\sigma^2 = np(1-p) = 4 \times 10\%(1-10\%) = 0.36$$

$$\sigma = 0.60$$

As with the mean, we could also use the probabilities from the table:

$$\sigma^2 = \sum_{i=0}^{4} p_i(x_i - \mu)^2$$

$$= 65.61\% \times 0.16 + 29.16\% \times 0.36 + 4.86\% \times 2.56 + 0.36\% \times 6.76 + 0.01\% \times 12.96$$

$$= 0.36$$

Again, this is consistent with our earlier result.

Figure 8.3 shows binomial distributions with $p = 0.50$, for $n = 4$, 16, and 64.

Monte Carlo Simulation

In practice, it is unlikely that all of the bonds in a portfolio will be identical, and default events are likely to be correlated. Not only are defaults correlated in general, but bonds with similar or related issuers are likely to have even more highly correlated defaults.

FIGURE 8.3 Binomial Probability Density Functions

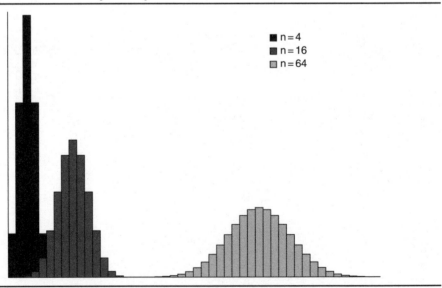

Corporate issuers may be more highly correlated if they are in the same industry or geography. Sovereign issuers may be more highly correlated if they are geographically close or linked by trading patterns.

Perhaps the simplest and most flexible approach to modeling correlated defaults is to use a Monte Carlo simulation. The disadvantage of using a Monte Carlo simulation is that, because default events are rare, a large number of trials must be run. This can lead to long calculation times.

When modeling defaults in a Monte Carlo simulation, the event of default for any given bond is normally modeled as a Bernoulli random variable, zero or one. This Bernoulli random variable is created from a standard uniform random variable (the default output of most programming languages' random number generators, and the RAND function in Excel). If the draw from the standard uniform variable is less than or equal to the default rate, then the bond defaults. If it is greater than the default rate, the bond does not default.

A slight complication can arise when trying to make defaults correlated. It is relatively easy to produce correlated standard normal variables. Because of this, it is tempting to first create a set of correlated standard normal variables and then convert these standard normal variables to standard uniform variables using the standard normal cumulative distribution function (CDF). The only problem is that correlation is not preserved under this nonlinear transformation. In other words, if the correlation between two normal variables is 50% and we convert them to uniform variables using the normal CDF, the correlation between the resulting uniform variables will not be 50%. It will be close, but it will not be exactly 50%.

Figure 8.4 shows the difference in correlations as a function of the correlation between the two normal variables. When two normal variables are negatively correlated, the two uniform variables produced from them will have a slightly higher correlation. For example, if two normal variables are −60% correlated, then the two uniform variables produced will be approximately −58% correlated. When two normal variables are positively correlated, the two uniform variables will tend to be less highly correlated. Only if the two normal variables are perfectly correlated, perfectly negatively correlated, or have zero correlation, will the correlation of two uniform variables will be the same. This error function can be closely approximated by a sine function. Equation 8.20 provides an approximation that reduces the maximum discrepancy from approximately 1.81% to 0.28%. Here ρ_{NN} is the correlation between the two normal variables and ρ_{UU} is the correlation between the resulting uniform variables.

$$\rho_{NN} \cong \rho_{UU} + 0.01813 \times \sin(\rho_{UU}\pi) \tag{8.20}$$

If necessary, additional terms can be employed to further reduce the error.

FIGURE 8.4 Correlation when Transforming Normal Variables to Uniform Variables

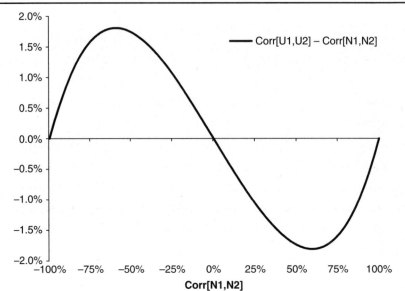

FIGURE 8.4 Correlation when Transforming Normal Variables to Uniform Variables

REDUCING CREDIT RISK

There are a number of ways in which a lender can reduce the credit risk from a borrower. Careful research and monitoring can help reduce unexpected credit losses. No matter how much research a lender does, though, default is always a possibility. Here we discuss five approaches to reducing credit risk.

The first method for reducing credit risk is to restrict the activity of the borrower. At the start of the chapter, we mentioned that bonds often include covenants that restrict what the bond issuer can and cannot do. Breaching a covenant is normally considered a default event. In our discussion of the Merton model, we described how equity holders can be viewed as being long a call option on the value of the firm. All other things being equal, increased volatility increases the value of a long option position. All else being equal, equity holders would like to see the firm increase its volatility. The bondholders, on the other hand, have effectively sold a put on the value of the firm. They would rather see the firm reduce the volatility of the value of the firm. Bond covenants are a way to mitigate this inherent conflict of interest between equity holders and bondholders. By restricting what the firm can do, the covenants limit the potential volatility of the firm, and reduce the bondholders' credit risk. Bondholders, in return for this reduction in risk, will be willing to pay more for the firm's bonds. This basic approach of restricting the behavior of the borrower can be employed in any setting. Banks can place covenants on loans to businesses, and brokers can place limits on the investment activities of investment firms and individuals to whom they extend margin.

Another way to limit credit risk is to have the borrower back the loan with collateral. Collateral is property that the borrower owns. In the event of default, depending on the terms of the loan, the property may be either turned over to the lender or sold, with the proceeds from the sale being used to pay back the loan. When mortgage lenders provide a mortgage to a homeowner, the home is almost always used as collateral for the mortgage loan. If the homeowner stops making payments, the mortgage lender can take possession of the home. Similarly, cars normally serve as collateral for auto loans. Manufacturers might use factories and equipment as collateral to secure bank loans. Corporations may use a portfolio of securities or real property to collateralize bond issues. If a bond issuer issues both collateralized and noncollateralized bonds, all else being equal, the collateralized bonds will have a lower yield because they entail less risk.

A large firm or municipality may borrow money from many different sources including suppliers, banks, and bondholders. In the event of default or bankruptcy, lenders are rarely treated equally. Some are considered to be more senior, and their claims are settled first. Others are considered to be junior, or subordinate, and their claims are settled later. A firm can specify the seniority of debt when the debt is issued. A corporation could issue both senior and subordinated bonds. In the event of default, the senior bondholders would be paid before the subordinated bondholders. Because of this, all else being equal, senior bonds will have a lower yield than subordinated bonds.

Netting is a popular mechanism employed by financial firms to reduce credit risk. Pretend you are the risk manager of an investment fund. Further pretend that your fund has purchased an at-the-money call on the S&P 500 from CR Bank, and sold an at-the-money call on the Dow Jones Industrial Average (DJIA) back to CR Bank. The notionals of the two trades are similar in size. The two indexes have similar standard deviations, and are highly correlated. Because your fund is both long and short similar calls, you conclude that the combined market risk of these two trades is very low. Now suppose that both indexes increase throughout the year and that at expiration both options are worth $1 million. That is, your firm owes CR Bank $1 million for the DJIA call, and CR Bank owes your firm $1 million for the S&P 500 call. Now suppose that CR Bank declares bankruptcy the same day that the options expire. In theory, they could try to claim the $1 million from you for the DJIA call (after all, you entered into a contract with them that said you would pay them in this scenario), but not pay you for the S&P 500 call (they could claim that other creditors are more senior than your firm and they need to pay back those other firms first). To avoid this sort of situation, most firms enter into netting agreements. With a netting agreement in place, a firm has to settle all contracts with a counterparty or none. In the case just mentioned, if a netting agreement were in place, and these were the only outstanding trades between your firm and CR Bank, then CR Bank would have to net its $1 million gain against its $1 million loss. The result would be no net payment and no loss for your firm.

Futures contracts are attractive to investors for a number of reasons, including the fact that they are listed on public exchanges, and that their contract terms are standardized. They also have very little credit risk. A forward contract, by contrast, can entail substantial credit risk. This is because all futures transactions are mediated by a clearinghouse. The clearinghouse, in turn, typically has margin requirements and daily settlement. Every futures contract or forward contract has two sides, a buyer and a seller. These contracts are a zero-sum game. Any profit made by the buyer is a loss to the seller, and vice versa. With futures contracts, the clearinghouse steps between the buyer and the seller. Rather than dealing with each other directly, the buyer of a futures contract buys the contract from the clearinghouse, which in turn tries to sell the contract to another market participant. Importantly, all payments go through the clearinghouse. If you buy or sell a futures contract, you only have to worry about the creditworthiness of the clearinghouse. The clearinghouse tries to reduce its overall credit risk, by maintaining little or no net exposure. The clearinghouse does this by maintaining an equal number of buyers and sellers for each type of contract. The clearinghouse typically also reduces its credit risk to each counterparty with margin requirements. That is, the clearinghouse requires each buyer or seller to maintain a certain amount of cash or securities, which serves as collateral for any potential payments. Most clearinghouses also require daily settlement. Rather than waiting until the futures contract expires to exchange payments, the contracts are marked to market, and appropriate payments are made from or to the clearinghouse at the end of each day. For example, if you buy a futures contract and the contract decreases in value by $10 the first day, you might transfer $10 to the clearinghouse. If the contract increased in value by $10 the next day, the clearinghouse might pay you back $10. In this way, the most that the clearinghouse can lose is one day's profit. In practice, the precise rules for daily settlement are usually more complicated, but the basic idea is the same.

Clearinghouses, netting, seniority, collateral, and covenants are all mechanisms designed to reduce credit risk. The legal agreements that underlie these mechanisms can be complicated. In attempting to reduce its credit risk, a firm may end up increasing its legal risk, a type of operational risk.

END-OF-CHAPTER QUESTIONS

1. What is the present value of a two-year bond with an annual coupon of 10% and a $1,000 notional? Assume there is no probability of default and that the risk-free rate is 5%.

2. A one-year bond has a 4% coupon and a notional of $100. There is a 12% probability that the bond will default. The expected recovery rate is 20%. What is the present value of the bond? Assume a risk-neutral valuation. The risk-free rate is also 4%.

3. A two-year bond with a 10% coupon and a notional of $100 is selling for $85. What is the yield of this bond?

4. A one-year zero-coupon bond with a 19% probability of defaulting currently has a market price of $72. The risk-free rate is 5%. What risk premium are investors demanding to accept the credit risk of this bond? Assume 100% LGD.

5. A company has $2,076 of debt outstanding and a market capitalization of $1,924. All of the debt matures in exactly one year. What is the probability that the company will default? Ignore drift and assume that the volatility of the enterprise value is 40%.

6. A bond portfolio contains 40 identical bonds, each with a 5% probability of defaulting. Defaults are independent. What is the probability that exactly four bonds default?

9

LIQUIDITY RISK

In a crisis, liquidity can often make the difference between survival and disaster for a financial firm. We begin this chapter by defining liquidity risk before introducing measures and models that can help manage liquidity risk.

WHAT IS LIQUIDITY RISK?

In financial risk management, when we talk about liquidity risk we are talking about the risk that a firm will not be able to buy or sell a security in the desired quantity near the current market price. In the worst-case scenario there will be no liquidity, and the firm will not be able to buy or sell at any price.

When we look at market risk, we typically assume that there is *a price* at which each security trades. In practice there is never really a single price. Even for very liquid securities there is always a bid-ask spread (sometimes referred to as the bid-offer spread). The spread is the difference between the highest price at which somebody is willing to buy (the bid) and the lowest price at which somebody is willing to sell (the ask). The quoted market price is likely either the last traded price, or the midpoint between the bid and the ask. If we want to sell a security, the bid is the best price that we will get. If we want to sell a large quantity of a security, our average price might be well below the bid. The more we try to sell, the lower the price we will have to accept. Similarly, the more we try to buy the more we are likely to pay on average.

Beyond this standard definition of liquidity risk, we can also think about liquidity risk in broader terms. Financial firms must constantly balance an internal demand for liquidity (cash) against the external supply of liquidity. The more narrow definition of liquidity given in the preceding paragraph covers just one aspect of this external supply of liquidity.

The Demand for Liquidity

Implicit in our narrow definition of liquidity risk is that we will need to buy and sell securities in the future. All firms require cash in order to conduct business. Farmers require cash to buy seeds and equipment and to pay laborers. Manufacturers require cash to buy raw materials, to purchase machines, and to pay workers. An investment fund, likewise, may require cash to pay trading fees, to rebalance its portfolio, or to meet the liquidity needs of investors.[1] Collectively we can refer to these needs for cash as *cash-flow uses* or as the *internal demand for liquidity*.

The internal demand for liquidity driven by trading fees is likely to be negligible and highly predictable for most funds. For exchange-traded securities, fees and commissions are likely to be explicit, set at a fixed dollar amount or a fixed percentage for each trade. For securities that trade over the counter, there are often no explicit fees; rather, the fees are incorporated into the bid-ask spread. This has traditionally been how foreign exchange (FX) markets work for large institutional investors.

The internal demand for liquidity driven by the need to rebalance the portfolio can be driven by changes in risk or changes in the investment outlook. Even in the absence of trading, the composition of a portfolio will change over time as security prices rise and fall. This will cause the risk of the portfolio to change as well. Changes in the market environment may also cause us to change our assessment of risk. If risk increases significantly, we many have to reduce positions (sell long positions, cover short positions), increase hedges (which may entail buying or selling securities), or rotate positions (decrease some positions and increase others). If risk is too low we may want to increase risk (remember the objective of risk management is not to eliminate risk), which will also involve adjusting positions. Our investment outlook will also change over time. As new information becomes available, a portfolio manager may decide to change the overall size of a portfolio or to rotate capital between different positions. If many market participants change their outlook at the same time, market dynamics can become very complicated as everybody tries to buy or sell securities as quickly as possible at the best price, realizing that all the other participants are trying to do the same.

---

[1] In the case of mutual funds and hedge funds, it is important that we differentiate between the investment fund and the fund advisor. Though we often confuse the terms in everyday speech, a mutual fund or hedge fund is a legal entity that contains the assets of the fund. The fund is managed by the fund advisor, a separate legal entity, who earns fees (e.g., management fees, incentive fees) for managing the fund. Technically, the investment fund does not pay employees; rather, the fund pays fees to the advisor, who in turn pays its employees.

The demand for liquidity, driven by the cash-flow needs of investors, is likely to vary from firm to firm. An insurance firm will manage an asset portfolio, whose proceeds are used to pay policy claims. If policy claims spike (e.g., due to a natural disaster), the insurer may have to liquidate part of its investment portfolio. A university endowment may need to liquidate part of its portfolio if the university for which it is managing funds requires more cash. The university's cash-flow demands may in turn be driven by changes in tuition subsidies, research grants, or capital projects. Mutual funds and hedge funds may face considerable uncertainty over cash-flow demand due to investor redemptions. The distribution of redemptions over time will depend greatly on the number of investors the fund has, the types of investors it has, and how often investors can liquidate.

A popular statistic for summarizing demand for liquidity is known as cash flow at risk (CFVaR). Similar to VaR, CFVaR measures the maximum possible cash-flow demand over a given time horizon at a given confidence level. For example, if the 99% CFVaR over one month is $5 million, this means that there is only a 1% probability that cash-flow demand will be greater than $5 million. CFVaR is also sometimes referred to as liquidity at risk (LaR).

The overall demand for liquidity varies significantly from firm to firm and can be challenging to model. Because of this, the financial literature tends to focus on the supply of liquidity but, for a risk manager, understanding the demand for liquidity is equally important.

The Supply of Liquidity

In finance, when we talk about liquidity risk, we tend to focus exclusively on our ability to buy and sell securities in the market. Indeed, this is consistent with the narrow definition of liquidity risk that was given at the beginning of the chapter. While liquidating positions is one way for financial firms to raise cash, there are other ways. Financial firms may be able to raise cash from new investors or to borrow money from other financial firms, central banks, or government agencies. As with the demand for liquidity, these other sources of liquidity tend to vary significantly from firm to firm and can be difficult to model.

Because these other sources of liquidity are difficult to model, we tend to focus on the market supply of liquidity, the liquidity derived from our ability to buy and sell securities. For any given financial firm, the market supply of liquidity is largely determined by other market participants. If we are trying to sell a security, the supply is defined by how much of that security other firms are willing to buy and at what price. Likewise, when we are trying to buy a security, liquidity supply is defined by how much of that security sellers are willing to sell and at what price. While models for the market supply of liquidity are not as standard as market- and credit-risk models, there are a number of approaches that practitioners have developed to measure liquidity risk. The rest of this chapter explores some of these approaches.

SIMPLE LIQUIDITY MEASURES

We begin by exploring some relatively simple liquidity measures. These measures fail to fully capture all aspects of liquidity risk, but they are easy to calculate and understand.

Weighted Average Days Volume

One of the simplest and most widely used measures of portfolio liquidity is the weighted average days' volume, often referred to simply as the average days' volume for a single security. For a single security, the average days' volume is simply the number of units (shares, contracts, etc.) owned by a firm divided by the average daily trading volume of the security. For example, if you own 10 million shares of XYZ and the average daily trading volume of XYZ is 2 million shares, then you own five days' volume of XYZ. For short positions, we need to use the absolute value of the number of units. If you are short 20,000 bond futures, and the average daily volume is 40,000 contracts, then you have exposure to $+0.5$ days' volume, not -0.5 days'.

Notice that we used the ambiguous term *average* in describing this measure. Practitioners are divided on using the mean or the median when calculating average trading volumes. On the one hand, trading volumes often spike around news events, producing highly skewed distributions. Because of this, the median will tend to be more stable and more conservative. On the other hand, if these volume spikes are fairly common, or our trading horizon is sufficiently long, the mean may provide a better indication of how difficult it will be to liquidate a position. Because of this, and because average daily volume is such a commonly used expression, we will continue to use *average* to describe this particular statistic.

To get the weighted average days' volume for a portfolio of securities we can calculate a weighted average based on each position's absolute market value. If a portfolio contains n securities, and the total market value and average days' volume of the ith security are v_i and $\overline{d}_i$, respectively, then the portfolio's weighted average days' volume, $\overline{d}_{Portfolio}$, is

$$\overline{d}_{Portfolio} = \frac{\sum\limits_{i=1}^{n} |v_i|\overline{d}_i}{\sum\limits_{i=1}^{n} |v_i|} = \frac{\sum\limits_{i=1}^{n} |x_i p_i|\dfrac{|x_i|}{\overline{q}_i}}{\sum\limits_{i=1}^{n} |x_i p_i|} \tag{9.1}$$

where x_i is the number of units owned of the ith security, with price, p_i, and average daily volume, $\overline{q}_i$.

SAMPLE PROBLEM

Question:

Calculate the weighted average days' volume of a portfolio that is long 20 million shares of MSFT and short 10 million shares of GOOG. Assume MSFT's closing price is $50 and its average daily trading volume is 40 million shares. Assume GOOG's closing price is $500 and its average daily trading volume is 10 million shares.

Answer:

The portfolio's average days' volume of MSFT is 0.5, and of GOOG is 1.0:

$$\overline{d}_{MSFT} = \frac{|20\text{ million}|}{40\text{ million}} = 0.5$$

$$\overline{d}_{GOOG} = \frac{|-10\text{ million}|}{10\text{ million}} = 1.0$$

The absolute market value of the MSFT position is $1,000 million. The absolute market value of the GOOG position is $5,000 million. Using Equation 9.1, we get the portfolio's overall weighted average days' volume, 0.92.

$$\overline{d}_{Portfolio} = \frac{\$1\text{ MM} \times 0.5 + \$5\text{ MM} \times 1.0}{\$1\text{ MM} + \$5\text{ MM}} = \frac{\$500 + \$5}{\$6} = 0.92$$

Notice that even though we own more shares of MSFT, the portfolio's weighted average days' volume is closer to that of GOOG. This is because GOOG represents 83% of the gross market value of the portfolio due to its higher share price.

One way to interpret the weighted average days' volume is that if we own five days' volume of a security, then it would take us five days to liquidate our position in that security if we traded the current average daily volume of the security every day for five days. The average daily volume for a particular security is the average daily volume for all market participants, though. It is unlikely that one firm could trade the average daily volume for the entire market for any length of time without significantly impacting the security's price. An easy solution to this problem is to imagine what would happen if you could only liquidate a certain percentage of the average daily volume. For example, if you limited yourself to 20% of average daily volume then it would take 25 days to trade out of 5 days' volume of a security (25 = 5 / 20%). Even though it requires some interpretation, because it is simple and easy to understand, reporting the weighted average days' volume using 100% of the average daily volume is still very popular.

Up until this point we have suggested measuring a security's volume based on the number of units (shares, bonds, etc.) that have traded historically. Traditionally, this unit volume is how volume has been measured and quoted. An alternative is to measure dollar volume.

If 1,000 shares of XYZ traded yesterday and the average price was $15, then we could say that the volume was 1,000 shares or $15,000. Dollar volumes can make comparing the liquidity of different securities easier. Dollar volumes are also likely to be robust to stock splits (Raw unit volumes would not typically be robust to splits, but they are often adjusted for splits to remedy this.). When prices are trending up or down, it is possible that unit or dollar volumes will be more stable. There are theoretical arguments to be made for both measures.

The advantage of using weighted average days' volume to summarize liquidity is that it is easy to calculate and easy to understand. That said, weighted average days' volume is incredibly simplistic and leaves out many aspects of liquidity risk, which may be important. Weighted average days' volume works best when a portfolio is composed of similar securities with similar risk characteristics and similar trading volumes. If a firm has a mix of highly liquid and highly illiquid securities, or if it has a mix of high-volatility and low-volatility securities, then we are likely to have to look beyond weighted average days' volume in order to accurately gauge liquidity risk.

Liquidity Schedule

A liquidity schedule shows how quickly a portfolio can be liquidated. Table 9.1 provides an example. Here 40% of the portfolio can be liquidated within one day, and the entire portfolio can be liquidated within four days.

To create a liquidity table, we need to make an assumption about how quickly we can liquidate individual positions. As with weighted average days' volume, there is no universally agreed-upon value. In practice a risk manager may look at more than one scenario, for example, a fast liquidation scenario and a slow liquidation scenario. Once we have decided on a liquidation rate, we calculate how much of each position we can liquidate each day. The standard approach for adding positions across the portfolio is to use gross market value. In Table 9.1, the fact that we can liquidate 60% of the portfolio within two days would typically mean that we can liquidate 60% of the gross market value within two days.

TABLE 9.1 Liquidity Schedule

Day	% Liquidated
1	40%
2	60%
3	80%
4	100%

SAMPLE PROBLEM

Question:

You are asked to calculate a liquidity schedule for a portfolio containing $100 million each of PTR and XOM. From previous work you know that the PTR position represents 0.50x the average daily volume of PTR and that the XOM position represents 0.25x the average daily volume of XOM. Assume that you can liquidate 10% of the average daily volume each day.

Answer:

If we can liquidate 10% of the average daily volume each day, then it will take us 5 days to liquidate the PTR position and 2.5 days to liquidate the XOM position. Looked at another way, we will be able to sell, at most, $20 million of PTR and $40 million of XOM each day. For PTR,

$$\frac{0.5 \text{ daily volume}}{10\% \text{ daily volume/day}} = 5 \text{ days}$$

$$\frac{\$100 \text{ million}}{5 \text{ days}} = \frac{\$20 \text{ million}}{\text{day}}$$

Using these values, we begin to construct our liquidation table. First, we insert our per day liquidity values. The only tricky part here is that on the third day there is only $20 million of XOM left to sell, so rather than selling $40 million, we sell $20 million. We then add these values together to get the total sold each day. We add these values to get the cumulative amount sold at the end of each day. We then turn this into a percentage of gross exposure by dividing by $200 million, the total initial gross market value of the portfolio. This last column in the table is our liquidation schedule.

Day	Per Day			Cumulative	
	PTR ($MM)	XOM ($MM)	Total ($MM)	Total ($MM)	% Liquidated
1	$20	$40	$60	$60	30%
2	$20	$40	$60	$120	60%
3	$20	$20	$40	$160	80%
4	$20		$20	$180	90%
5	$20		$20	$200	100%

A liquidity schedule is only slightly more complicated to calculate for a portfolio than the weighted average days' volume. When the liquidity of positions varies greatly within a portfolio, a liquidity schedule provides a more accurate picture of the supply of liquidity. Consider, for example, two portfolios each with two equal-sized positions. In the first portfolio both positions represent 10 days of average daily volume. In the second portfolio, the first position represents 1 day's volume and the second represents 19. In both cases, the weighted average days' volume is 10, but the liquidity schedules would be very different. Which portfolio is better? It depends on the expected liquidity requirements. If you need to liquidate the entire portfolio as quickly as possible, then the first portfolio is better. If it is more important that you can liquidate up to half of the portfolio quickly, then the second is better.

The liquidity schedule is more granular than the weighted average days' volume, but the standard liquidity schedule still omits many details. As we've described it, the liquidity schedule ignores market risk. Imagine two portfolios, Portfolio A and Portfolio B, each containing two positions of equal size. In Portfolio A, the first position is illiquid and has market risk, while the second position is liquid and has low market risk. In Portfolio B, there is also one liquid and one illiquid position, but the illiquid position has low market risk and the liquid position has high market risk. Even though the liquidity schedule of the two portfolios will be very similar, if we need to reduce market risk quickly, then Portfolio B will be better. If the market risk of securities varies greatly, we may need a risk measure that combines market risk and liquidity risk.

We may also need to consider how securities are related to each other. For example, what if we only have two positions, a very *illiquid* long equity position and a very liquid short futures hedge? If we liquidate the hedge first, without selling the long position, market risk could increase significantly. If we want to avoid a sharp increase in market risk, we will only be able to liquidate the hedge as fast as we can liquidate the long equity position. A more comprehensive approach to modeling liquidity would incorporate this market-risk dynamic as well. We will explore this idea further when we discuss optimal liquidation later in the chapter. Before that, though, we examine liquidity measures that focus not on how fast positions can be liquidated, but on the costs associated with liquidation. Up until now we have been asking, "How much can we sell without having too much of an impact on price?" These models turn the question around and ask, "Given how much we want to sell, how much will it cost us?"

LIQUIDITY COST MODELS

Our standard market-risk model is based on market prices, which are often the midpoint of the bid-ask spread. When we go to sell a security, we will not receive this market price, but the ask price, which is slightly lower. This lower price will act to reduce our profit and loss (P&L). We can add this potential loss into the profit distribution due to market risk. We can then calculate the liquidity-adjusted value at risk (LVaR), which should not be confused with the previously mentioned liquidity at risk (LaR).

If we try to sell too much, we may push down the price and our profits further. In the first section we will ignore this potential source of loss and assume we can trade as much as we want at the current bid or ask price. In other words, we will assume that the price at which we can buy and sell securities is exogenous, and not impacted by our actions. In the second section, when we look at endogenous models, we will incorporate the potential impact of our own behavior on security prices.

Exogenous Liquidity Models

The difference between the market price and the price where we can buy or sell is equal to half the bid-ask spread. Given the bid-ask spread, the LVaR for a single unit of a security is just the standard VaR plus half the bid-ask spread. For n units of the security, we simply multiply the spread by n.

$$\text{LVaR} = \text{VaR} + n\frac{1}{2}(P_{\text{ask}} - P_{\text{bid}}) \tag{9.2}$$

Equation 9.2 is true for both long and short positions. The bid-ask spread, $P_{\text{ask}} - P_{\text{bid}}$, is always positive; therefore, LVaR is always greater than the VaR.

For extremely liquid securities, under normal market conditions, the bid-ask spread might be relatively stable. For less liquid securities, or in unsettled markets, the bid-ask spread may fluctuate significantly. Rather than using a fixed bid-ask spread, then, it may be appropriate to model the spread as a random variable. As with the distribution of market returns used to calculate our standard VaR, we can use either parametric or non-parametric distributions to model the bid-ask spread.

When adding spread adjustments to our market risk distribution, it may be necessary to consider the correlation between spreads and market returns. In severe down markets, spreads will often widen. Depending on whether we are long or short, this correlation may make LVaR worse or better, compared to an assumption of no correlation. Spreads may also increase as market volatility increases.

In Equation 9.2, we specified the bid-ask spread as the difference between the ask price and the bid price. For example, if the bid and ask prices were $9.90 and $10.10, respectively, then the bid-ask spread would be $0.20. Quoting spreads in dollar terms like this is common practice in financial markets. When modeling spreads, though, it might be more appropriate to use percentage spreads. A percentage spread is just the dollar spread divided by the midpoint price of the security. In this example, $0.20 divided by the mid-price, $10.00, would be a 2% spread. Are percentage spreads more stable over time and across securities? If two securities are similar in all respects, except one is trading at $200 and one is trading at $2, shouldn't the dollar spread of the security trading at $200 be 100 times as great?

In theory, we might expect percentage spreads to be more stable. In practice because securities trade in discrete increments, and because there are fixed costs associate with trading a unit of a security, the distribution of dollar spreads may in fact be more stable. This is another factor to consider when specifying a model.

Endogenous Liquidity Models

Financial securities, just like all other goods and services, are subject to the law of supply and demand. The higher the price of a security, the more sellers will be willing to sell, increasing the supply, but the less buyers will be willing to buy, decreasing the demand.[2] When the price of a security is lower, supply will decrease and demand will increase. If we could see the prices and associated quantities at which all market participants are willing to buy and sell a security, we could form partial supply and demand curves.[3]

Figure 9.1 shows an example of a partial supply and demand curve for a security. Unlike the supply and demand curves that you might be familiar with from economics textbooks, these partial curves represent only the buyers and sellers who are unwilling to trade at the current price. These buyers and sellers represent potential liquidity in the market. The small gap between the two leftmost points on each curve represents the bid-ask spread. Because securities trade in discrete units (e.g., currently U.S. stocks trade in one-cent increments) when we look closely at these curves, they appear jagged. In the top half of Figure 9.1, we can see this clearly. If we zoom out, though, as in the bottom half of the figure, the curves start to look smooth. As we will see, even when markets are discrete, we often base our models on these smooth approximations.

A popular functional form for supply and demand curves is to choose constant elasticity. The elasticity, λ, is the percentage change in quantity divided by the percentage change in price:

$$\lambda = \frac{dQ/Q}{dP/P} \tag{9.3}$$

In normal markets, the elasticity of demand is negative, and the elasticity of supply is positive. If the elasticity of demand were -2, then a 10% reduction in a security's price would

---

[2] For many securities, bonds, and equities, the ultimate supply is fixed. Unless a company sells more shares or more bonds, this ultimate supply will not change. What we are referring to here is not this ultimate supply, but the supply that is available to trade in the market, which can change very quickly.

[3] In some markets we refer to Level I and Level II quotes. Level I represents the bid and ask prices. Level II represents the best bid and ask prices along with quantities for all market makers. We could base supply and demand curves off these Level II quotes, but to get the full supply and demand curves, we would need not just the best bids and asks, but how much the market makers were willing to buy or sell at any price, plus this same information from non–market makers.

FIGURE 9.1 Partial Supply and Demand Curves

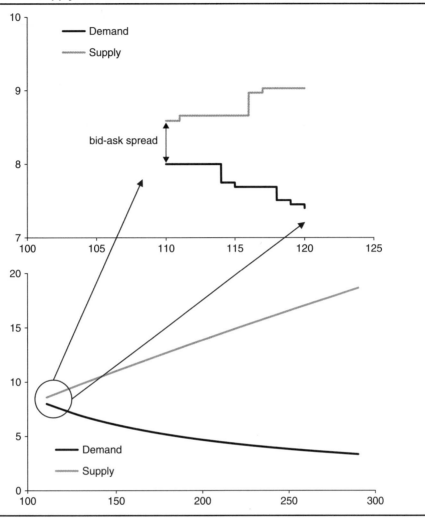

correspond to a 20% increase in the demand for the security. In order for the elasticity to remain constant as P and Q change, the demand curve must be of the form

$$P = \left(\frac{Q}{\alpha} \right)^{1/\lambda} \tag{9.4}$$

where α is a constant. For the demand curve, if elasticity is extremely negative then a significant increase in sales will entail only a negligible impact on price. If the elasticity is closer to zero, then a small increase in sales will result in a large impact on price. Once we know the elasticity of demand, it is a simple matter to calculate the impact of a given trade on the price of the security. This can then be translated into a loss, which can be added to the market VaR to arrive at the LVaR.

LVaR is a compelling statistic for a number of reasons. It defines liquidity risk in terms of its impact on P&L, and it provides us with a single number which captures both market and liquidity risk. It is not without its disadvantages, though. Spreads may be difficult to esti-mate for illiquid securities—the very securities that may pose the most liquidity risk—and estimating the supply or demand functions can be extremely difficult, even for liquid secu-rities. The uncertainty surrounding estimates of the liquidity adjustment could potentially swamp the overall estimate, turning a meaningful VaR statistic into a difficult-to-interpret LVaR statistic. In practice, LVaR is rarely a replacement for VaR; rather, it is reported in addition to VaR.

The impact of liquidation on P&L will be significantly impacted by what quantity is traded and by how quickly the trades are carried out. A meaningful LVaR needs to take into account what percentage of the portfolio might be liquidated in a crisis, and how quickly. As with exogenous models, endogenous models can be deterministic or stochastic. Also, as with exogenous models, endogenous models can take into account other variables such as market returns.

Even though the name is very similar to VaR, LVaR is fundamentally different. Whereas we can backtest VaR, comparing it to actual P&L on a regular basis, large liquidations are likely to happen infrequently. LVaR is likely to be very difficult to backtest.

Volume-Weighted Average Price

When executing trades, traders often refer to the volume-weighted average price (VWAP). The VWAP is just the average trade price for a security over a certain time span, weighted by the number of shares traded at each price. For example, over the course of an hour, if 10 shares trade at $90 and 30 shares trade at $110, then the VWAP would be $(10 \times \$90 + 30 \times \$110)/(10 + 30) = \$105$. As an investor, if you go to buy shares and your weighted average price is significantly above the market's VWAP, then you may wonder if your executing broker is doing a good job. Maybe your executing broker tried to buy the shares too quickly and pushed the price up in the process.

In an effort to guarantee a fair price for their clients, many executing brokers will offer to buy and sell at the VWAP (or very close to it). In order to provide this service, the executing broker needs to have a firm grasp on the supply and demand for each security. For large investors, the ability to place VWAP orders can significantly reduce uncertainty around trade execution.

OPTIMAL LIQUIDATION

When trying to liquidate a portfolio or part of a portfolio, there is always a trade-off between reducing risk and reducing liquidation costs. If we trade out of positions too quickly, we are likely to move the market, which will negatively impact our P&L. If we trade more slowly, we may be able to trade closer to the market price, but the market may start to move against us. Up until now, the speed at which we have liquidated has always been somewhat arbitrary. For example, with liquidity schedules, we typically assume an arbitrary percentage of average daily volume, which determines how long it takes to liquidate the portfolio. With LVaR models, the standard approach is to choose an arbitrary liquidation horizon, which, in turn, determines the liquidation cost. The idea behind optimal liquidation is to let the model choose the time horizon, so that risk reduction and liquidation costs are balanced.

We start with a simple scenario. Imagine you are faced with a choice: You are long $100 of XYZ. Tomorrow there is a 50/50 chance that the price of XYZ will either increase or decrease by 10%. You can either sell the entire position today, or sell half today and half tomorrow. On either day, you can sell up to $55 at 2% below the market price. If you sell the $100 in one day you will need to sell at 4% below the market price. What should you do?

As summarized in Figure 9.2, if you sell everything today you are guaranteed to get $96. If you only sell 50% today you have a 50/50 chance of ending up with $102.90 or $93.10. This is an expected payout of $98. If you wait, you are better off on average, but you could be worse off. In this scenario, no choice is necessarily better than the other. Which is better depends on personal preference. More specifically, as we will see when we discuss behavioral finance, the choice depends on how risk averse you are. If you are extremely risk averse you will choose $96 with certainty. If you are less risk averse, you will choose to accept more risk for a slightly higher expected return. Determining the appropriate level of risk aversion to apply can make the optimal liquidation difficult to determine in practice.

FIGURE 9.2 Optimal Liquidation

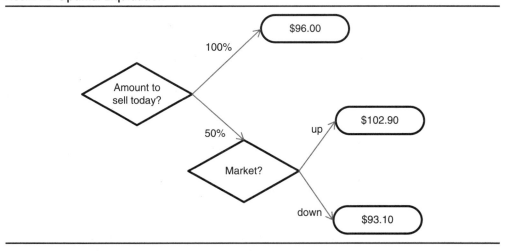

Full-blown scenario analysis can be extremely complex. As with LVaR, we can use exogenous spreads or endogenous spreads, and consider the correlation of liquidity risk to other risk factors.

END-OF-CHAPTER QUESTIONS

1. The following table contains price and volume data over 15 days for shares of AAPL. What is the 15-day average trading volume in terms of shares? What is the 15-day average dollar volume? Calculate both values based on both the mean and the median.

	Volume (millions of shares)	Price ($)
5/23/2017	20	153.80
5/24/2017	19	153.34
5/25/2017	19	153.87
5/26/2017	22	153.61
5/30/2017	20	153.67
5/31/2017	24	152.76
6/1/2017	16	153.18
6/2/2017	28	155.45
6/5/2017	25	153.93
6/6/2017	27	154.45
6/7/2017	21	155.37
6/8/2017	21	154.99
6/9/2017	65	148.98
6/12/2017	72	145.42
6/13/2017	34	146.59

2. You own 2 million shares of IBM. The current price of IBM is $80 and the average daily volume of IBM is 4 million shares. How many days' volume of IBM do you own?

3. In addition to the IBM shares from Question 2, assume you are short 3 million shares of MSFT. MSFT's current price is $50 and the average daily volume of MSFT is 6 million shares. Construct a liquidity schedule for this portfolio assuming 20% of average daily volume.

4. A trader has $1,000 to invest. The trader can either buy 1,000 shares of ABC at $1, or buy 1 share of XYZ, for $1,000. The bid-ask spread for ABC is $0.01, and for XYZ

is \$1. Both stocks have an annualized return standard deviation of 16%. What is the one-day 95% LVaR for each of these choices. For this question, assume that returns are normally distributed and that there are 256 business days per year.

5. Assume the demand function for XYZ exhibits a constant elasticity of −4. The current demand in the market is 10 million shares, and the current price of XYZ is \$64. If you try to sell an additional 2.5 million shares, by how much will the price of XYZ decrease? What will the proceeds from the sale be? Use Equation 9.3 to get your answer.

10

BAYESIAN ANALYSIS

Bayesian analysis is an extremely broad topic. In this chapter we introduce Bayes' theorem and other concepts related to Bayesian analysis. We will begin to see how Bayesian analysis can help us tackle some very difficult problems in risk management. We start with a quick review of conditional probability.

CONDITIONAL PROBABILITY

In risk management, we are often concerned with the relationship between financial variables. For example, we might want to know the probability of our portfolio having a negative return after a market crash, or the probability that a bond will default if the economy enters a downturn. We might even ask, "What is the probability that the stock market will be up *given* that it is raining?" We can write this conditional probability as

$$P[\text{market up} \mid \text{rain}] = p \tag{10.1}$$

The vertical bar signals that the probability of the first argument is conditional on the second. You would read Equation 10.1 as "The probability of 'market up' given 'rain' is equal to p."

Using this conditional probability, we can calculate the probability that it will rain *and* that the market will be up:

$$P[\text{market up and rain}] = P[\text{market up} \mid \text{rain}] \times P[\text{rain}] \tag{10.2}$$

For example, if there is a 10% probability that it will rain tomorrow, and the probability that the market will be up *given* that it is raining is 40%, then the probability of rain and the market being up is 4%: 40% × 10% = 4%.

From a statistics standpoint, it is just as valid to calculate the probability that it will rain and that the market will be up as follows

$$P[\text{market up and rain}] = P[\text{rain | market up}] \times P[\text{market up}] \qquad (10.3)$$

As we will see, even though the right-hand sides of Equations 10.2 and 10.3 are mathematically equivalent, how we interpret them can often be different.

We can also use conditional probabilities to calculate unconditional probabilities. On any given day, either it rains or it does not rain. The probability that the market will be up, then, is simply the probability of the market being up when it is raining plus the probability of the market being up when it is not raining. We have

$$P[\text{market up}] = P[\text{market up and rain}] + P[\text{market up and } \overline{\text{rain}}]$$

$$= P[\text{market up | rain}] \times P[\text{rain}] + P[\text{market up | } \overline{\text{rain}}] \times P[\overline{\text{rain}}]$$

$$(10.4)$$

Here we have used a bar over "rain" to signify logical negation; $\overline{\text{rain}}$ can be read as "not rain."

In general, if a random variable X has n possible outcomes, $x_1, x_2, \ldots, x_n$, then the unconditional probability of Y can be calculated as

$$P[Y] = \sum_{i=1}^{n} P[Y|x_i]P[x_i] \qquad (10.5)$$

If the probability of the market being up on a rainy day is equal to the probability of the market being up on a day with no rain, then we say that the market is conditionally independent of rain. If the market is conditionally independent of rain, then the probability that the market is up given that it is raining must be equal to the unconditional probability of the market being up. We can see this mathematically by replacing the conditional probability of the market being up given no rain with the conditional probability of the market being up given rain in Equation 10.4. (We can do this only because we are assuming that these two conditional probabilities are equal.) We then have

$$P[\text{market up}] = P[\text{market up | rain}] \times P[\text{rain}] + P[\text{market up | rain}] \times P[\overline{\text{rain}}]$$

$$= P[\text{market up | rain}] \times (P[\text{rain}] + P[\overline{\text{rain}}]) \qquad (10.6)$$

$$= P[\text{market up | rain}]$$

In the last line of Equation 10.6, we rely on the fact that the probability of rain plus the probability of no rain is equal to one. Either it rains or it does not rain.

In Equation 10.6 we could just have easily replaced the conditional probability of the market being up given rain with the conditional probability of the market being up given no rain. If the market is conditionally independent of rain, then it is also true that the probability that the market is up, given that it is not raining, must be equal to the unconditional probability of the market being up:

$$P[\text{market up}] = P[\text{market up} \mid \overline{\text{rain}}] \tag{10.7}$$

If the market is independent of rain, then the probability that the market will be up and that it will rain must be equal to the probability of the market being up multiplied by the probability of rain. To see why this must be true, we simply substitute the last line of Equation 10.6 into Equation 10.2, to get

$$P[\text{market up and rain}] = P[\textit{market up} \mid \textit{rain}] \times P[\text{rain}]$$

$$= P[\textit{market up}] \times P[\text{rain}] \tag{10.8}$$

Remember that Equation 10.8 is true only if the market being up and rain are independent. If the weather somehow affects the stock market, however, then the conditional probabilities might not be equal. We could have a situation where

$$P[\text{market up} \mid \text{rain}] \neq P[\text{market up} \mid \overline{\text{rain}}] \tag{10.9}$$

In this case, the weather and the stock market are no longer independent. We can no longer multiply their probabilities together to get their joint probability.

OVERVIEW OF BAYESIAN ANALYSIS

The foundation of Bayesian analysis is Bayes' theorem. Bayes' theorem is named after the 18th-century English mathematician Thomas Bayes, who first described the theorem. During his life, Bayes never actually publicized his eponymous theorem. Bayes' theorem might have been confined to the dustheap of history had not a friend submitted it to the Royal Society two years after his death.

Bayes' theorem itself it incredibly simple. For two random variables, A and B, Bayes' theorem states that

$$P[A|B] = \frac{P[B|A]P[A]}{P[B]} \tag{10.10}$$

In the next section we'll derive Bayes' theorem and explain how to interpret Equation 10.10. As we will see, the simplicity of Bayes' theorem is deceptive. It can be applied to a wide range of problems, and its application can often be quite complex.

Bayesian analysis is used in a number of fields. It is most often associated with computer science and artificial intelligence, where it is used in everything from spam filters to machine translation and the software that controls self-driving cars. The use of Bayesian analysis in finance and risk management has grown in recent years, a trend that will likely continue.

BAYES' THEOREM

Assume we have two bonds, Bond A and Bond B, each with a 10% probability of defaulting over the next year. Further assume that the probability that both bonds default is 6%, and that the probability that neither bond defaults is 86%. It follows that the probability that only Bond A *or* Bond B defaults is 4%. We can summarize all of this information in a probability matrix as shown in Table 10.1. As required, the rows and columns of the matrix add up, and the sum of all the probabilities is equal to 100%.

In the probability matrix, notice that the probability of both bonds defaulting is 6%. This is higher than the 1% probability we would expect if the default events were independent (10% × 10% = 1%). The probability that neither bond defaults, 86%, is also higher than what we would expect if the defaults were independent (90% × 90% = 81%). In the real world, because bond issuers are often sensitive to broad economic trends, bond defaults are often highly correlated.

We can also express features of the probability matrix in terms of conditional probabilities. What is the probability that Bond A defaults, given that Bond B has defaulted? Bond B defaults in 10% of the scenarios, but the probability that both Bond A and Bond B default is only 6%. In other words, Bond A defaults in 60% of the scenarios in which Bond B defaults. We write this as

$$P[A|B] = \frac{P[A \text{ and } B]}{P[B]} = \frac{6\%}{10\%} = 60\% \qquad (10.11)$$

Notice that the conditional probability is different from the unconditional probability. The unconditional probability of default is 10%.

$$P[A] = 10\% \neq 60\% = P[A|B] \qquad (10.12)$$

It turns out that Equation 10.11 is true in general. By rearranging this equation, we can see that it is equivalent to Equation 10.2, that is

$$P[A \text{ and } B] = P[A|B]P[B] \qquad (10.13)$$

In other words, the probability of both A and B occurring is just the probability that A occurs, given B, multiplied by the probability of B occurring. What's more, the ordering of

TABLE 10.1 Probability Matrix

		Bond A		
		No Default	Default	
Bond B	No Default	86%	4%	90%
	Default	4%	6%	10%
		90%	10%	100%

A and *B* doesn't matter. We could just as easily write:

$$P[A \text{ and } B] = P[B|A]P[A] \qquad (10.14)$$

The right-hand side of both of these equations are equal to P[*A* and *B*]; therefore, P[*A*|*B*]P[*B*] = P[*B*|*A*]P[*A*]. Dividing both sides by P[*B*] leads us to Bayes' theorem,

$$P[A|B] = \frac{P[B|A]P[A]}{P[B]} \qquad (10.15)$$

The following sample problem shows how Bayes' theorem can be applied to a very interesting statistical question.

SAMPLE PROBLEM

Question:

Imagine there is a disease that afflicts 1 in every 100 people in the population. A new test, which is 99% accurate, has been developed to detect the disease. That is, for people with the disease, the test correctly indicates that they have the disease in 99% of cases. Similarly, for those who do not have the disease, the test correctly indicates that they do not have the disease in 99% of cases.

If a person takes the test and the result of the test is positive, what is the probability that he or she actually has the disease?

Answer:

While not exactly financial risk, this is a classic example of how conditional probability can be far from intuitive. This type of problem is also far from being an academic curiosity. A number of studies have asked doctors similar questions. The results are often discouraging. The physicians' answers vary widely and are often far from correct.

If the test is 99% accurate, it is tempting to guess that there is a 99% chance that the person who tests positive actually has the disease. In fact, 99% is a very bad guess. The correct answer is that there is only a 50% chance that a person who tests positive actually has the disease.

To calculate the correct answer, we first need to calculate the unconditional probability of a positive test. This is simply the probability of a positive test being produced by somebody with the disease plus the probability of a positive test being produced by somebody without the disease. Using a "+" to represent a positive test result, this can be calculated as

$$P[+] = P[+ \text{ and have disease}] + P[+ \text{ and } \overline{\text{have disease}}]$$

$$= P[+|\text{have disease}] \times P[\text{have disease}] + P[+|\overline{\text{have disease}}] \times P[\overline{\text{have disease}}]$$

$$= 99\% \times 1\% + 1\% \times 99\%$$

$$= 2\% \times 99\%$$

Here we use the line above "have disease" to represent logical negation. In other words, P[$\overline{\text{have disease}}$] is the probability of not having the disease.

We can then calculate the probability of having the disease given a positive test using Bayes' theorem,

$$P[\text{have disease}|+] = \frac{P[+|\text{have disease}]P[\text{have disease}]}{P[+]}$$

$$= \frac{99\% \times 1\%}{2\% \times 99\%}$$

$$= 50\%$$

The reason the answer is 50% and not 99% is because the disease is so rare. Most people don't have the disease, so even a small number of false positives overwhelms the number of actual positives. It is easy to see this in a matrix. Assuming 10,000 trials:

		Actual		
		+	−	
Test	+	99	99	198
	−	1	9,801	9,802
		100	9,900	10,000

If you check the numbers, you'll see that they work out exactly as described: 1% of the population with the disease, and 99% accuracy in each column. In the end, though, the number of positive test results is identical for the two populations, 99 in each. This is why the probability of actually having the disease given a positive test is only 50%.

In order for a test for a rare disease to be meaningful, it has to be extremely accurate. In the case just described, 99% accuracy was not nearly accurate enough.

Bayes' theorem is often described as a procedure for updating beliefs about the world when presented with new information. For example, pretend you have a coin that you believe is fair, with a 50% chance of landing heads or tails. If you flip the coin 10 times and it lands heads each time, you might start to suspect that the coin is not fair. Ten heads in a row could happen, but the odds of seeing 10 heads in a row is only 1:1,024 for a fair coin: $(1/2)^{10} = 1/1,024$. How do you update your beliefs after seeing 10 heads? If you believed there was a 90% probability that the coin was fair before you started flipping, then after seeing 10 heads, your belief that the coin is fair should probably be somewhere between 0% and 90%. You believe it is less likely that the coin is fair after seeing 10 heads (so less than 90%), but there is still some probability that the coin is fair (so greater than 0%). As the following sample problem will make clear, Bayes' theorem provides a framework for deciding exactly what our new beliefs should be.

SAMPLE PROBLEM

Question:

You are an analyst at Astra Fund of Funds. Based on an examination of historical data, you determine that all fund managers fall into one of two groups. Stars are the best managers. The probability that a star will beat the market in any given year is 75%. Ordinary, non-star managers, by contrast, are just as likely to beat the market as they are to underperform it. For both types of managers, the probability of beating the market is independent from one year to the next.

Stars are rare. Of a given pool of managers, only 16% turn out to be stars. A new manager was added to your portfolio three years ago. Since then, the new manager has beaten the market every year. What was the probability that the manager was a star when the manager was first added to the portfolio? What is the probability that this manager is a star now? After observing the manager beat the market over the past three years, what is the probability that the manager will beat the market next year?

Answer:

We start by summarizing the information from the problem and introducing some notation. The probability that a manager beats the market given that the manager is a star is 75%, or

$$P[B|S] = 75\% = \frac{3}{4}$$

The probability that a non-star manager will beat the market is 50%, or

$$P[B|\overline{S}] = 50\% = \frac{1}{2}$$

At the time the new manager was added to the portfolio, the probability that the manager was a star was the same as the probability of any manager being a star, 16%. The unconditional probability was

$$P[S] = 16\% = \frac{4}{25}$$

To answer the second part of the question, we need to find $P[S|3B]$, the probability that the manager is a star, given that the manager has beaten the market three years in a row. We can find this probability using Bayes' theorem,

$$P[S|3B] = \frac{P[3B|S]P[S]}{P[3B]}$$

We already know $P[S]$. Because outperformance is independent from one year to the next, the other part of the numerator, $P[3B|S]$, is just the probability that a star beats the market in any given year to the third power,

$$P[3B|S] = \left(\frac{3}{4}\right)^3 = \frac{27}{64}$$

The denominator is the unconditional probability of beating the market for three years. This is just the weighted average probability of three market-beating years over both types of managers:

$$P[3B] = P[3B|S]P[S] + P[3B|\bar{S}]P[\bar{S}]$$

$$= \left(\frac{3}{4}\right)^3 \frac{4}{25} + \left(\frac{1}{2}\right)^3 \frac{21}{25} = \frac{27}{64}\frac{4}{25} + \frac{1}{8}\frac{21}{25} = \frac{69}{400}$$

Putting it all together, we get our final result,

$$P[S|3B] = \frac{P[3B|S]P[S]}{P[3B]} = \frac{\frac{27}{64}\frac{4}{25}}{\frac{69}{400}} = \frac{9}{23} = 39\%$$

Our updated belief about the manager being a star, having seen the manager beat the market three times, is 39%, a significant increase from our prior belief of 16%. A star is much more likely to beat the market three years in a row—more than three times as likely—so it makes sense that we believe our manager is more likely to be a star now.

Even though it is much more likely that a star will beat the market three years in a row, we are still far from certain that this manager is a star. In fact, at 39%, the odds are more likely that the manager is *not* a star. As was the case in the medical-test example, the reason has to do with the overwhelming number of false positives. There are so many non-star managers that some of them are bound to beat the market three years in a row. The real stars are simply outnumbered by these lucky non-star managers.

Next, we answer the final part of the question. The probability that the manager beats the market next year is just the probability that a star would beat the market plus the probability that a non-star would beat the market, weighted by our new beliefs. Our updated belief about the manager being a star is 39% = 9/23, so the probability that the manager is not a star must be 61% = 14/23, or

$$P[B] = P[B|S]P[S] + P[B|\bar{S}]P[\bar{S}]$$

$$= \frac{3}{4} \times \frac{9}{23} + \frac{1}{2} \times \frac{14}{23}$$

$$= 60\%$$

The probability that the manager will beat the market next year falls somewhere between the probability for a non-star (50%) and for a star (75%), but is closer to the probability for a non-star. This is consistent with our updated belief that there is only a 39% probability that the manager is a star.

When using Bayes' theorem to update beliefs, we often refer to prior and posterior beliefs and probabilities. In the preceding sample problem, the prior probability was 16%. That is, *before* seeing the manager beat the market three times, our belief that the manager was a star was 16%. The posterior probability for the sample problem was 39%. That is, *after* seeing the manager beat the market three times, our belief that the manager was a star was 39%.

We often use the terms *evidence* and *likelihood* when referring to the conditional probability on the right-hand side of Bayes' theorem. In the sample problem, the probability of beating the market, assuming that the manager was a star, $P[3B|S] = 27/64$, was the likelihood. In other words, the likelihood of the manager beating the market three times, assuming that the manager was a star, was 27/64.

$$\text{posterior} \longrightarrow P[S|3B] = \frac{\overset{\text{likelihood}}{\overbrace{P[3B|S]}}P[S] \longleftarrow \text{prior}}{P[3B]} \qquad (10.16)$$

BAYESIANS VERSUS FREQUENTISTS

Pretend that, as an analyst, you are given daily profit data for a fund that has had positive returns for 560 of the past 1,000 trading days. What is the probability that the fund will generate a positive return tomorrow? Without any further instructions, it is tempting to say that the probability is 56%: 560/1,000 = 56%. In the previous sample problem, though, we were presented with a portfolio manager who beat the market in three out of three years. Shouldn't we have concluded that the probability that the portfolio manager would beat the market the following year was 100% (3/3 = 100%), and not 60%? How can both answers be correct?

Taking three out of three positive results and concluding that the probability of a positive result next year is 100%, is known as the frequentist approach. The conclusion is based only on the observed frequency of positive results. Prior to this chapter, we had been using the frequentist approach to calculate probabilities and other parameters.

The Bayesian approach, which we have been exploring in this chapter, also counts the number of positive results. The conclusion is different because the Bayesian approach starts with a prior belief about the probability of a positive outcome.

Which approach is better? It's hard to say. Within the statistics community there are those who believe that the frequentist approach is always correct. However, there are also those who believe the Bayesian approach is always superior.

Proponents of Bayesian analysis often point to the absurdity of the frequentist approach when applied to small data sets. Observing three out of three positive results and concluding that the probability of a positive result next year is 100% suggests that we are absolutely certain and that there is no possibility of a negative result. Clearly this is not right.

Proponents of the frequentist approach often point to the arbitrariness of Bayesian priors. In the portfolio manager example, we started our analysis with the assumption that 16% of managers were stars. In another example we assumed that there was a 90% probability that a coin was fair. How did we arrive at these priors? In most cases, the prior is either subjective or based on frequentist analysis. This also does not seem right.

Perhaps unsurprisingly, most practitioners tend to take a more balanced view, realizing that there are situations that lend themselves to frequentist analysis and others that lend themselves to Bayesian analysis. Situations in which there is very little data, or in which the signal-to-noise ratio is extremely poor, often lend themselves to Bayesian analysis. When we have lots of data, the conclusions of frequentist analysis and Bayesian analysis are often very similar, and the frequentist results are often easier to calculate.

In the example with the portfolio manager, we had only three data points. Using the Bayesian approach for this problem made sense. In the example where we had 1,000 data points, most practitioners would probably utilize frequentist analysis. In risk management, performance analysis and stress testing are examples of areas where we often have very little data, and the data we do have is very noisy. These areas are likely to lend themselves to Bayesian analysis.

MANY-STATE PROBLEMS

In the two previous sample problems, each variable could exist in only one of two states: a person either had the disease or did not have the disease; a manager was either a star or a non-star. We can easily extend Bayesian analysis to any number of possible outcomes. For example, suppose rather than stars and non-stars, we believe there are three types of managers: underperformers, in-line performers, and outperformers. The underperformers beat the market only 25% of the time, the in-line performers beat the market 50% of the time, and the outperformers beat the market 75% of the time. Initially we believe that a given manager is most likely to be an in-line performer, and is less likely to be an underperformer or an outperformer. More specifically, our prior belief is that a manager has a 60% probability of being an in-line performer, a 20% chance of being an underperformer, and a 20% chance of being an outperformer. We can summarize this as

$$P[p = 0.25] = 20\%$$

$$P[p = 0.50] = 60\% \qquad (10.17)$$

$$P[p = 0.75] = 20\%$$

Now suppose a manager beats the market two years in a row. What should our updated beliefs be? We start by calculating the likelihoods, the probability of beating the market two years in a row, for each type of manager,

$$P[2B|p = 0.25] = \left(\frac{1}{4}\right)^2 = \frac{1}{16}$$

$$P[2B|p = 0.50] = \left(\frac{1}{2}\right)^2 = \frac{4}{16} \tag{10.18}$$

$$P[2B|p = 0.75] = \left(\frac{3}{4}\right)^2 = \frac{9}{16}$$

The unconditional probability of observing the manager beat the market two years in a row, given our prior beliefs about p, is

$$
\begin{aligned}
P[2B] &= 20\%\frac{1}{16} + 60\%\frac{4}{16} + 20\%\frac{9}{16} \\
&= \frac{2}{10}\frac{1}{16} + \frac{6}{10}\frac{4}{16} + \frac{2}{10}\frac{9}{16} \\
&= \frac{44}{160} = 27.5\%
\end{aligned}
\tag{10.19}
$$

Putting this all together and using Bayes' theorem, we can calculate our posterior belief that the manager is an underperformer:

$$P[p = 0.25|2B] = \frac{P[2B|p = 0.25]P[p = 0.25]}{P[2B]} = \frac{\frac{1}{16}\frac{2}{10}}{\frac{44}{160}} = \frac{1}{22} = 4.55\% \tag{10.20}$$

Similarly, we can show that the posterior probability that the manager is an in-line performer is 54.55%, or

$$P[p = 0.50|2B] = \frac{P[2B|p = 0.50]P[p = 0.50]}{P[2B]} = \frac{\frac{4}{16}\frac{6}{10}}{\frac{44}{160}} = \frac{12}{22} = 54.55\% \tag{10.21}$$

and that the posterior probability that the manager is an outperformer is 40.91%, or

$$P[p = 0.75|2B] = \frac{P[2B|p = 0.75]P[p = 0.75]}{P[2B]} = \frac{\frac{9}{16}\frac{2}{10}}{\frac{44}{160}} = \frac{9}{22} = 40.91\% \tag{10.22}$$

As we would expect, given that the manager beat the market two years in a row, the posterior probability that the manager is an outperformer has increased, from 20% to 40.91%, and the posterior probability that the manager is an underperformer has decreased, from 20% to 4.55%. Even though the probabilities have changed, the sum of the probabilities is still equal to 100% (the percentages seem to add to 100.01%, but that is only a rounding error):

$$\frac{1}{22} + \frac{12}{22} + \frac{9}{22} = \frac{22}{22} = 1 \tag{10.23}$$

At this point it is worth noting a useful shortcut. Notice that for each type of manager, the posterior probability was calculated as

$$P[p = x | 2B] = \frac{P[2B | p = x]P[p = x]}{P[2B]} \tag{10.24}$$

In each case, the denominator on the right-hand side is the same, $P[2B]$, or $44/160$. We can then rewrite this equation in terms of a constant, c,

$$P[p = x | 2B] = cP[2B | p = x]P[p = x] \tag{10.25}$$

We also know that the sum of all the posterior probabilities must equal one:

$$\sum_{i=1}^{3} cP[2B | p = x_i]P[p = x_i] = c \sum_{i=1}^{3} P[2B | p = x_i]P[p = x_i] = 1 \tag{10.26}$$

In our current example we have

$$c \left(\frac{1}{16} \frac{2}{10} + \frac{4}{16} \frac{6}{10} + \frac{9}{16} \frac{2}{10} \right) = c \frac{2 + 24 + 18}{160} = c \frac{44}{160} = 1$$

$$c = \frac{160}{44} \tag{10.27}$$

We can then use this to calculate each of the posterior probabilities. For example, the posterior probability that the manager is an underperformer is

$$P[p = 0.25 | 2B] = cP[2B | p = 0.25]P[p = 0.25] = \frac{160}{44} \frac{1}{16} \frac{2}{10} = \frac{1}{22} \tag{10.28}$$

In the current example this might not seem like much of a shortcut, but, as we will see, with continuous distributions this approach can make seemingly intractable problems very easy to solve.

SAMPLE PROBLEM

Question:

Using the same prior distributions as in the preceding example, what would the posterior probabilities be for an underperformer, an in-line performer, or an outperformer if instead of beating the market two years in a row, the manager had beat the market in 6 of the next 10 years?

Answer:

For each possible type of manager, the likelihood of beating the market 6 times out of 10 can be determined using a binomial distribution:

$$P[6B | p] = \binom{10}{6} p^6 (1 - p)^4$$

Using our shortcut, we first calculate the posterior probabilities in terms of an arbitrary constant, c. If the manager is an underperformer,

$$P[p = 0.25|6B] = cP[6B|p = 0.25] \times P[p = 0.25]$$

$$= c \binom{10}{6} \left(\frac{1}{4}\right)^6 \left(\frac{3}{4}\right)^4 \times \frac{2}{10}$$

$$= c \binom{10}{6} \frac{2 \times 3^4}{10 \times 4^{10}}$$

Similarly, if the manager is an in-line performer or outperformer, we have

$$P[p = 0.50|6B] = c \binom{10}{6} \frac{6 \times 2^{10}}{10 \times 4^{10}}$$

$$= c \binom{10}{6} \frac{2 \times 3^6}{10 \times 4^{10}}$$

Because all of the posterior probabilities sum to one, we have

$$P[p = 0.25|6B] + P[p = 0.50|6B] + P[p = 0.75|6B] = 1$$

$$c \binom{10}{6} \frac{2 \times 3}{10 \times 4^{10}} (3^3 + 2^{10} + 3^5) = 1$$

$$c \binom{10}{6} \frac{2 \times 3}{10 \times 4^{10}} 1{,}294 = 1$$

$$c = \frac{1}{\binom{10}{6}} \frac{10 \times 4^{10}}{2 \times 3} \frac{1}{1{,}294}$$

This may look unwieldy, but, as we will see, many of the terms will cancel out before we arrive at the final answers. Substituting back into the equations for the posterior probabilities, we have

$$P[p = 0.25|6B] = c \binom{10}{6} \frac{2 \times 3^4}{10 \times 4^{10}} = \frac{3^3}{1{,}294} = \frac{27}{1{,}294} = 2.09\%$$

$$P[p = 0.50|6B] = c \binom{10}{6} \frac{6 \times 2^{10}}{10 \times 4^{10}} = \frac{2^{10}}{1{,}294} = \frac{1024}{1{,}294} = 79.13\%$$

$$P[p = 0.75|6B] = c \binom{10}{6} \frac{2 \times 3^6}{10 \times 4^{10}} = \frac{3^5}{1{,}294} = \frac{243}{1{,}294} = 18.78\%$$

In this case, the probability that the manager is an in-line performer has increased from 60% to 79.13%. The probability that the manager is an outperformer decreased slightly from 20% to 18.78%. It now seems very unlikely that the manager is an under-performer (2.09% probability compared to our prior belief of 20%).

> While the calculations looked rather complicated, using our shortcut saved us from actually having to calculate many of the more complicated terms. For more complex problems, and especially for problems involving continuous distributions, this shortcut can be extremely useful.

This sample problem involved three possible states. The basic approach for solving a problem with four, five, or any finite number of states is exactly the same, only the number of calculations increases. The end-of-chapter questions include one question with four possible states. Because the calculations are highly repetitive, it is often much easier to solve these problems using a spreadsheet or computer program. The online content includes an example involving 11 possible states.

CONTINUOUS DISTRIBUTIONS

In the limit, as we increase the number of possible states, our prior and posterior distributions converge to continuous distributions. Our fundamental equation, Bayes' theorem, remains the same, only now the prior and posterior probabilities are replaced with prior and posterior probability density functions (PDFs):

$$P[A|B] = \frac{P[B|A]P[A]}{P[B]} \quad \rightarrow \quad f(A|B) = \frac{g(B|A)f(A)}{\displaystyle\int_{-\infty}^{+\infty} g(B|A)f(A)dA} \tag{10.29}$$

Here $f(A)$ is the prior PDF, $f(A|B)$ is the posterior PDF, and $g(B|A)$ is the likelihood. We can also mix discrete and continuous distributions. If the prior distribution is continuous, then the posterior distribution will almost always be continuous, but the likelihood can easily be discrete or continuous. Finally, the integral in the denominator represents the unconditional probability of B, $P[B]$. Calculating $P[B]$ through integration is analogous to how we calculated $P[B]$ for a discrete distribution by summing across all of the possible states.

Just as we did for the discrete case, we can rewrite Equation 10.29 using our shortcut from the previous section. For a constant, c, it must be true that

$$f(A|B) = c \times g(B|A)f(A) \tag{10.30}$$

For a discrete posterior distribution, it is necessary that all of the possible posterior distributions sum to one. In the continuous case, the analogous requirement is that the integral of the posterior PDF over the relevant range be equal to one:

$$\int_{-\infty}^{+\infty} f(A|B)dA = 1 \tag{10.31}$$

In other words, we require that the posterior distribution be a proper distribution. Substituting Equation 10.30 into Equation 10.31, we have

$$c \int_{-\infty}^{+\infty} g(B|A)f(A)\,dA = 1 \tag{10.32}$$

We will put this result to use in the following sample problem.

SAMPLE PROBLEM

Question:

As in the preceding sample problem, assume that we observe a portfolio manager beat the market in 6 out of 10 years. Instead of assuming that there are two or three types of managers, though, we assume that the manager can beat the market anywhere between 0% and 100% of the time. Prior to observing the manager, we believed that the manager was equally likely to be anywhere between 0% and 100%. That is, our prior distribution was a uniform distribution between 0% and 100%. Our prior PDF, $f(p)$, is

$$f(p) = 1 \quad 0 \le p \le 1$$

What is the posterior distribution after observing the manager beat the market in 6 out of 10 years?

Answer:

As in the preceding sample problem, the likelihood is described by a binomial distribution,

$$g(6B|p) = \binom{10}{6} p^6 (1-p)^4$$

In the preceding equation and what follows, we assume $0 \le p \le 1$. For a constant, c, the posterior probability density function is then

$$f(p|6B) = c \times g(6B|p)f(p)$$

$$= c \times \binom{10}{6} p^6 (1-p)^4 \times 1$$

$$= c \times \binom{10}{6} p^6 (1-p)^4$$

Next, we note that the number of combinations is independent of p. Because of this, we can rewrite the posterior distribution in terms of a new constant, k,

$$f(p|6B) = k \times p^6 (1-p)^4 \quad \text{where} \quad k = c \binom{10}{6}$$

The next step is the tricky part. The PDF for the beta distribution can be written as

$$\beta(p; a, b) = \frac{1}{B(a,b)} p^{a-1} (1-p)^{b-1} \quad 0 \le p \le 1$$

Here, B(a, b) is the incomplete beta function.[1] Both our posterior distribution and the beta distribution are nonzero from zero to one, and, because they are distributions, the integral of their PDFs over this range must be equal to one:

$$\int_0^1 k \times p^6(1-p)^4 dp = 1 = \int_0^1 \frac{1}{B(a,b)} p^{a-1}(1-p)^{b-1} dp$$

Taking the constants out of the integrals and rewriting the exponents, we have

$$k \int_0^1 p^{7-1}(1-p)^{5-1} dp = \frac{1}{B(a,b)} \int_0^1 p^{a-1}(1-p)^{b-1} dp$$

If we set a equal to 7 and b equal to 5, it is clear that k must equal 1/B(7,5) in order for the two sides of the equation to be equal. Replacing k in our previous equation for the posterior distribution, we arrive at our final answer. The posterior distribution of our beliefs after seeing the manager beat the market in 6 out of 10 years is a beta distribution, $\beta(p; 7, 5)$:

$$f(p|6B) = \frac{1}{B(7,5)} p^6(1-p)^4$$

The prior and posterior distributions are shown in Figure 10.1.

The posterior distribution has a mode of 0.60 and a mean of 0.58. Extreme values (below 0.2 and above 0.9) are very unlikely for the posterior distribution.

FIGURE 10.1 Prior and Posterior Distributions

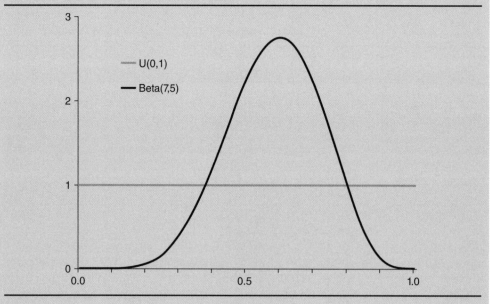

---

[1] The beta distribution is actually quite useful. If you are not familiar with the beta distribution or the incomplete beta function, do not feel bad. Both functions are relatively complicated and can be difficult to calculate. That said, many statistical packages will be able to calculate values for these functions. This is a perfect example of how Bayes' theorem, which seems very simple at first, can lead to very complex results. For an overview of the beta distribution, see Miller (2014).

The uniform distribution is a special case of the beta distribution, where both parameters, *a* and *b*, are equal to one. In the sample problem, then, both the prior and posterior distributions are beta distributions. This is not a coincidence. In general, if the prior distribution is a beta distribution, and the likelihood function follows a binomial distribution, then the posterior distribution will also be a beta distribution. More precisely, if we start with a beta distribution $\beta(x; a, b)$ and then observe *n* trials, of which *k* are successful and $(n - k)$ are unsuccessful, the posterior distribution will be $\beta(x; a + k, b + n - k)$. We simply add the number of successful trials to the first parameter of the beta distribution and add the number of unsuccessful trials to the second.

SAMPLE PROBLEM

Question:

As in the previous sample problem, assume we are observing a portfolio manager whose probability of beating the market can range from 0% to 100%. Instead of believing that all probabilities are equally likely, though, our prior distribution puts more weight on probabilities closer to 50%. More specifically, our prior distribution is a beta distribution, $\beta(x; 2, 2)$, as depicted in Figure 10.2. After 20 years, the portfolio manager has beaten the market only 9 times. What is the posterior distribution for the portfolio manager?

FIGURE 10.2 Beta Distribution

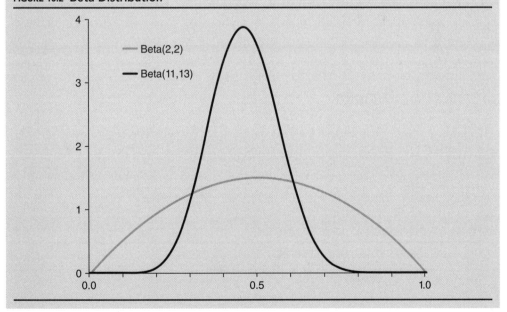

Answer:

Even though the problem seems complex, almost no calculation is required in this case. Adding the number of successes (9) to the first parameter, and the number of failures (11) to the second parameter, we arrive at our final answer: a posterior distribution of $\beta(x; 11,13)$.

As expected, the posterior distribution has a mean and median below 50%, and the most extreme probabilities are even less likely than they were prior to the observations.

It is not always the case that the prior and posterior distributions are of the same type. When both the prior and posterior distributions *are* of the same type, we say that they are conjugate distributions. As we just saw, the beta distribution is the conjugate distribution for the binomial likelihood distribution. Here is another useful set of conjugates: The normal distribution is the conjugate distribution for the normal likelihood when we are trying to estimate the distribution of the mean, and the variance is known.

Conjugate distributions are extremely easy to work with and make calculating posterior distributions very simple. This latter fact was extremely appealing before the widespread use of computers. Unfortunately, real-world problems need not involve conjugate distributions. The real world is not obligated to make our statistical calculations easy. In practice, prior and posterior distributions may be nonparametric and require numerical methods to solve. While all of this makes Bayesian analysis involving continuous distributions more complex, these are problems that are easily solved by computers. One reason for the increasing popularity of Bayesian analysis has to do with the rapidly increasing power of computers in recent decades.

BAYESIAN NETWORKS

A Bayesian network illustrates the causal relationship between different random variables. Figure 10.3 shows a Bayesian network with two nodes that represent the economy, E, and a stock, S. The arrow between them indicates that E causes S. If the arrow were pointing the other way, then the relationship would be reversed, with S causing E.

FIGURE 10.3 Bayesian Network with Two Nodes

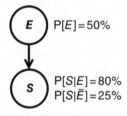

$P[E] = 50\%$

$P[S|E] = 80\%$
$P[S|\bar{E}] = 25\%$

In this simple example, both E and S are discrete random variables, which can be either up or down. Figure 10.3 also shows three probabilities: the probability that E is up, $P[E]$; the probability that S is up given that E is up, $P[S|E]$; and the probability that S is up given that E is not up, $P[S|\overline{E}]$. Three other probabilities, $P[\overline{E}]$, $P[\overline{S}|E]$, and $P[\overline{S}|\overline{E}]$, can easily be determined using the first three probabilities. For example, $P[\overline{E}]$, the probability that E is not up, is just $1 - P[E]$, or 50%. Similarly, $P[\overline{S}|E] = 20\%$, and $P[\overline{S}|\overline{E}] = 75\%$.

Using Bayes' theorem, we can also calculate $P[E|S]$. This is the probability that E is up, given that we have observed S being up,

$$P[E|S] = \frac{P[S|E]P[E]}{P[S]} = \frac{P[S|E]P[E]}{P[S|E]P[E] + P[S|\overline{E}]P[\overline{E}]} \qquad (10.33)$$

From a causation standpoint, $P[E|S]$ is the reverse of $P[S|E]$. Even though we can assign numerical values to both $P[S|E]$ and $P[E|S]$, most people find it more natural to think about $P[S|E]$. This is because human brains are wired to move from causes to effects, and not the other way around. If we believe that the state of the economy determines the performance of stocks, then it seems much more logical to ask, "What is the probability that the stock will be up, given that the economy is up?" It seems strange to ask the reverse, "What is the probability that the economy was up, given that the stock is up?" Our hunter-gatherer ancestors were more likely to ask, "What is the probability that the woolly mammoth will die if I hit it with a spear?" than to ask, "What is the probability that I hit the woolly mammoth with a spear, given that it is dead?" In Bayesian statistics, we refer to these two alternative modes of evaluating a network as causal reasoning and diagnostic reasoning. Causal reasoning, $P[S|E]$, follows the cause-and-effect arrow of our Bayesian network. Diagnostic reasoning, $P[E|S]$, works in reverse.

For most people, causal reasoning is much more intuitive than diagnostic reasoning. Diagnostic reasoning is one reason why people often find Bayesian logic to be confusing. Bayesian networks do not eliminate this problem, but they do implicitly model cause and effect, allowing us to differentiate easily between causal and diagnostic relationships.

Bayesian networks are extremely flexible. Figure 10.4 shows a network with seven nodes. Nodes can have multiple inputs and multiple outputs. For example, node B influences both nodes D and E, and node F is influenced by both nodes C and D.

In a network with n nodes, where each node can be in one of two states (for example, up or down), there are a total of 2^n possible states for the network. As we will see, an advantage of Bayesian networks is that we will rarely have to specify 2^n probabilities in order to define the network. For example, in Figure 10.3 with two nodes, there are four possible states for the network, but we only had to define three probabilities.

FIGURE 10.4 Bayesian Network with Seven Nodes

FIGURE 10.4 Bayesian Network with Seven Nodes

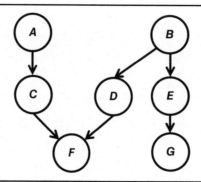

BAYESIAN NETWORKS VERSUS CORRELATION MATRICES

Figure 10.5 shows two networks, each with three nodes. In each network E is the economy and $S1$ and $S2$ are two stocks. In the first network, on the left, $S1$ and $S2$ are directly influenced by the economy. In the second network, on the right, $S1$ is still directly influenced by the economy, but $S2$ is only indirectly influenced by the economy, being directly influenced only by $S1$. In the first example, we might imagine that $S1$ and $S2$ represent the stocks of large, diverse corporations whose performance is largely determined by the state of the economy. In the second example, we might imagine that $S1$ is still the stock of a large, diverse company, but that $S2$ is now the stock of a supplier whose largest customer is $S1$. In the second network, $S2$ is still influenced by E, but the influence is indirect.

For each network in Figure 10.5 there are eight possible states: $2^3 = 8$. Given the probabilities supplied, we can figure out the entire joint distribution for each network; that is, we can figure out the probability of each state. For example, in the first network, the probability of E, $S1$, and $S2$ occurring together is 25.20%,

$$P[E, S1, S2] = P[E]P[S1|E]P[S2|E] = 60\% \times 70\% \times 60\% = 25.20\% \qquad (10.34)$$

FIGURE 10.5 Two Bayesian Networks with Three Nodes Each

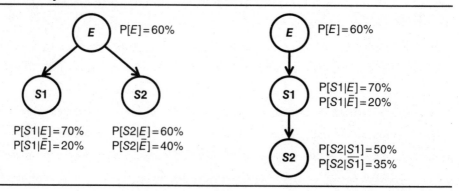

TABLE 10.2 Probabilities of Networks

E	S1	S2	Network 1	Network 2
0	0	0	19.20%	20.80%
0	0	1	12.80%	11.20%
0	1	0	4.80%	4.00%
0	1	1	3.20%	4.00%
1	0	0	7.20%	11.70%
1	0	1	10.80%	6.30%
1	1	0	16.80%	21.00%
1	1	1	25.20%	21.00%
			100.00%	**100.00%**

Table 10.2 shows all eight probabilities for both networks. In the table, the occurrence of an event is signified by a 1, and an event not occurring by a 0. For example, the probability of E, $S1$, and $S2$ occurring, $P[E, S1, S2]$, can be found in the last row of the table where E, $S1$, and $S2$ are all equal to 1. You should check all of the remaining values in the table to ensure that you understand how they are calculated.

As with any random variable, we can calculate the mean, standard deviation, and variance of E, $S1$, and $S2$. Also, because we know the joint distribution of all three variables, we can calculate their covariances and correlations as well. For example, the mean of $S1$ in both networks is 50%:

$$E[S1] = E[S1|E]P[E] + E[S1|\overline{E}]P[\overline{E}]$$

$$= 70\% \times 60\% + 20\% \times (1 - 60\%) \tag{10.35}$$

$$= 50\%$$

SAMPLE PROBLEM

Question:

Using the probabilities for the first network in Figure 10.5, calculate the covariance between E and $S1$.

Answer:

Using our equation for covariance from Chapter 3, the covariance of E and $S1$ is

$$\sigma_{E,S1} = E[(E - E[E])(S1 - E[S1])] = E[E \times S1] - E[E]E[S1]$$

We already know $E[S1]$ from Equation 10.35. We could calculate $E[E]$ in a similar fashion. Alternatively, we could read the values and probabilities straight from the joint probability distribution in Table 10.2. The equation is longer, but the process is more mechanical and much easier to automate.

$$E[E] = 19.20\% \times 0 + 12.80\% \times 0 + 4.80\% \times 0 + 3.20\% \times 0 + 7.20\% \times 1$$

$$+10.80\% \times 1 + 16.80\% \times 1 + 25.20\% \times 1$$

$$= 7.20\% + 10.80\% + 16.80\% + 25.20\%$$

$$= 60\%$$

In the second line of the preceding equation, we see that calculating $E[E]$ is equivalent to adding up all the probabilities in Table 10.2, where E is equal to 1. We can calculate $E[E \times S1]$ in a similar fashion. $E \times S1$ is equal to 1 only if both E and S are equal to 1, which is true for only the last two lines of Table 10.2. Therefore,

$$E[E \times S1] = 16.80\% + 25.20\% = 42.00\%$$

Putting this all together, we have our final answer,

$$\sigma_{E,S1} = E[E \times S1] - E[E]E[S1] = 42.00\% - 60.00\% \times 50.00\% = 12.00\%$$

The complete covariance matrices are provided in Figure 10.6. Calculating these covariance matrices and the corresponding correlation matrices is left as an exercise at the end of the chapter.

Not surprisingly, given the similarity of the Bayesian networks from which they were derived, the covariance matrices are very similar to each other. E, $S1$, and $S2$ are all positively correlated with each other in both cases.

One advantage of Bayesian networks is that they can be specified with very few parameters, relative to other approaches. In the preceding example, we were able to specify each network using only five probabilities, but each covariance matrix contains six nontrivial entries, and the joint probability table, Table 10.2, contains eight entries for each network. As networks grow in size, this advantage tends to become even more dramatic.

Another advantage of Bayesian networks is that they are more intuitive. It is hard to have much intuition for entries in a covariance matrix or a joint probability table. Given the scenarios described in this example, it makes sense that the entries in the covariance

FIGURE 10.6 Covariance Matrices

Network 1				Network 2			
	E	*S1*	*S2*		*E*	*S1*	*S2*
E	24%	12%	5%	*E*	24%	12%	2%
S1	12%	25%	2%	*S1*	12%	25%	4%
S2	5%	2%	25%	*S2*	2%	4%	24%

matrices are positive, but beyond that it is difficult say much. What if we were worried that we had accidentally reversed the data for the two networks? An equity analyst covering the two companies represented by $S1$ and $S2$ might be able to look at the Bayesian networks and say that the linkages and probabilities seem reasonable, but it would be much more difficult for the analyst to know if the two covariance matrices had been reversed.

Because Bayesian networks are more intuitive, they might be easier to update in the face of a structural change or regime change. In the second network, where we have described $S2$ as being a supplier to $S1$, suppose that $S2$ announces that it has signed a contract to supply another large firm, thereby making it less reliant on $S1$? With the help of our equity analyst, we might be able to update the Bayesian network immediately (for example, by decreasing the probabilities $P[S2|S1]$ and $P[\overline{S2}|\overline{S1}]$), but it is not as obvious how we would directly update the covariance matrices.

END-OF-CHAPTER QUESTIONS

1. The probability that gross domestic product (GDP) decreases is 20%. The probability that unemployment increases is 10%. The probability that unemployment increases given that GDP has decreased is 40%. What is the probability that GDP has decreased given that unemployment has increased?

2. An analyst develops a model for forecasting bond defaults. The model is 90% accurate. In other words, of the bonds that actually default, the model identifies 90% of them; likewise, of the bonds that do not default, the model correctly predicts that 90% will not default. You have a portfolio of bonds, each with a 5% probability of defaulting. Given that the model predicts that a bond will default, what is the probability that it actually defaults?

3. As a risk analyst, you are asked to look at EB Corporation, which has issued both equity and bonds. The bonds can either be downgraded, be upgraded, or have no change in rating. The stock can either outperform the market or underperform the market. You are given the following probability matrix from an analyst who had worked on

		Equity		
		Outperform	**Underperform**	
Bonds	**Upgrade**	W	5%	**15%**
	No Change	45%	X	**65%**
	Downgrade	Y	15%	Z
		60%	**40%**	

the company previously, but some of the values are missing. Fill in the missing values. What is the conditional probability that the bonds are downgraded, given that the equity has underperformed?

4. Your firm is testing a new quantitative strategy. The analyst who developed the strategy claims that there is a 55% probability that the strategy will generate positive returns on any given day. After 20 days the strategy has generated a profit only 10 times. What is the probability that the analyst is right and the actual probability of positive returns for the strategy is 55%? Assume that there are only two possible states of the world: Either the analyst is correct, or the strategy is equally likely to gain or lose money on any given day. Your prior assumption was that these two states of the world were equally likely.

5. Your firm has created two equity baskets. One is procyclical, and the other is countercyclical. The procyclical basket has a 75% probability of being up in years when the economy is up, and a 25% probability of being up when the economy is down or flat. The probability of the economy being down or flat in any given year is only 20%. Given that the procyclical index is up, what is the probability that the economy is also up?

6. You are an analyst at Astra Fund of Funds, but instead of believing that there are two or three types of portfolio managers, your latest model classifies managers into four categories. Managers can be underperformers, in-line performers, stars, or superstars. In any given year, these managers have a 40%, 50%, 60%, and 80% chance of beating the market, respectively. In general, you believe that managers are equally likely to be any one of the four types of managers. After observing a manager beat the market in three out of five years, what do you believe the probability is that the manager belongs in each of the four categories?

7. You have a model that classifies Federal Reserve statements as either bullish or bearish. When the Fed makes a bullish announcement, you expect the market to be up 75% of the time. The market is just as likely to be up as it is to be down or flat, but the Fed makes bullish announcements 60% of the time. What is the probability that the Fed made a *bearish* announcement, given that the market was up?

8. You are monitoring a new strategy. Initially, you believed that the strategy was just as likely to be up as it was to be down or flat on any given day, and that the probability of being up was fairly close to 50%. More specifically, your initial assumption was that the probability of being up, p, could be described by a beta distribution, $\beta(4, 4)$. Over

the past 100 days, the strategy has been up 60 times. What is your new estimate for the distribution of the parameter p? What is the probability that the strategy will be up the next day?

9. For the Bayesian network in Figure 10.7, each node can be in one of three states: up, down, or no change. How many possible states are there for the entire network? What is the minimum number of probabilities needed to completely define the network?

FIGURE 10.7 **Three-State Network**

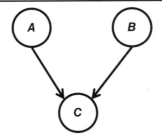

10. Calculate the correlation matrix for Network 1, the network on the left, in Figure 10.6. Start by calculating the covariance matrix for the network.

11. Calculate the correlation matrix for Network 2, the network on the right, in Figure 10.6. Start by calculating the covariance matrix for the network.

11

BEHAVIORAL ECONOMICS AND RISK

Understanding human behavior can help us understand how people make financial decisions. In this chapter we introduce several topics in behavioral economics and discuss their relevance to risk management.

UTILITY FUNCTIONS

What is a dollar worth? For most of this book we have framed financial scenarios in terms of dollars (and euro and yen and yuan), but the value of a dollar is ultimately subjective. People want money because money can be used to buy things which make them happy. If we are going to understand the financial decisions that people make, and the value that they place on financial assets, then we are going to have to understand what makes people happy.

Unfortunately measuring happiness is a lot harder than measuring dollars. We cannot observe happiness directly, and what makes people happy can vary significantly between people and over time. Fortunately, when we look at large numbers of people, patterns do emerge.

The branch of economics that studies how people's subjective preferences are used to make decisions is known as behavioral economics. The equivalent field in finance is known as behavioral finance. Academics refer to the subjective value that individuals derive from goods and services as utility. Economic agents are utility maximizers. Faced with a decision people choose the path which they believe will result in the highest level of utility.

Most goods and services exhibit what is referred to as declining marginal utility. The more we consume of something the less utility we derive from each additional unit. As an example, imagine a family in the suburbs purchasing their first car. Owning a car will allow them to do many things that they could not do before they owned a car. They are likely to derive considerable utility form their first car. What if they purchase a second car? The second car will allow them to do things that they could not do when they had only one car, but the difference in not as great as the difference between not owning a car and owning one car. The second car increases their overall utility, but not as much as the first car did. A third car would increase their utility by an even smaller amount. The marginal utility of each additional car decreases with each additional car. The same is true of pizza slices, vacation homes, clothing, and most goods and services.

One way to visualize this is by plotting a utility function, as in Figure 11.1, which shows the relationship between consumption and utility. Figure 11.1 displays all the attributes of a typical utility function. First, as pictured here, utility is zero for zero consumption and positive for positive consumption. Second, the curve is upward sloping, utility increases as consumption increases. Finally, the curve is concave, as consumption increases the curve rises less and less quickly, the curve display diminishing marginal utility.

Economists generally assume that utility is time-separable, that is they assume that they can look at any given hour, day, month, or year and evaluate a consumer's utility during that period based solely on their consumption during that period. It's as if the consumer starts each day with a clean slate. Utility in one period does not impact utility in the next period, and utility, unlike money, cannot be transferred from one period to the next.

FIGURE 11.1 Utility Function

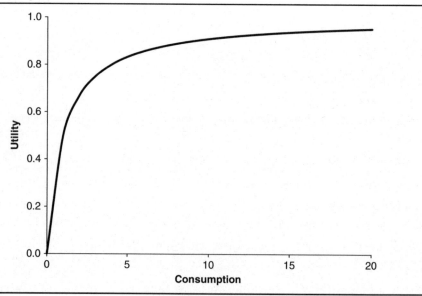

One consequence of declining marginal utility is that people may try to smooth consumption over time. If we assume that utility is time-separable, and marginal utility is declining then consuming two units this year and two units next year is going to be more satisfying than consuming four units this year and no units next year. This will lead people to borrow money when times are tough, and to save money when times are good. Most people earn less money when they are young. In order to smooth consumption over a lifetime people will borrow money when they are young (college loans, home mortgages, and credit card debt), to be paid off when they are older. In effect they are transferring money from their higher earning future selves to their less productive younger selves.

In the realm of investments, this desire to smooth consumption may lead investors to prefer assets whose returns are less correlated with their own income and less correlated with the returns of other assets. For this reason, an airline pilot may decide not to invest in airline stocks (or even to short airline stocks). This desire to avoid highly correlated investments may conflict with the desire of employers to align employee interests through stock options, or of employees to invest in industries that they understand well.

To fully model consumers' intertemporal decisions, we also need to take into account the fact that individuals prefer current utility over future utility. Just as we can discount future cash flows to evaluate the present value of a financial asset, we can discount the utility of future consumption to derive the present value of that utility. Because consumers prefer current utility, they require compensation to forego consumption. This is why investors require interest even on risk-free investments.

SAMPLE PROBLEM

Question:

From previous work, we know that Mr. Arrow's utility function can be approximated by the following formula:

$$U_t = 1 - e^{-\alpha C_t}$$

Here U_t is the utility Mr. Arrow receives at time t from consuming C_t; α is a constant. You can easily confirm that this utility function displays decreasing marginal utility when α is positive, by confirming that the first derivative of this function is positive and the second is negative.

Assume that Mr. Arrow must split one unit of consumption between this year and next year and that consumption must be non-negative in both years. How should he split this unit of consumption in order to maximize the present value of his utility? Assume that $\alpha = 0.50$, and that Mr. Arrow discounts future utility at a constant rate of $r = 4\%$. Treat all consumption as occurring on the first day of the year.

Answer:

Because there is only one unit of consumption, if Mr. Arrow consumes C_1 this year, he must consume $(1 - C_1)$ next year. The total present value of utility from both periods is

$$PV[U] = (1 - e^{-\alpha C_1}) + e^{-r}(1 - e^{-\alpha(1-C_1)})$$

To find the maximum, we start by taking the first derivative of this equation,

$$\frac{dPV[U]}{dC_1} = \alpha e^{-\alpha C_1} - \alpha e^{-r-\alpha(1-C_1)}$$

We can confirm that setting this equation to zero will return the maximum by calculating the second derivative,

$$\frac{d^2PV[U]}{dC_1^2} = -\alpha^2 e^{-\alpha C_1} - \alpha^2 e^{-r-\alpha(1-C_1)} < 0$$

The second derivate is clearly less than zero for all positive values of α, when C_1 is between zero and one, as in this problem. Setting the first derivative to zero and solving, we have

$$\alpha e^{-\alpha C_1^*} = \alpha e^{-r-\alpha(1-C_1^*)}$$

$$-\alpha C_1^* = -r - \alpha(1 - C_1^*)$$

$$C_1^* = \frac{\alpha + r}{2\alpha}$$

This answer makes sense. If r were equal to zero, that is if utility next period were as valuable as utility this period, then consumption would equal ½ in both periods. In our case where the discount rate is 4% and α is 0.50, the consumption in the first period is 0.54 and in the second period is 0.46:

$$C_1^* = \frac{0.50 + 0.04}{2 \times 0.50} = 0.54$$

$$C_2^* = 1 - C_1^* = 0.46$$

The optimal split has consumption being close to equal in both periods. It is slightly higher in the first period due to the fact that future utility is discounted.

Loss Aversion

When economists first started thinking about utility functions, they specified utility functions in terms of consumption. This made sense. Rather than trying to accumulate wealth, people were trying to enjoy as much utility as possible during their lives. There might be ups and downs, but the point was to maximize overall utility.

When economists started to examine how people *actually* behave, though, they noticed that people often reacted very differently to positive and negative changes in consumption. More specifically, for most people losses seem to be more psychologically damaging than gains are beneficial. This phenomenon is known as loss aversion. In certain situations, this can lead to seemingly illogical conclusions. For example, a person that wins $10 and then immediately loses $10 might feel worse off even though their overall financial situation has not changed.

Figure 11.2 depicts a utility function, which displays loss aversion. Notice how the steepness of the curve changes at the origin. The curve is noticeably steeper for negative changes in consumption than it is for positive changes.

In financial markets, the probability of observing a loss often depends on how frequently you look. Take for example a fund for which the log returns are normally distributed with an annualized mean and standard deviation of 14% and 10%, respectively. Assume that daily returns are independent. The probability of seeing a loss on any given day is then close to 50%, but the probability of seeing a loss over five years is close to zero. Table 11.1 shows the exact probabilities over various time horizons.

If investors display loss aversion then investors could make themselves happier simply by looking at their portfolios less frequently. Benartzi and Thaler (1995) suggested that in reality investors may look at their portfolios too frequently, causing them to avoid assets such as equities, which are prone to losses in the short term, but are very likely to deliver significant positive returns in the long run. They dubbed this behavior myopic loss aversion.

FIGURE 11.2 Loss Aversion

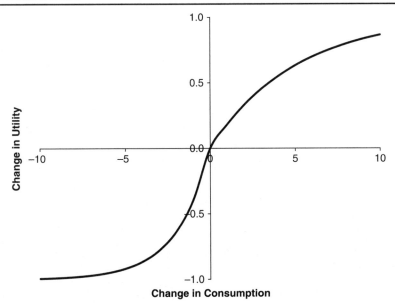

TABLE 11.1 Probability of Observing a Loss over Various Time Horizons

Time	P[Loss]
1 day	46.5%
1 month	34.3%
1 year	8.1%
5 years	0.1%

UTILITY UNDER UNCERTAINTY

Economic agents are described as being risk averse if they need to be compensated for entering into a fair bet. A fair bet is a bet with an expected payout of zero. For example, if a game offered a 50/50 chance of winning or losing $100, a risk-averse person would not play this game. A mildly risk-averse individual might play the game if you gave them $1, while an extremely risk averse person might not play the game even if you gave them $90.

Rather than thinking about how much we would need to compensate a risk-averse individual, we can think in terms of the total expected payout of a bet or game. A risk-averse individual will only play a risky game if the total expected payout is positive. Risk-seeking individuals would play a game with a negative expected payout and would actually pay to play a fair game. Risk-neutral agents are indifferent to fair bets, will always play games with positive expected payouts and avoid games with negative expected payouts.

If investors display declining marginal utility, then they will be risk averse. This is because an equal gain will increase utility less than an equal loss will decrease utility. This will leave the investor worse off, on average, when entering into a fair bet. We typically think of investors as being risk averse.

SAMPLE PROBLEM

Question:

Pretend an investor initially plans to consume $1,000 and is offered the chance to invest in an option which will gain $100 with probability p and lose $100 with probability $(1 - p)$. Also assume that the investor's utility, U, is a function of consumption, C, such that

$$U = \frac{(C + 1)^{1-\theta} - 1}{1 - \theta}$$

Here, θ is a constant, which controls the level of risk aversion. What would the probability of gaining $100 have to be in order to leave the investor indifferent to investing in the option, assuming θ is equal to 5? 20?

Answer:

We need to find the probability, p, such that the investor's utility is equal when consuming \$1,000 with certainty or investing in the option. The utility of \$1,000 with certainty is

$$U_C = \frac{1{,}001^{1-\theta} - 1}{1 - \theta}$$

If the investor invests in the option, the expected utility is the weighted average utility from consuming \$1,100 with probability p, and \$900 with probability $(1 - p)$,

$$U_O = p\frac{1{,}101^{1-\theta} - 1}{1 - \theta} + (1 - p)\frac{901^{1-\theta} - 1}{1 - \theta}$$

Setting the two equal and solving for p, we have

$$\frac{1{,}001^{1-\theta} - 1}{1 - \theta} = p\frac{1{,}101^{1-\theta} - 1}{1 - \theta} + (1 - p)\frac{901^{1-\theta} - 1}{1 - \theta}$$

$$1{,}001^{1-\theta} = p \times 1{,}101^{1-\theta} + (1 - p) \times 901^{1-\theta}$$

$$p = \frac{1{,}001^{1-\theta} - 901^{1-\theta}}{1{,}101^{1-\theta} - 901^{1-\theta}}$$

When θ equals 5, p equals 62%. This gives the option an expected profit of \$24.63. If θ is equal to 20, then p is equal to 88%, and the expected profit of the option is \$76.89. When θ is equal to 20, the investor is extremely risk averse. Even if the option leaves the investor better off in 88% of scenarios, and only results in a 10% reduction in consumption in 12% of scenarios, the investor would be just as likely to not invest in this option as to invest.

As mentioned, behavioral economists and psychologists have shown that peoples' attitudes toward risk can be very different when dealing with losses rather than gains (see Kahneman and Tversky, 1984). While we typically think of investors as being risk averse, when dealing with scenarios where losses are involved people actually tend to display risk seeking behavior. Given the choice between losing \$100 with certainty, and taking a 50/50 option that loses either \$60 or \$150, most people will choose the 50/50 option, even though the expected payout is a loss of \$105. This risk-seeking behavior for negative outcomes was depicted in Figure 11.2, where the utility function is convex for negative outcomes.

While we do see this type of behavior, on average, when it comes to financial decisions, investors seem to be extremely risk averse. In 1985, Mehra and Prescott published an article that examined how investors allocate their investment portfolios between relatively risky equities and relatively safe investments such as government bonds. Historically, over long periods, the equity premium, the performance of equities over risk-free bonds, has almost always been positive. Despite this, investors allocate considerable portions of their invest-ment portfolios to government bonds. As Mehra and Prescott saw it, this behavior could only be explained by an unbelievable degree of risk aversion. The result was so unexpected, that they dubbed it the "equity premium puzzle". Since then, various theories have been proposed to explain the equity premium puzzle. Some focus on data, while others focus on behavioral models. In the end, most of these new theories move the needle only slightly. The average investor may not be irrationally risk averse, but they are still likely to be very risk averse in most circumstances.

Low-Probability Events

While people are generally risk averse for positive outcomes and risk seeking for negative out-comes there is one important exception. When it comes to low-probability events, the exact opposite is typically true. This is why people are willing to pay a lot for insurance (avoiding the risk of a low-probability negative outcome), and purchase lottery tickets (assuming the risk of a very low-probability positive outcome).

As an explanation for this behavior, Kahneman and Tversky (1984) suggest that, when assessing probabilities, people behave as if extremely rare events are much more likely to occur than they actually are, and as if events that are almost certain are less likely to occur than they actually are. Kahneman and Tversky depict this as in Figure 11.3, where the probability that we appear to use when we make decisions, the decision weight, is seen as a

FIGURE 11.3 The Perception of Low-Probability Events

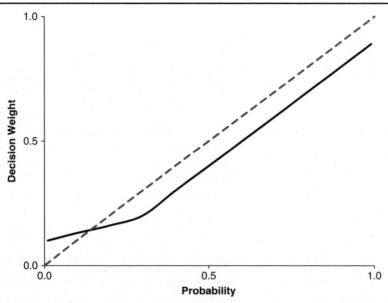

function of the actual probability. For extremely unlikely events such as winning the lottery or collecting on insurance, the decision weight is greater than the actual probability. People act as if the events are more likely than they really are.

For financial investors, this tendency to act as if rare events are more probable than they actually are may lead investors to over-hedge, or to pay too much for far out-of-the-money options. In general, investors choose less-risky investment portfolios than we might otherwise expect. In addition to extreme loss aversion, this may be because they believe that rare crashes are much more likely than they actually are. When it comes to specific investments, though, investors often choose highly risky assets, such as Internet stocks, possibly because they believe that the very low probability of massively outperforming the market is much more likely than it actually is.

Relative Utility

In the earliest utility models, utility was both time-separable and independent for each individual. In other words, a person's happiness this year was supposed to be independent of what they consumed last year and independent of what other people were consuming. In reality, people care about how their consumption this year compares to last year. They prefer consumption to increase over time. People also tend to judge their well-being relative to those around them.

The idea that people prefer their consumption to increase over time is referred to as habit formation. A person's habit level is a function of past levels of consumption. Unlike in previous examples, the order of consumption matters. Ignoring the impact of discounting, all else being equal, a person that consumes \$100,000 this year and \$200,000 next year will be happier than if they consume \$200,000 this year and \$100,000 next year. How consumers weigh absolute consumption versus relative consumption in their overall utility is difficult to say. If habit formation is very strong, though, then consumers in rapidly growing emerging markets might be happier than consumers in stagnant developed markets, even if the absolute level of consumption of the emerging market consumers is significantly lower.

In the simplest models, habit level is equated with last period's consumption. A slightly more complex way to model an individual's habit level would be to assume exponentially declining weights. For example,

$$H_t = \sum_{i=i}^{t} \delta^i C_{t-i} \qquad (11.1)$$

where δ is a constant such that $0 < \delta < 1$. In reality, habit level is likely to be a complex function of past consumption. If a consumer's habit level changes slowly over time, then a sharp drop in consumption levels can have a lasting impact on a consumer's subjective sense of well-being. For example, take a consumer with an initial habit level of $100,000. If the consumer's consumption drops by $50,000, and then increases $60,000, they may still be below their habit level, even though their consumption increased in the most recent period.

To the extent that investment losses might force a reduction in consumption, habit formation may lead investors to choose less risky portfolios, and to avoid investments that are highly correlated with other sources of income. It might also dampen the desire of younger workers to smooth consumption by borrowing against higher expected future earnings.

In the United States and many other countries, wealthy individuals tend to have more volatile consumption levels because more of their income is tied to investment income or corporate profits. This higher volatility can increase the probability of decreases in consumption levels. So, while these wealthy individuals will benefit from their higher absolute level of consumption, this benefit is likely to be tempered somewhat by higher volatility in consumption.

The idea that consumers not only care about their absolute level of consumption but their consumption relative to those around them is often referred to by economists as "catching up with the Joneses." This is a deliberate play on the more common expression "keeping up with the Joneses," and a fancy way of saying that people can often be jealous. If a person's utility from consumption is impacted by the consumption of other people around them, then a person whose consumption increases might be less happy if their neighbor's consumption increases more. At the same time, if this effect is strong enough, then a consumer might not feel any worse off after a drop in consumption, as long as everybody else's consumption falls as well.

A natural question when considering catching up with the Joneses is, "Who are the Joneses?" Do we evaluate our consumption relative to our neighbors, relative to the average consumption level within our country, or relative to the average global consumption level? The answer is likely to be a weighted average of many different groups. A worker living in Manhattan and consuming $57,000 in 2016, might feel poor relative to the average New Yorker, even though their consumption is in line with the United States' GDP per capita, and is significantly higher than world GDP per capita of roughly $11,000.

Similar to other aspects of utility, consuming less than one's peers is likely to hurt considerably more than consuming more feels good. Consuming $100 less and then $100 more than your peers is likely to leave you feeling worse off than if you had consumed the same amount as your peers in both periods.

A basic tenant of finance is that, all else being equal, investors prefer more diversified portfolios, and that investors will seek out investments that have a low correlation with their existing portfolio. Interestingly, from a risk-management standpoint, if catching up with the Joneses is very strong, then we might not feel so bad if we suffer a big loss to our investment portfolio during a market crash, when everybody else is also suffering, and we might feel extremely bad if we suffer a modest loss when the market is up and most of our friends are making money in their investment portfolios. In other words, if catching up with the Joneses is extremely important to our overall utility, then the best strategy for investors may be to invest in a portfolio that is substantially similar to the portfolios of their peers, that is, a portfolio that is highly correlated with the market. This might also lower the appeal of alternative investments, which are supposed to have a low correlation with the overall market.

HEURISTICS AND BIASES

Every day we must make thousands of decisions, many of which are probabilistic in nature: Will I make it to work on time if I hit the snooze button? Which road will get me to work faster? Which project should I work on first? Which lunch option is healthiest? And on and on and on. To make these decisions we could develop complex models and analyze lots of data, but in reality we simply don't have the time or the resources. Instead we rely on heuristics, rules of thumb, and patterns that allow us to quickly reduce complex problems to simple ones. These heuristics often work well (if they didn't we wouldn't use them), but they are not perfect. In a seminal paper, Kahneman and Tversky (1974) point out a number of ways in which heuristics can be biased, leading to systematic errors in decision making.

Representativeness

Pretend you are in a room with 30 portfolio managers, and that somebody tells you that all of the "good" managers have black hair. You are then introduced to a portfolio manager, who just happens to have black hair. What is the probability that the portfolio manager is good? Many people would believe that the manager is extremely likely to be good. After all, you were just told that all of the good managers have black hair and this manager has black hair. We are ignoring two important facts when reaching this conclusion, however: 1) What percentage of the portfolio managers in the room are good, and 2) What percentage of the "bad" portfolio managers also have black hair. What if only two portfolio managers are good, and half the bad portfolio managers also have black hair? In this case there are 14 portfolio managers with black hair who are bad, and only 2 who are good. There is only a 1-in-8 chance that the portfolio manager we were introduced to is in fact good.

   As we know from the last chapter, the proper way to evaluate these problems is to use Bayesian analysis.

$$P[\text{good}|\text{black hair}] = \frac{P[\text{black hair}|\text{good}]P[\text{good}]}{P[\text{black hair}]} = \frac{1.00 \times 2/30}{16/30} = \frac{1}{8} \qquad (11.2)$$

As we also know from the last chapter, Bayesian analysis is far from intuitive, especially when it involves diagnostic reasoning. Evidence from many studies suggests that people consistently ignore this type of logic, instead relying almost solely on how representative the object is of the population. Even risk managers and people with backgrounds in statistics make this mistake.

The previous example, where hair color was associated with being a good or bad portfolio manager was intentionally contrived. While hair color might not be associated with portfolio-manager performance, investors do try to differentiate between good and bad portfolio managers. More realistically, we might expect good managers to have graduated from a top university and to have strong convictions. Because of this, when we meet a portfolio manager that graduated from Princeton and is very opinionated, we will be tempted to conclude that there is a high probability that the portfolio manager is a good portfolio manager. If good portfolio managers are rare, or bad portfolio managers are also likely to display these characteristics, our estimate will be far from accurate. Representativeness can often lead us astray in these types of situations.

Availability

What is the probability that a plane will crash, that a business project will succeed, or that we will enjoy eating at a certain restaurant? When deciding to board a plane, to fund a project, or to make a reservation at a restaurant, we need to assess these probabilities. People rarely rely on formal statistical models when making these decisions in real life. One way in which people estimate the probability of an event occurring is by seeing how easily they can recall examples of similar events. If it is easy for them to recall similar events, they judge the event to be highly probable. If they struggle to recall similar events, they judge the event to be highly unlikely. There is a certain logic to this approach. Pretend you have been working at a company for a long time, and you have worked on a large number of projects. If only 10% of these projects succeeded, then when you try to recall projects, it should be relatively simple for you to remember specific projects that failed, and more difficult to remember projects that succeeded. This approach works well in many cases, but can easily fail for rare and extreme events, or for events that are far from our everyday experience. When trying to assess the probability that a plane will crash, we will likely give a higher estimate if we have recently read a story about a plane crash. This bias is likely to be made worse by the fact that the news story will have likely focused exclusively on the crash, without mentioning how many planes landed safely that day, or how long it has been since the last plane crash. News stories are inevitably about the rare and extreme, and rarely about the common and mundane.

We may underestimate the probability of events that are far from our everyday experience. Globally, what percentage of people speak more than one language? If you live in West Virginia (where 2.3% of the population speaks a language other than English at home, according to the 2010 Census), you might have a hard time thinking of people you know who speak more than one language. If you live in New York City, you may find it much easier to recall people who speak more than one language (41% of students in New York City speak a language other than English at home). People living in West Virginia and New York City certainly realize that their homes are not perfectly representative of the entire world, and they may use other data when arriving at an estimate. Nonetheless, their estimates are likely to be heavily influence by how easily they can recall individuals they know who speak a foreign language.

Availability certainly plays a role in financial decisions. It is well known that sales of insurance policies to homeowners increase after a natural disaster such as an earthquake, flood, or hurricane. Investors may expect that extremely positive and extremely negative returns for individual stocks are more likely, since the media are more likely to report on these outliers (this could be one more reasons why people seem to be so risk averse with their portfolio allocations). Analysts may underestimate the probability of bankruptcy or fraud if it has been a long time since they have come across such events. At the same time, risk managers may underestimate the risk from extremely rare or unusual events for which they have had little direct experience.

In risk management, availability might not always lead us astray. In many financial markets, volatility displays significant serial correlation. Financial markets tend to go through extended periods of above-average and below-average volatility. The GARCH model, which we explored in Chapter 2, is designed to exhibit this type of behavior. To the extent that extreme moves in the market lead us to believe that more extreme moves are likely in the near future, our intuition is correct.

Anchoring

How much does the average person weigh? To answer this question, you might start with your own weight, and then adjust this figure up or down depending on whether you think you weigh more or less than the average person. Psychologists refer to this initial estimate as an anchor. The potential problem with this process is that people seem to be susceptible to spurious anchors, and tend not to adjust far enough. If the initial anchor is above the actual value, this incomplete adjustment will cause people to overestimate the true value. If the initial anchor is below the actual value, the incomplete adjustment will cause people to underestimate the true value.

As an example, suppose you were asked to estimate the average salary of a starting risk analyst in New York City. If right before this, you were told that the GDP per capita in Bangladesh was $1,700 per year, you would be likely to underestimate the starting salary. Even though per capita GDP in Bangladesh has nothing to do with the starting salary of a risk analyst in New York you are likely to start with $1,700, and adjust upwards. Your adjustment is likely to be too small, leading to an underestimation. Similarly, if you had been asked to estimate the population of New York City (8 million+) immediately before estimating the average risk analyst's salary, you would likely overestimate the value. In controlled studies, people have been shown to be influenced by completely random numbers generated by dice or spinning wheels.

Kahneman and Tversky suggest that when it comes to estimating the magnitude of rare financial events, people are likely to underestimate the magnitude due to anchoring. For example, pretend that at the start of each month, you ask somebody to estimate the 10% one-month VaR level for the Nikkei. After 100 months you would expect to observe 10 exceedances of their VaR estimates, but in reality you are likely to observe fewer. This is because, in coming up with the 10% one-month VaR estimate, the person likely started with the current level of the Nikkei and then made an incomplete adjustment down from there.

The Endowment Effect

When evaluating the value of a security that is already in their portfolio, a natural anchor for a portfolio manager is the price at which they purchased the security. If the security has fallen in value since it was purchased, the portfolio manager may be inclined to view the security as undervalued. If the security has risen in value, the portfolio manager may be inclined to view the security as overvalued. Because of this, portfolio managers may hold on to losers too long and sell winners too early. In this type of decision, portfolio managers might also be influenced by the endowment effect (Thaler, 1980). The endowment effect describes the tendency of people to want to hold on to what they already have. The endowment effect can be so strong that people will refuse to sell an object at a price that they previously refused to buy at. A person might say that they are unwilling to pay more than $50 for a shirt, but if you give them the shirt they may not want to sell it back to you for even $100. This suggests that portfolio managers may be tempted to hold on to winners for too long as well.

A WORD OF CAUTION

There is something fascinating about the illogical behavior induced by heuristic biases. As mentioned at the start of the section though, even though they might not always work, heuristics do tend to work. If they didn't, we wouldn't use them. John List, among others, has argued that biases might be even less important in the real world than much of the research in behavioral finance has suggested (see, for example, Levitt and List, 2007). Behavioral finance researchers often rely on laboratory experiments, where university students are presented with extremely contrived problems. List's studies suggest that these laboratory results are often at odds with behavior seen in real-world settings. While biases certainly have some role to play in financial decision making, we should not overestimate their importance (which would be a bias in itself).

It has also been pointed out that the vast majority of behavioral finance studies have been carried out in the United States and Western Europe, and that the university students who account for the vast majority of the participants in these studies are far from being representative of all humanity. In 2010, a group of researches coined the term WEIRD (Western, educated, industrialized, rich, and democratic) to highlight just how atypical these study participants tend to be, not just in behavioral finance but in psychology in general (Henrich et al., 2010).

END-OF-CHAPTER QUESTIONS

1. You are offered the opportunity to invest in an option with a 60% chance of gaining $100, and a 40% chance of losing $25. How much would you be willing to pay for this option if you were risk averse? Risk neutral? Risk seeking?

2. Assume that a consumer's utility can be described by the following utility function:

$$U = 1 - e^{-\alpha C}$$

where α is a constant and C is the level of consumption. Currently the consumer's consumption is uncertain, varying between zero and one with equal probability. In other words, the consumer's current level of consumption can be described by a standard uniform distribution. How much would you have to offer the consumer, with certainty, to leave the consumer just as well off if α is equal to 5?

3. You are the owner of a widget factory that is expected to generate $100 in profits over the next 12 months. Unfortunately, your factory is in a flood plain. There is a small chance that a flood will cause damage that will entirely wipe out your profit. To be more specific, you estimate that there is a 99% probability that you will earn $100, and a 1% probability that there will be a flood and you will earn $0. Assume that your utility is based solely on your earnings according to

$$U = \frac{(C+1)^{1-\theta} - 1}{1 - \theta}$$

where C is the earnings from the factory over the next 12 months. How much would you be willing to pay for flood insurance that would pay you $100 in the event of a flood if $\theta = 0.50$? What if $\theta = 2.0$?

4. In the previous question, what would you have been willing to pay for insurance if the factory was expected to earn $1,000 if there is no flood. In the event of a flood, you would still earn $0, but the insurance would pay $1,000. How much would you be willing to pay for the insurance now? Assume $\theta = 0.50$.

5. Consider an investor who is subject to habit formation, where the investor's habit level is a simple weighted average of consumption in the previous three periods,

$$H_t = \frac{4}{7}C_{t-1} + \frac{2}{7}C_{t-2} + \frac{1}{7}C_{t-3}$$

and the investors utility in any period is

$$U_t = \sqrt{\frac{C_t}{H_t}}$$

The investor consumed $105 last year, $95 the year before that, and $90 the year before that. The investor is considering two potential investments. An investment in GRW will allow the investor to consume $110 this year, and $120 next year. An investment in DCL, is just the reverse, allowing the investor to consume $120 this year, and $110 the following year. Assume that the discount rate is zero. Which investment will provide the investor with the most utility over the next two years?

6. You are the chief risk officer for a large pension fund. In a recent meeting, the manager of the fund's equity portfolio, explained how she planned to shift the portfolio away from large retail companies and toward smaller technology firms. After the meeting, you remember that a number of stores have recently closed in your area, and that a business magazine that you and the portfolio manager both read recently ran an article about "hot new tech companies". What heuristic biases might the portfolio manager want to consider when making her allocation decision?

APPENDIX A

MAXIMUM LIKELIHOOD ESTIMATION

Imagine you flip a coin twice. The first time it lands on heads and the second time it lands on tails. What is the probability that it will land on heads if you flip the coin a third time? Forget for the moment that we are working with an extremely small sample size. Intuitively, the answer is 50%. When you flipped the coin the first two times, it landed on heads 50% of the time (one out of two trials), so you expect the coin to land on heads 50% of the time it the future as well.

Intuition is easy in this case, but how can we answer this question more formally? One way to formalize this process would be to use expectations. It is not too difficult to show that the mean number of heads observed is an unbiased estimator of the probability of landing on heads. Though we might not always think about it in these terms, we are often doing something similar to this when we estimate the parameters of a probability distribution.

A not-so-obvious way to go about this problem—but one that turns out to be extremely flexible—is to ask: If the probability of heads had been 10%, what is the likelihood that we would have observed the coin landing on heads and then on tails. What if the probability had been 20%? Or 30%? If the probability of landing on heads had been 10%, then the probability of observing heads and then tails would have been the probability of landing on heads multiplied by the probability of landing on tails, $10\% \times (1 - 10\%) = 9\%$. If the probability had been 20% it would have been $20\% \times (1 - 20\%) = 16\%$. In general, if the probability of landing on heads had been p, then the probability of observing heads followed by tails would have been $p \times (1 - p)$. We could graph this function for all possible values of p from zero to one, as in Figure A.1. As can be seen in the graph, the function

247

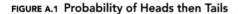

FIGURE A.1 Probability of Heads then Tails

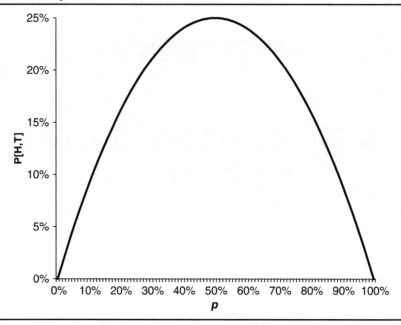

reaches a maximum at $p = 50\%$. In other words, of all the possible values that p could take, observing heads and then tails would have been most likely if p had been 50%.

Mathematically, we could find this maximum by finding the place where the derivative of the function is equal to zero. If we define the likelihood function, L, as the probability of observing heads followed by tails, then we have

$$L = p(1 - p) \tag{A.1}$$

Taking the derivative with respect to p and setting it to zero, we get

$$\frac{dL}{dp} = 1 - 2p$$

$$1 - 2p^* = 0$$

$$p^* = \frac{1}{2} \tag{A.2}$$

This is consistent with our earlier answer. This process of defining the likelihood function and then finding the maximum value for the function is the essence of maximum likelihood estimation (MLE).

So why would we go to all this trouble when it seems much easier to obtain the answer using other methods? It turns out that in risk management we often run into distributions where we know the probability density function (PDF), but where there is no explicit solution for finding the parameters of the distribution. In these situations, MLE may be the most practical method available for estimating parameters. In other cases, explicit solutions may exist, but they may be just as complicated as MLE.

One advantage of MLE is that it is extremely flexible. Once you learn how to apply it to one problem, it is very easy to apply it to others. The rest of this appendix provides two slightly more complex examples of how to apply MLE. Both of these have explicit solutions. When the solution to the MLE equations is not obvious, numerical methods can be applied, making MLE even more flexible. Excel's Solver can be used to find the maximum of an MLE equation. Newton-Raphson or similar methods can be used when programming. Brute force approaches, while less elegant, are often sufficient.

Continuing with the previous example, how would we generalize A.1 to any number of coin flips? Assume we have n coin flips and we observe h heads, followed by $(n - h)$ tails. The likelihood equation would then be

$$L = p^h (1 - p)^{n-h} \tag{A.3}$$

In this case, taking the derivative of the equation directly is not difficult, but in more difficult cases it can often be easier to take the log of L first. Because the logarithm is a monotonic increasing function, the maximum of $\ln(L)$ and L will occur at the same point. In this case we have

$$\ln(L) = h \ln(p) + (n - h) \ln(1 - p) \tag{A.4}$$

The derivative with respect to p is

$$\frac{d \ln(L)}{dp} = \frac{h}{p} - \frac{n - h}{1 - p} \tag{A.5}$$

Setting the derivative equal to zero, we get our final solution:

$$\frac{h}{p^*} - \frac{n - h}{1 - p^*} = 0$$

$$p^* = \frac{h}{n} \tag{A.6}$$

As we might have guessed, the MLE estimator for the probability of observing heads is equal to the percentage of heads observed, h/n. You should confirm for yourself that you obtain the same result by taking the derivative of Equation A.3 directly.

What if we have more than one parameter? The basic approach is the same, but instead of taking one derivative, we need to take the partial derivative with respect to each parameter separately. Take for example the normal probability density function,

$$f(x) = \frac{1}{\sigma \sqrt{2\pi}} e^{-\frac{1}{2}\left(\frac{x-\mu}{\sigma}\right)^2} \tag{A.7}$$

If we have n observations, $x_1, x_2, \ldots, x_n$, then the appropriate likelihood function is

$$L = \prod_{i=1}^{n} \frac{1}{\sigma\sqrt{2\pi}} e^{-\frac{1}{2}\left(\frac{x_i-\mu}{\sigma}\right)^2} \tag{A.8}$$

This time, taking the log of the likelihood equation makes matters considerably easier.

$$\ln(L) = -\frac{1}{2\sigma^2} \sum_{i=1}^{n} (x_i - \mu)^2 - n\ln(\sigma) - \frac{n}{2}\ln(2\pi) \tag{A.9}$$

At this point, some people prefer to work with the negative of $\ln(L)$. Finding the minimum of the negative of $\ln(L)$ is equivalent to finding the maximum of $\ln(L)$. It saves a lot of minus signs, but for this example we proceed with $\ln(L)$, first taking the partial derivative with respect to μ.

$$\frac{\partial \ln(L)}{\partial \mu} = \frac{1}{\sigma^2} \sum_{i=1}^{n}(x_i - \mu) \tag{A.10}$$

Setting this equal to zero, we have

$$\frac{1}{\sigma^2} \sum_{i=1}^{n}(x_i - \mu^*) = 0$$

$$\sum_{i=1}^{n}(x_i - \mu^*) = 0$$

$$\sum_{i=1}^{n} x_i - \sum_{i=1}^{n} \mu^* = \sum_{i=1}^{n} x_i - n\mu^* = 0$$

$$\mu^* = \frac{1}{n} \sum_{i=1}^{n} x_i \tag{A.11}$$

As we would expect, the MLE estimate for μ is simply the mean of the observed values.

Next, rather than solving for σ directly, we solve for σ^2,

$$\frac{\partial \ln(L)}{\partial (\sigma^2)} = \frac{1}{2\sigma^4} \sum_{i=1}^{n} (x_i - \mu)^2 - n\frac{1}{2\sigma^2} \tag{A.12}$$

Setting this equal to zero we have

$$\frac{1}{2(\sigma^{2*})^2} \sum_{i=1}^{n} (x_i - \mu)^2 - n\frac{1}{2\sigma^{2*}} = 0$$

$$\frac{1}{\sigma^{2*}} \sum_{i=1}^{n} (x_i - \mu)^2 - n = 0$$

$$\sigma^{2*} = \frac{1}{n} \sum_{i=1}^{n} (x_i - \mu)^2 \tag{A.13}$$

The right-hand side of Equation A.13 is simply the population variance. The MLE estimator for σ^2 is simply the population variance. In general, standard MLE will produce the population parameter, not the sample estimate. However, in finance, as discussed in Chapter 2, more often than not, we require the sample estimate. In some cases, the population and sample parameter are the same (as is the case with the mean), or there is a well-known method for adjusting the parameter (as is the case with standard deviation and variance). In other cases, transforming the population parameter into a sample estimate can be more complicated.

Using MLE to prove that the mean and variance are good estimators for the parameters μ and σ^2 of the normal distribution may have seemed complicated, but the alternative of using expectations operator is equally, if not more, difficult, requiring the solution to two nonstandard integrals. In the case of the normal distribution, both MLE and expectations provide explicit parameter estimates. In more difficult cases, MLE is often the most practical method for estimating parameters.

APPENDIX B

COPULAS

The following is a summary of the properties of various named copulas. Formulas are given in terms of two cumulative distribution functions (CDFs), but these definitions can be extended to any number of variables. The following notation is used for each copula:

- g: the generator function for the copula
- g^{-1}: inverse of the generator function
- C: the copula in terms of two CDFs, u and v
- C_1: the marginal CDF of the copula, $\frac{\partial C}{\partial u}$
- c: the copula's density function
- τ: Kendall's tau
- ρ: Spearman's rho

Clayton

$$g^{-1} = (1 + t)^{-1/\alpha}$$

$$g = t^{-\alpha} - 1$$

$$C = (u^{-\alpha} + v^{-\alpha} - 1)^{-1/\alpha}$$

$$C_1 = \frac{\partial C}{\partial u} = u^{-(\alpha+1)}(u^{-\alpha} + v^{-\alpha} - 1)^{-\frac{1+\alpha}{\alpha}}$$

$$v = u\left(C_1^{-\frac{\alpha}{1+\alpha}} + u^{\alpha} - 1\right)^{-1/\alpha}$$

$$c = (1 + \alpha)(uv)^{-(\alpha+1)}(u^{-\alpha} + v^{-\alpha} - 1)^{-\frac{1+2\alpha}{\alpha}}$$

$$\alpha > 0$$

$$\tau = \frac{\alpha}{\alpha + 2}$$

Farlie-Gumbel-Morgenstern (FGM)

$$C = uv[1 + \alpha(1 - u)(1 - v)]$$

$$C_1 = v(1 + \alpha - 2\alpha u) + v^2\alpha(2u - 1)$$

$$c = 1 + \alpha(1 - 2u)(1 - 2v)$$

$$-1 \leq \alpha \leq +1$$

$$\tau = \frac{2}{9}\theta$$

$$\rho = \frac{1}{3}\alpha$$

Frank

$$g^{-1} = \frac{1}{-\alpha}\ln[1 - (1 - e^{-\alpha})e^{-t}]$$

$$g = -\ln\left(\frac{1 - e^{-\alpha t}}{1 - e^{-\alpha}}\right)$$

$$C = -\frac{1}{\alpha}\ln\left[1 + \frac{(e^{-\alpha u} - 1)(e^{-\alpha v} - 1)}{e^{-\alpha} - 1}\right]$$

$$C_1 = \frac{\partial C}{\partial u} = \frac{(e^{-\alpha u} - 1)(e^{-\alpha v} - 1) + (e^{-\alpha v} - 1)}{(e^{-\alpha u} - 1)(e^{-\alpha v} - 1) + (e^{-\alpha} - 1)}$$

$$v = -\frac{1}{\alpha}\ln\left[1 + \frac{C_1(e^{-\alpha} - 1)}{1 + (e^{-\alpha u} - 1)(1 - C_1)}\right]$$

$$c = \alpha(1 - e^{-\alpha})\frac{e^{-\alpha(u+v)}}{[(e^{-\alpha u} - 1)(e^{-\alpha v} - 1) + (e^{-\alpha} - 1)]^2}$$

$$\alpha \neq 0$$

$$\tau = 1 - \frac{4}{\alpha}\left[1 - \frac{1}{\alpha}\int_0^\alpha \frac{t}{e^t - 1}dt\right]$$

$$\rho = 1 - \frac{12}{\alpha}\left[\frac{1}{\alpha}\int_0^\alpha \frac{t}{e^t - 1}dt - \frac{1}{\alpha^2}\int_0^\alpha \frac{t^2}{e^t - 1}dt\right]$$

Gumbel

$$g^{-1} = e^{-t^{1/\alpha}}$$

$$g = (-\ln t)^\alpha$$

$$C = e^{-[(-\ln u)^\alpha + (-\ln v)^\alpha]^{\frac{1}{\alpha}}}$$

$$C_1 = \frac{\partial C}{\partial u} = \frac{1}{u}(-\ln u)^{\alpha-1}C[(-\ln u)^\alpha + (-\ln v)^\alpha]^{\frac{1-\alpha}{\alpha}}$$

$$c = \frac{1}{uv}[(\ln u)(\ln v)]^{\alpha-1}C[(-\ln u)^\alpha + (-\ln v)^\alpha]^{\frac{1-2\alpha}{\alpha}}[\alpha - 1 + ((-\ln u)^\alpha + (-\ln v)^\alpha)^{1/\alpha}]$$

$$\alpha \geq 1$$

$$\tau = \frac{\alpha - 1}{\alpha}$$

Independent

$$g^{-1} = e^{-t}$$
$$g = -\ln t$$
$$C = uv$$
$$C_1 = \frac{\partial C}{\partial u} = u$$
$$v = C_1$$
$$c = 1$$
$$\tau = 0$$
$$\rho = 0$$

Joe

$$g^{-1} = 1 - (1 - e^{-t})^{1/\alpha}$$
$$g = -\ln[1 - (1 - t)^\alpha]$$
$$C = 1 - [(1 - u)^\alpha + (1 - v)^\alpha - (1 - u)^\alpha(1 - v)^\alpha]^{1/\alpha} = 1 - D^{1/\alpha}$$
$$c = (1 - u)^{\alpha-1}(1 - v)^{\alpha-1}D^{\frac{1-2\alpha}{\alpha}}(1 - \alpha - D)$$
$$\alpha \geq 0$$
$$\tau = 1 - 4\sum_{i=1}^{\infty} \frac{1}{i(\alpha i + 2)(\alpha(i - 1) + 2)}$$

ANSWERS TO END-OF-CHAPTER QUESTIONS

CHAPTER 2

1. Mean = 3%; standard deviation = 6.84%.

2. Series #1: Mean = 0, standard deviation = 39, skewness = 0.
   Series #2: Mean = 0, standard deviation = 39, skewness = −0.63.

3. Series #1: Mean = 0, standard deviation = 17, kurtosis = 1.69.
   Series #2: Mean = 0, standard deviation = 17, kurtosis = 1.

4. The mean, μ, is

$$\mu = \int_0^6 x \frac{x}{18} dx = \left[\frac{x^3}{3 \times 18} \right]_0^6 = \frac{6^3}{3 \times 18} - \frac{0^3}{3 \times 18} = \frac{6^2}{3^2} = 4$$

The variance, σ^2, is then

$$\sigma^2 = \int_0^6 (x-4)^2 \frac{x}{18} dx = \frac{1}{18} \int_0^6 (x^3 - 8x^2 + 16x) dx$$

$$\sigma^2 = \frac{1}{18} \left[\frac{1}{4} x^4 - \frac{8}{3} x^3 + 8x^2 \right]_0^6 = \frac{6^2}{18} \left(\frac{1}{4} 6^2 - \frac{8}{3} 6 + 8 \right)$$

$$\sigma^2 = 2(9 - 16 + 8) = 2$$

5. We need to find h, such that

$$\sum_{i=0}^{h-1} \delta^i = \frac{1}{2} \sum_{i=0}^{n-1} \delta^i = \frac{1}{2} \frac{1 - \delta^n}{1 - \delta} = \frac{1 - \delta^h}{1 - \delta}$$

Solving, we find

$$0.5(1 - \delta^n) = 1 - \delta^h$$

$$\delta^h = 0.5 + 0.5\delta^n$$

$$h \ln(\delta) = \ln(0.5 + 0.5\delta^n)$$

$$h = \frac{\ln(0.5 + 0.5\delta^n)}{\ln(\delta)}$$

Alternatively, the formula for the half-life can be expressed as

$$h = \frac{\ln(0.5) + \ln(1 + \delta^n)}{\ln(\delta)}$$

6. We start by computing decay factors and values for x^2.

t	0	1	2	3	4	5	6	7
x	11	84	30	73	56	58	52	35
δ	0.6983	0.7351	0.7738	0.8145	0.8574	0.9025	0.9500	1.0000
x^2	121	7,056	900	5,329	3,136	3,364	2,704	1,225

For the mean, using Equation 2.25, we have

$$\hat{\mu}_t = \frac{1 - \delta}{1 - \delta^n} \sum_{i=0}^{n-1} \delta^i x_{t-i} = 0.15 \times 336.86 = 50.04$$

For the variance, using Equation 2.35, we have

$$\hat{\sigma}_t^2 = A \sum_{i=0}^{n-1} \delta^i x_{t-i}^2 - B\hat{\mu}_t^2 = 0.17 \times 19826.75 - 1.15 \times 50.04^2 = 505.18$$

Finally, we can take the square root of our answer for the variance, to get the standard deviation, 22.48.

7. We start by calculating the following values:

t	0	1	2	3	4	5
x	0.04	0.84	0.28	0.62	0.42	0.46
δ_1	1.0000	1.0000	1.0000	1.0000	1.0000	1.0000
δ_2	0.9044	0.9135	0.9227	0.9321	0.9415	0.9510
δ_3	0.3487	0.3874	0.4305	0.4783	0.5314	0.5905

t	6	7	8	9	10
x	0.66	0.69	0.39	0.99	0.37
δ_1	1.0000	1.0000	1.0000	1.0000	1.0000
δ_2	0.9606	0.9703	0.9801	0.9900	1.0000
δ_3	0.6561	0.7290	0.8100	0.9000	1.0000

We then use Equation 2.25 to calculate our estimates of the mean: mean (no decay) = 0.5236; mean (decay = 0.99) = 0.5263; mean (decay = 0.90) = 0.5486.

8. We start by expanding the table from our answer to question 7:

t	0	1	2	3	4	5
x	0.04	0.84	0.28	0.62	0.42	0.46
δ_1	1.0000	1.0000	1.0000	1.0000	1.0000	1.0000
δ_2	0.9044	0.9135	0.9227	0.9321	0.9415	0.9510
δ_3	0.3487	0.3874	0.4305	0.4783	0.5314	0.5905
x^2	0.0016	0.7056	0.0784	0.3844	0.1764	0.2116
$(x - E[x])^2$	0.233904	0.100086	0.059359	0.009286	0.01074	0.00405

t	6	7	8	9	10
x	0.66	0.69	0.39	0.99	0.37
δ_1	1.0000	1.0000	1.0000	1.0000	1.0000
δ_2	0.9606	0.9703	0.9801	0.9900	1.0000
δ_3	0.6561	0.7290	0.8100	0.9000	1.0000
x^2	0.4356	0.4761	0.1521	0.9801	0.1369
$(x - E[x])^2$	0.018595	0.027677	0.017859	0.217495	0.023604

In the last line, we have used our estimate of the mean (no decay) from the previous problem.

For the first estimator with no decay factor, we can use Equation 2.19 to calculate the variance:

$$\hat{\sigma}_x^2 = \frac{1}{n-1} \sum_{i=1}^{n} (x_i - \hat{\mu}_x)^2 = \frac{1}{11-1} 0.7227 = 0.0723$$

For the second and third estimators, we use Equation 2.35 and our estimates of the mean from the previous question:

$$\hat{\sigma}_t^2 = A \sum_{i=0}^{n-1} \delta^i x_{t-i}^2 - B\hat{\mu}_t^2 = 0.11 \times 3.58 - 1.10 \times 0.5263^2 = 0.0716$$

$$\hat{\sigma}_t^2 = A \sum_{i=0}^{n-1} \delta^i x_{t-i}^2 - B\hat{\mu}_t^2 = 0.16 \times 2.49 - 1.11 \times 0.5486^2 = 0.0681$$

Taking the square root of the variances, we arrive at our final answers: standard deviation (no decay) = 0.2688; standard deviation (decay = 0.99) = 0.2676; standard deviation (decay = 0.90) = 0.2610.

9. The new estimates are 10.10%, 9.82%, and finally 9.78%. These can be found as follows:

$$\hat{\mu}_t = 0.02x_t + 0.98\hat{\mu}_{t-1}$$

$$\hat{\mu}_1 = 0.02 \times 15\% + 0.98 \times 10\% = 10.10\%$$

$$\hat{\mu}_2 = 0.02 \times (-4\%) + 0.98 \times 10.10\% = 9.82\%$$

$$\hat{\mu}_3 = 0.02 \times 8\% + 0.98 \times 9.82\% = 9.78\%$$

10. The half-lives are:

$$h_{200} = \frac{\ln(0.5 + 0.5 \times 0.95^{200})}{\ln(0.95)} = 13.5127$$

$$h_{1,000} = \frac{\ln(0.5 + 0.5 \times 0.95^{1,000})}{\ln(0.95)} = 13.5134$$

11. The half-life of the EWMA estimator is approximately 11.11 days. A rectangular window with 22 days would have the most similar half-life, 11 days.

$$h_{32} = \frac{\ln(0.5 + 0.5 \times 0.96^{32})}{\ln(0.96)} = 11.11$$

12. $1 - 0.96^{50} = 87\%$.

13. We can use our updating rule,

$$\hat{\sigma}_t^2 = (1 - \delta)r_t^2 + \delta\hat{\sigma}_{t-1}^2$$

to calculate successive estimates of the variance. The estimate of the standard deviation is just the square root of the variance estimator:

t	0	1	2	3	4	5	6
r		−5%	18%	16%	−2%	5%	−10%
$E[\sigma^2]$	0.010000	0.009625	0.010764	0.011506	0.010950	0.010528	0.010501
$E[\sigma]$	10%	9.81%	10.37%	10.73%	10.46%	10.26%	10.25%

The final estimate of the standard deviation is approximately 10.25%.

CHAPTER 3

1. We take the approximation for dV as a given, as an equality, and take the expectations of both sides:

$$E[dV] = \widetilde{\Delta}E[R] + \frac{1}{2}\widetilde{\Gamma}E[R^2] + \theta dt$$

Because R has a mean of zero, $E[R] = 0$ and the variance is equal to $E[R^2]$.

$$\sigma^2 = E[R^2] + E[R]^2 = E[R^2] + 0^2 = E[R^2]$$

Substituting back into our previous equation, we have

$$E[dV] = \widetilde{\Delta}0 + \frac{1}{2}\widetilde{\Gamma}\sigma^2 + \theta dt = \frac{1}{2}\widetilde{\Gamma}\sigma^2 + \theta dt$$

2. The most likely day for the next exceedance is tomorrow. This is something of a trick question. It is tempting to guess that the next exceedance is equally likely to occur on any future day. In fact, if the probability of an exceedance on any given day is α, then the probability of an exceedance tomorrow is α, but the probability that the *next* exceedance is the day after tomorrow is $(1-\alpha)\alpha$. This is because in order for the *next* exceedance to be the day after tomorrow, two things have to happen. First, there must be no exceedance tomorrow. Second, there must be an exceedance the day after tomorrow. The probability of these two events are $(1-\alpha)$ and α, respectively, so the probability that both happen is $(1-\alpha)\alpha$. Because $(1-\alpha)$ is less than one, $(1-\alpha)\alpha<\alpha$. For example, if we are calculating the 95% VaR, then $\alpha = 5\%$. The probability that the next exceedance is tomorrow is 5%, and the probability that the next exceedance is the day after tomorrow is $5\% \times 95\% = 4.75\%$. The probability continues to decline further out. The probability that the next exceedance happens in n day is, $(1-\alpha)^{(n-1)}\alpha$, which is likewise always less than α.

3. Five percent of 256 is 12.8, so the 95% VaR is between the 12th and 13th worst returns. Because we do not know the distribution between the 12th and 13th worst returns, we use the 12th. The one-day 95% VaR is -16%, or a loss of 16%.

4. In order to calculate the hybrid VaR, we need to calculate weights for the returns. For each return, the corresponding weight is 0.99^t. We can convert this to a percentage weight by dividing by the total weight, $92.37 = (1 - 0.99^{256})/(1 - 0.99)$. Starting with the worst return, we then sum these percentage weights to get the cumulative percentage weight until we reach 5%. This time, 5% occurs between the 7th and 8th worst returns. The 7th worst return, −20%, is our one-day 95% VaR. Many of the worst returns have occurred recently, so it is not surprising that the hybrid VaR is worse than the historical VaR.

	t	*R*	**wt**	**%wt**	**cum. %**
1	42	−35%	0.6557	0.71%	0.71%
2	83	−29%	0.4342	0.47%	1.18%
3	10	−26%	0.9044	0.98%	2.16%
4	23	−25%	0.7936	0.86%	3.02%
5	3	−24%	0.9703	1.05%	4.07%
6	58	−21%	0.5583	0.60%	4.67%
7	188	−20%	0.1512	0.16%	4.84%
8	103	−19%	0.3552	0.38%	5.22%
9	131	−18%	0.2680	0.29%	
10	12	−16%	0.8864	0.96%	
11	116	−16%	0.3117	0.34%	
12	245	−16%	0.0852	0.09%	
13	150	−15%	0.2215	0.24%	
14	56	−14%	0.5696	0.62%	
15	61	−14%	0.5417	0.59%	
16	31	−13%	0.7323	0.79%	
17	69	−13%	0.4998	0.54%	
18	95	−13%	0.3849	0.42%	
19	161	−13%	0.1983	0.21%	
20	35	−12%	0.7034	0.76%	

5. For a normal distribution, 5% of the weight is less than −1.64 standard deviations from the mean. The 95% VaR can be found as: 0.40% − 1.64 × 2.30% = −3.38%. Because of our quoting convention for VaR, the final answer is VaR = 3.38%.

6. To find the 95% VaR, we need to find v, such that:

$$\int_{-100}^{v} p\, d\pi = 0.05$$

Solving, we have:

$$\int_{-100}^{v} \frac{1}{200} d\pi = \left[\frac{\pi}{200} \right]_{-100}^{v} = \frac{v+100}{200} = 0.05$$

$$v = -90$$

The VaR is a loss of 90. Alternatively, we could have used geometric arguments to arrive at the same conclusion. In this problem, the PDF describes a rectangle with a base of 200 units and a height of 1/200. As required, the total area under the PDF (base multiplied by height) is equal to one. The leftmost fraction of the rectangle, from −100 to −90, is also a rectangle, with a base of 10 units and the same height, giving an area of 1/20, or 5% of the total area. The edge of this area is our VaR, as previously found by integration.

7. To find the 95% VaR, we need to find v, such that

$$0.05 = \int_{15}^{v} p \, d\pi$$

By inspection, half the distribution is below 5, so we need only bother with the first half of the function,

$$0.05 = \int_{-15}^{v} \left(\frac{3}{80} + \frac{1}{400} \pi \right) d\pi$$

$$= \left[\frac{3}{80} \pi + \frac{1}{800} \pi^2 \right]_{-15}^{v}$$

$$= \frac{3}{80} (v + 15) + \frac{1}{800} \left(v^2 - 15^2 \right)$$

$$= \frac{3}{80} (v + 15) + \frac{1}{800} \left(v^2 - 225 \right)$$

Rearranging terms,

$$v^2 + 30v + 185 = 0$$

We can solve this using the quadratic equation:

$$v = \frac{-30 \pm \sqrt{900 - 4 \times 185}}{2} = -15 \pm 2\sqrt{10}$$

Because the distribution is not defined for $\pi < -15$, we can ignore the negative, giving us the final answer of

$$v = -15 + 2\sqrt{10} \approx -8.68$$

The one-day 95% VaR for Pyramid Asset Management is approximately 8.68.

8. To answer this question, we need to first calculate the delta of the put option. We can do this by using put-call parity. Assume the price of a call is C, the price of a put is P. For a call and put with the same expiration on a non-dividend paying stock, put-call parity states

$$C - P = S - Xe^{-rT}$$

Taking the derivative of both sides with respect to S, we have

$$\Delta_C - \Delta_P = 1$$

Or, rearranging terms,

$$\Delta_P = \Delta_C - 1$$

Assuming the same underlying, same expiration and same strike, as in the question, if the delta of the call option is 0.50, then the delta of the put must be -0.50.

The 95% VaR corresponds to the bottom 5% of returns. For a normal distribution 5% of the distribution is less than 1.64 standard deviations below the mean. We can get this result from a lookup table, a statistics application, or a spreadsheet. For example, in Excel = NORM.S.INV(0.05) would give us -1.64, the negative sign indicating that the result is below the mean. Given the standard deviation of 2%, this corresponds to a -3.28% return for XYZ.

For the call option, the delta-adjusted exposure is $\$100 \times 0.50 = \$50$. In other words, for small changes in the underlying price, owning one call option is like owning $50 worth of stock. The one-day 95% VaR of the call option is then a loss of $1.64: $50 \times -3.28\% = -\$1.64$.

For the put option, the delta-adjusted exposure is $\$100 \times -0.50 = -\$50$. In other words, for small changes in the underlying price, owning one put option is equivalent to being short $50 worth of stock. Now, if you are long a put, the worst thing that can happen is that the stock price goes up, not down. To calculate the 95% VaR of the put, we shouldn't use the 5th percentile of the normal distribution, but the 95th percentile. Because the normal distribution is symmetric, if the 5th percentile is -1.64 standard deviations from the mean then the 95th percentile is $+1.64$. So rather than -3.28%, we should use $+3.28\%$. The one-day 95% VaR of the put option is then a loss of $1.64: $-\$50 \times 3.28\% = -\$1.64$. Notice that the call option and put option, because they have the same absolute delta-adjusted exposure both have the same VaR.

For the portfolio as a whole, the VaR is zero. This might seem strange given that the call and put both have positive VaR in isolation, but remember, VaR is not additive. The reason the portfolio VaR is zero is that the delta-adjusted exposure of the portfolio is zero, $-\$50 + \$50 = \$0$. For small changes in the underlying price, the portfolio value will not change significantly.

In reality, this portfolio is not free of risk. This combination of a put and a call is often referred to as a straddle. It can be thought of as a bet on volatility. The straddle will make money if the underlying price increases or decreases significantly. Conversely, you will lose money if the stock stays near the strike price of the options. Even if the stock price doesn't change, a change in implied volatility could significantly alter the value of the straddle. A straddle can lose money both in the short run and long run. Even though the delta-normal VaR is zero, this portfolio is not risk free.

9. The VaR of the call and the put in isolation are $1.64, just as in the previous equation. This is because the absolute delta-adjusted exposures are the same. Similarly, the VaR of the portfolio is the same, $0, because the delta-adjusted exposure is zero.

Just as before, even though the delta-adjusted VaR of this portfolio is zero, this portfolio is not risk free. The portfolios are not equally risky. This portfolio, where we are short both options is much riskier. As a risk manager, alarm bells should always go off when you see a short option position. If you are long a call or put, the worst-case scenario is that the value of the option goes to zero. If you are long an option, the most you can lose is the current value of the option. If you are short a call option, though, the potential loss is unlimited (if you are short a put option, the worst-case scenario is for the underlying price to go to zero; the potential loss is limited, but it could still be very significant). Because of this, the worst-case scenario for a short straddle is worse than the worst-case scenario of a long straddle. Most risk managers would therefore view the short straddle as significantly riskier.

CHAPTER 4

1. Positive homogeneity requires that multiplying all outcomes by a constant, c, also increases the risk measure by c. For a random variable, X, the variance is defined as

$$\sigma_X^2 = E[(X - E[X])^2]$$

Multiplying all the outcomes of X by c is the same as multiplying X by c. If we multiply X by c then we have

$$\sigma_{cX}^2 = E[(cX - E[cX])^2]$$
$$= E[(cX - cE[X])^2]$$
$$= E[(c(X - E[X]))^2]$$
$$= E[c^2(X - E[X])^2]$$
$$= c^2 E[(X - E[X])^2]$$
$$= c^2 \sigma_X^2$$

Taking the square root of both sides, we have

$$\sigma_{cX} = c\sigma_X$$

The standard deviation of cX is c times the standard deviation of X. This proves that standard deviation displays positive homogeneity.

2. The minimum expected shortfall of the portfolio is $-\$700$. Because expected shortfall is subadditive, we know that the expected shortfall of the portfolio will be at worst the sum of the expected shortfalls of the two securities separately.

3. In the previous chapter we found that the VaR for Box Asset Management was equal to a loss of 90. To find the expected shortfall, we can use Equation 4.3 as follows:

$$S = -\frac{1}{1-\gamma} \int_{-\infty}^{VaR} xf(x)dx$$

$$= -\frac{1}{0.05} \int_{-100}^{-90} \pi \frac{1}{200} d\pi$$

$$= -\frac{1}{20}[\pi^2]_{-100}^{-90}$$

$$= 95$$

The final answer, a loss of 95 for the expected shortfall, makes sense. The PDF in this problem is a uniform distribution, with a minimum at -100 or a loss of $+100$. Because it is a uniform distribution, all losses between the VaR, 90, and the maximum loss, 100, are equally likely; therefore, the mean loss, given a VaR exceedance, is halfway between 90 and 100.

4. We start by calculating the cumulative distribution function, $F(\pi)$, for Euler Fund:

$$F(x) = \int_{-0.10}^{x} f(\pi)d\pi$$

$$= c \int_{-0.10}^{x} e^{\pi} d\pi$$

$$= c[e^{\pi}]_{-0.10}^{x}$$

$$= c(e^x - e^{-0.10})$$

The value of the CDF at the maximum value of the function must be equal to one. We use this fact to calculate c,

$$F(10\%) = c(e^{0.10} - e^{-0.10}) = 1$$

$$c = \frac{1}{e^{0.10} - e^{-0.10}} = 4.99$$

We then proceed to calculate the one-day 95% VaR, the point where the CDF equals 5%:

$$F(VaR) = 4.99(e^{-VaR} - e^{-0.10}) = 0.05$$

$$VaR = -\ln\left(\frac{0.05}{4.99} + e^{-0.10}\right)$$

$$VaR = 0.08899$$

VaR is a loss of 8.899%. To find the expected shortfall, S, we proceed as follows:

$$S = -\frac{1}{0.05}\int_{-0.10}^{VaR} \pi f(\pi)d\pi$$

$$= -\frac{1}{0.05}\int_{-0.10}^{VaR} \pi c e^{\pi} d\pi$$

$$= -\frac{c}{0.05}[e^{\pi}(\pi - 1)]_{-0.10}^{VaR}$$

$$= 0.0945$$

The expected shortfall for Euler Fund is a loss of 9.45%.

FIGURE EOCQ.1 Euler Fund PDF and VaR

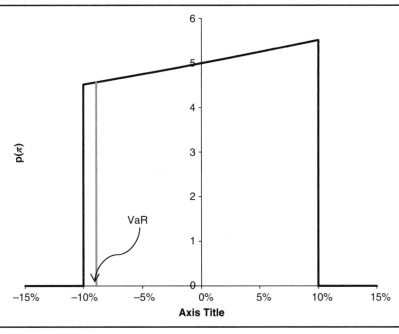

5. (b) Weibull, (c) Fréchet, and (e) Gumbel are distributions associated with extreme value theory.

6. Based on our discussion of translation invariance, we know that cash does not impact the value at risk (VaR) of a portfolio. Based on our discussion of positive homogeneity, we know that $800 of ABC will have a VaR 8 times the VaR of $100 of ABC. Therefore, the portfolio with $200 cash and $800 of ABC will have a one-day 95% VaR of $8 \times \$4 = \$32$.

7. If we have 1,000 data points in our simulation, then the one-day 99% VaR should correspond to the 10th worst loss, or 11%. The one-day 99% expected shortfall is just the average of the 10 worst losses, or 13%: (17% + 14% + 14% + 13% + 13% + 12% + 12% + 12% + 12% + 11%)/10 = 130%/10 = 13%.

8. If we change only the two worst losses, and the 10th worst loss remains the same, then the one-day 99% VaR is still 11%. We increased each of the two worst losses by 10%, though, so the sum of the 10 worst losses is now 150%. The one-day 99% expected shortfall, the average of the worst losses, is then 150%/10 = 15%.

   Changing the two worst returns had no impact on our estimate of VaR, but had a significant impact on our estimate of the expected shortfall. In practice, there is likely to be considerable uncertainty around extremely rare events. This is a perfect example of why VaR is more robust to outliers compared to expected shortfall.

9. We start by calculating the worst return in each of the eight years, as shown in the last row of the following table.

		Year							
		1	2	3	4	5	6	7	8
	1	6%	4%	4%	12%	−1%	−1%	−3%	1%
	2	7%	1%	−3%	2%	−2%	1%	1%	4%
	3	2%	−1%	6%	5%	1%	2%	4%	5%
	4	2%	1%	−5%	−2%	−3%	8%	−4%	3%
	5	−4%	0%	−6%	−2%	−6%	−4%	8%	−10%
	6	1%	−1%	−5%	4%	6%	3%	−15%	6%
Month	7	−23%	1%	−2%	−14%	−2%	4%	−13%	−7%
	8	−5%	6%	−1%	−7%	−1%	0%	4%	−9%
	9	1%	0%	8%	−5%	9%	−4%	−6%	9%
	10	6%	1%	5%	−3%	0%	3%	7%	−3%
	11	−1%	−2%	0%	−6%	−4%	−4%	1%	−3%
	12	3%	2%	−3%	0%	4%	0%	5%	−3%
	min	−23%	−2%	−6%	−14%	−6%	−4%	−15%	−10%

The mean of the minimums is then

$$\text{mean} = \frac{1}{8}(-23\% - 2\% - 6\% - 14\% - 6\% - 4\% - 15\% - 10\%)$$

$$= \frac{-80\%}{8} = -10\%$$

Therefore the expected worst monthly return next year is -10%.

CHAPTER 5

1. Using Equation 5.15, we can calculate the portfolio standard deviation,

$$\sigma_p^2 = \$100^2 \times 40\%^2 + (-\$100)^2 \times 30\%^2 + 2 \times \$100 \times (-\$100) \times 37.5\%$$

$$\times 40\% \times 30\%$$

$$\sigma_p^2 = \$100^2(0.16 + 0.09 - 0.09) = \$100^2(0.16)$$

$$\sigma_p = \$100 \times 40\% = \$40$$

The portfolio standard deviation is \$40. The standard deviation of the AAPL and XOM positions in isolation is \$40 and \$30, respectively. This can be found by multiplying the standard deviation of each security by the absolute exposure of each security.

2. One way to calculate the answer to this problem is to calculate the beta of each security. The dollar beta with respect to the S&P 500 for AAPL is \$100:

$$\beta_{AAPL} = \rho_{AAPL,SPX} \frac{\sigma_{AAPL}}{\sigma_{SPX}} = 50\% \frac{\$40}{20\%} = \$100$$

If the correlation between XOM and the S&P 500 is 80%, then the correlation between a short position in XOM and the S&P 500 is going to be -80%. The beta of XOM is then $-\$120$:

$$\beta_{XOM} = \rho_{XOM,SPX} \frac{\sigma_{XOM}}{\sigma_{SPX}} = -80\% \frac{\$30}{20\%} = -\$120$$

We can find the beta of the entire portfolio by adding the two position betas together. The beta of the entire portfolio is $\$100 + (-\$120) = -\$20$. To minimize the variance of the portfolio we would then buy \$20 of the S&P 500.

3. We can find the answer by substituting the values provided into the regression equation.

$$E[r_{ABC}|r_A, r_B] = 0.01 + 1.25 \times r_A + 0.34 \times r_B$$

$$= 0.01 + 1.25 \times 0.10 + 0.34 \times 0.50$$

$$= 0.01 + 0.125 + 0.17$$

$$= 0.305$$

The final answer is 30.5%.

4. Covariance $= 4.87\%$; correlation $= 82.40\%$.

5. First we note that the expected value of X_A plus X_B is just the sum of the means:

$$E[X_A + X_B] = E[X_A] + E[X_B] = \mu_A + \mu_B$$

Substituting into our equation for variance, and rearranging, we get

$$\sigma_{A+B}^2 = E[(X_A + X_B - E[X_A + X_B])^2]$$
$$= E[((X_A - \mu_A) + (X_B - \mu_B))^2]$$

Expanding the squared term and solving,

$$\sigma_{A+B}^2 = E[(X_A - \mu_A)^2 + (X_B - \mu_B)^2 + 2(X_A - \mu_A)(X_B - \mu_B)]$$
$$= E[(X_A - \mu_A)^2] + E[(X_B - \mu_B)^2 + 2E[(X_A - \mu_A)(X_B - \mu_B)]]$$

The first and second terms on the right-hand side are the variance of A and B, respectively. The last term is the covariance between them. Therefore,

$$\sigma_{A+B}^2 = \sigma_A^2 + \sigma_B^2 + 2\text{Cov}[X_A, X_B]$$

Using our definition of covariance, we can rewrite the covariance in terms of correlation and standard deviation, arriving at our final answer,

$$\sigma_{A+B}^2 = \sigma_A^2 + \sigma_B^2 + 2\rho_{AB}\sigma_A\sigma_B$$

6. From our definition of R^2, we have

$$R^2 = 1 - \frac{\text{RSS}}{\text{TSS}} = 1 - \frac{10.80\%}{13.50\%} = 20\%$$

The R^2 is 20%.

7. Using Equation 5.50, the corresponding F-statistic is,

$$F = \frac{R^2/(n-1)}{(1-R^2)/(t-n)} = \frac{20\%/(2-1)}{(1-20\%)/(50-2)} = 12$$

Using a spreadsheet or other program, we see that the probability associated with this F-statistic is 0.11%; that is, there is only a 0.11% chance that an F-statistic of this magnitude (or greater) would have happened by chance. The F-statistic is significant at the 95% confidence level.

8. We want to start by rewriting the equation for the covariance of X and Y,

$$\text{Cov}[X, Y] = E[(X - E[X])(Y - E[Y])]$$

Using our linear regression equation and making use of the OLS assumptions, we see that the second term can be expressed in terms of X, β, and ε:

$$Y - E[Y] = (\alpha + \beta X + \varepsilon) - E[\alpha + \beta X + \varepsilon]$$

$$= (\alpha + \beta X + \varepsilon) - (\alpha + \beta E[X] + E[\varepsilon])$$

$$= \beta(X - E[X]) + (\varepsilon - E[\varepsilon])$$

In the last line, because it is equal to zero, we could have removed the term $E[\varepsilon]$, but, as we will see, keeping this last term as it is, which expresses ε as a deviation from the mean, will be useful.

Substituting into our covariance equation,

$$Cov[X, Y] = E[(X - E[X])(\beta(X - E[X]) + (\varepsilon - E[\varepsilon]))]$$

$$= E[\beta(X - E[X])^2 + (X - E[X])(\varepsilon - E[\varepsilon])]$$

$$= \beta E[(X - E[X])^2] + E[(X - E[X])(\varepsilon - E[\varepsilon])]$$

The first expectation on the right-hand side is the variance of X, and the last term is the covariance of X and ε. We then have

$$Cov[X, Y] = \beta \sigma_X^2 + Cov[X, \varepsilon]$$

As we stated with Equation 5.28, one of the assumption of the OLS model is that X and ε are uncorrelated; therefore,

$$Cov[X, Y] = \beta \sigma_X^2$$

All that remains is to divide both sides by the variance of X, and to expand the correlation term,

$$\beta = \frac{Cov[X, Y]}{\sigma_X^2} = \frac{\rho_{XY}\sigma_X\sigma_Y}{\sigma_X^2} = \rho_{XY}\frac{\sigma_Y}{\sigma_X}$$

9. We can use our Cholesky decomposition algorithm to find the elements of the matrix

$$l_{11} = \sqrt{\sigma_{11}} = \sqrt{4} = 2$$

$$l_{21} = \frac{1}{l_{11}}\sigma_{21} = \frac{1}{2}14 = 7$$

$$l_{22} = \sqrt{\sigma_{22} - l_{21}^2} = \sqrt{50 - 7^2} = 1$$

$$l_{31} = \frac{1}{l_{11}}\sigma_{31} = \frac{1}{2}16 = 8$$

$$l_{32} = \frac{1}{l_{22}}\left(\sigma_{32} - l_{31}l_{21}\right) = \frac{1}{1}(58 - 8 \times 7) = 2$$

$$l_{33} = \sqrt{\sigma_{33} - l_{31}^2 - l_{32}^2} = \sqrt{132 - 8^2 - 2^2} = 8$$

We can express the full lower triangular matrix as:

$$\mathbf{L} = \begin{bmatrix} 2 & 0 & 0 \\ 7 & 1 & 0 \\ 8 & 2 & 8 \end{bmatrix}$$

We can verify this answer by noting that $\mathbf{LL}'$ is indeed equal to our original covariance matrix, Σ.

10. The expected return of XYZ is 6.01%,

$$E[r_{XYZ}|r_{index}] = E[\alpha + \beta r_{index} + \varepsilon|r_{index}]$$

$$= \alpha + \beta r_{index}$$

$$= 0.01\% + 1.20 \times 5.0\%$$

$$= 6.01\%$$

11. The expected value of r_{XYZ} is 0.07%,

$$E[r_{XYZ}] = E[\alpha + \beta r_{index} + \varepsilon]$$

$$= \alpha + \beta E[r_{inde}]$$

$$= 0.01\% + 1.20 \times 0.05\%$$

$$= 0.07\%$$

To calculate the variance of r_{XYZ}, we start by re-expressing the deviation from the mean for r_{XYZ}. If

$$r_{XYZ} = \alpha + \beta r_{index} + \varepsilon$$

and

$$E[r_{XYZ}] = \alpha + \beta E[r_{index}] + E[\varepsilon]$$

then

$$r_{XYZ} - E[r_{XYZ}] = \beta(r_{index} - E[r_{index}]) + (\varepsilon - E[\varepsilon])$$

The variance of r_{XYZ} is, then

$$\sigma_{XYZ}^2 = E[(r_{XYZ} - E[r_{XYZ}])^2]$$

$$= E[(\beta(r_{index} - E[r_{index}]) + (\varepsilon - E[\varepsilon]))^2]$$

$$= E[\beta^2(r_{index} - E[r_{index}]) + 2\beta(\varepsilon - E[\varepsilon])(r_{index} - E[r_{index}]) + (\varepsilon - E[\varepsilon])^2]$$

$$= \beta^2 E[(r_{index} - E[r_{index}])] + 2\beta E[(\varepsilon - E[\varepsilon])(r_{index} - E[r_{index}])]$$

$$+ E[(\varepsilon - E[\varepsilon])^2]$$

$$= \beta\sigma_{\text{index}}^2 + 2\beta\text{Cov}[r_{\text{index}}, \varepsilon] + \sigma_\varepsilon^2$$

$$= \beta\sigma_{\text{index}}^2 + \sigma_\varepsilon^2$$

$$= 0.000424$$

To get to the second to last line, we use the fact that the covariance between the regressor and the disturbance term is zero in a linear regression.

Taking the square root of the variance, we get a standard deviation of 2.06%.

12. We start by re-expressing the deviation from the mean for r_{XYZ}, similar to the previous question:

$$r_{\text{XYZ}} - E[r_{\text{XYZ}}] = \beta(r_{\text{index}} - E[r_{\text{index}}]) + (\varepsilon - E[\varepsilon])$$

We then substitute this into the equation for covariance,

$$\text{Cov}[r_{\text{XYZ}}, r_{\text{index}}] = E[(r_{\text{XYZ}} - E[r_{\text{XYZ}}])(r_{\text{index}} - E[r_{\text{index}}])]$$

$$= E[(\beta(r_{\text{index}} - E[r_{\text{index}}]) + (\varepsilon - E[\varepsilon]))(r_{\text{index}} - E[r_{\text{index}}])]$$

$$= E[\beta(r_{\text{index}} - E[r_{\text{index}}])^2 + (r_{\text{index}} - E[r_{\text{index}}])(\varepsilon - E[\varepsilon])]$$

$$= \beta E[(r_{\text{index}} - E[r_{\text{index}}])^2] + E[(r_{\text{index}} - E[r_{\text{index}}])(\varepsilon - E[\varepsilon])]$$

The first term on the right-hand side is the variance of r_{index}, while the second term is the covariance of r_{index} and the ε, which is zero. This gives us

$$\text{Cov}[r_{\text{XYZ}}, r_{\text{index}}] = \beta\sigma_{\text{index}}^2$$

The correlation is then

$$\rho = \frac{\text{Cov}[r_{\text{XYZ}}, r_{\text{index}}]}{\sigma_{\text{XYZ}}\sigma_{\text{index}}} = \frac{\beta\sigma_{\text{index}}^2}{\sigma_{\text{XYZ}}\sigma_{\text{index}}} = \beta\frac{\sigma_{\text{index}}}{\sigma_{\text{XYZ}}} = 1.20\frac{1.50\%}{2.06\%} = 87.42\%$$

CHAPTER 6

1. If you examine the data closely, you'll notice that Fund A and Fund B have both had the same returns, only in different orders. Because of this, the mean and standard deviation of their returns must be equal. We start by finding those quantities. Remember, we were asked to find the population coskewness, so we should calculate the populate standard deviation not the sample standard deviation. Also, because multiplying one or both variables by a constant will not change the coskewness, rather than using the percent values we use the values multiplied by 100 (so, 3 instead of 0.03). We have

$$\mu_A = \mu_B = \frac{1}{5}[-3 - 1 + 0 + 1 + 3] = 0$$

$$\sigma_A^2 = \sigma_B^2 = \frac{1}{5}[(-3-0)^2 + (-1-0)^2 + (0-0)^2 + (1-0)^2 + (3-0)^2]$$

$$= \frac{1}{5}[9 + 1 + 0 + 1 + 9]$$

$$= 4$$

$$\sigma_A = \sigma_B = 2$$

Next, we need to calculate the cross-central moment,

$$\mu_{AAB} = \frac{1}{5}[(-3-0)^2(-3-0) + (-1-0)^2(0-0)$$

$$+ (0-0)^2(3-0) + (1-0)^2(1-0) + (3-0)^2(-1-0)]$$

$$= \frac{1}{5}[-27 + 0 + 0 + 1 - 9]$$

$$= -7$$

Putting it all together, we arrive at our final answer, $-7/8$,

$$S_{AAB} = \frac{\mu_{AAB}}{\sigma_A^2 \sigma_B} = -\frac{7}{4 \times 2} = -\frac{7}{8}$$

2. Because the bonds are independent, and only because the bonds are independent, the probability of both bonds defaulting is the probability of one bond defaulting multiplied by the probability of the other bond defaulting. If we represent the first bond defaulting by A and the second by B, then in this case $P[A \text{ and } B] = P[A] \times P[B] = 10\% \times 10\% = 1\%$. Remember, we can only do this because A and B are independent. Similarly, the probability of neither bond defaulting is, $P[\overline{A} \text{ and } \overline{B}] = (1 - P[A])(1 - P[B]) = 90\% \times 90\% = 81\%$, where $\overline{A}$ can be read "not A." The probability of one bond defaulting is 18%. There are two ways for only one bond to default: A can default and B does not, or B can default and A does not. The probability of each of the events is 9%: $P[\overline{A} \text{ and } B] = (1 - P[A])P[B] = 90\% \times 10\% = 9\%$, and $P[A \text{ and } \overline{B}] = P[A](1 - P[B]) = 10\% \times 90\% = 9\%$. Therefore, the probability of just one bond defaulting is 9% + 9% = 18%. This is easy to see in a probability matrix.

		Bond A	
		Default	**No Default**
Bond B	**Default**	1%	9%
	No Default	9%	81%

As is required, the sum of all possible outcomes is equal to 100%, 1% + 81% + 18% = 100%.

3. We can calculate the probability that Option A ends up in the money by adding the up the probabilities in the left column of the probability matrix, $P[A_{ITM}] = 40\% + 20\% = 60\%$. Similarly, the probability that Option B is in the money is found by adding the entries in the first row $P[B_{ITM}] = 40\% + 10\% = 50\%$.

The probability that both options end up in the money is $P[B_{ITM}$ and $A_{ITM}] = 40\%$. If the options were independent, we would expect this joint probability to be $60\% \times 50\% = 30\%$. Therefore, Option A and B are not independent, $P[B_{ITM}$ and $A_{ITM}] \neq P[B_{ITM}] \times P[A_{ITM}]$.

4. The shape of the PDF resembles a truncated paraboloid, as shown in Figure 6.A1.

To see if X and Y are independent, we start by calculating the marginal distribution of X,

$$f_x(x) = \int_y f(x, t)dt$$

$$= \int_{-2}^{+2} c(8 - x^2 - t^2)dt$$

$$= c\left[8t - tx^2 - \frac{1}{3}t^3\right]_{-2}^{+2}$$

$$= 4c\left(\frac{20}{3} - x^2\right)$$

FIGURE FIGURE 6.A1 Joint Probability Density Function

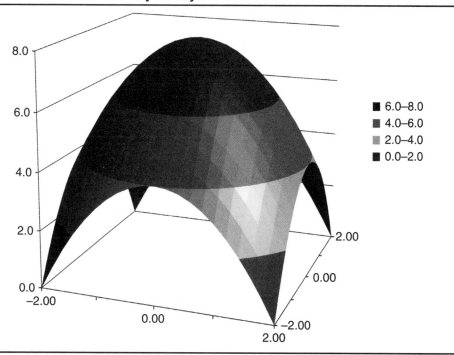

The marginal distribution of Y is

$$f_y(y) = \int_x f(t,y)dt$$

$$= \int_{-2}^{+2} c(8 - t^2 - y^2)dt$$

$$= c\left[8t - ty^2 - \frac{1}{3}t^3\right]_{-2}^{+2}$$

$$= 4c\left(\frac{20}{3} - y^2\right)$$

Putting the two together, we can see that the product of the marginal distributions does not equal the joint distribution.

$$f_x(x)f_y(y) = 16c^2\left(\frac{20}{3} - x^2\right)\left(\frac{20}{3} - y^2\right)$$

$$= \frac{1}{16^3}(400 - 60x^2 - 60y^2 + 9x^2y^2)$$

$$\neq f(x,y)$$

We conclude that X and Y are *not* independent.

5. The joint distribution in 6.10a is nonelliptical and the two variables are negatively correlated. The joint distribution in 6.10b is elliptical and the two variables are positively correlated.

6. To calculate Kendall's tau, we start by examining the concordance of all possible pairs of points. With three points there are three distinct pairs:

Pair	Concordant = +1, Discordant = −1
A, B	−1
A, C	−1
B, C	+1

One pair is concordant and two are discordant; therefore, Kendall's tau is −33%,

$$\tau = \frac{\text{\# of concordant points} - \text{\# of discordant points}}{\binom{n}{2}} = \frac{1 - 2}{3} = -33\%$$

To calculate Spearman's rho, we start by calculating the rank of each data point,

	X	Y	**Rank[X]**	**Rank[Y]**
A	70%	5%	1	3
B	40%	35%	2	1
C	20%	10%	3	2

The general formula for correlation is

$$\text{Corr}[X, Y] = \frac{\sum_{i=1}^{n} (x_i - \bar{x})(y_i - \bar{y})}{\sqrt{\sum_{i=1}^{n} (x_i - \bar{x})^2} \sqrt{\sum_{i=1}^{n} (y_i - \bar{y})^2}}$$

where $\bar{x}$ and $\bar{y}$ are the mean of X and Y respectively. To calculate Spearman's rho, we use not X and Y values, but their ranks. The mean of both Rank[X] and Rank[Y] is 2; therefore,

$$\rho_s = \frac{(1-2)(3-2) + (2-2)(1-2) + (3-2)(2-2)}{\sqrt{(1-2)^2 + (2-2)^2 + (3-2)^2} \sqrt{(3-2)^2 + (1-2)^2 + (2-2)^2}}$$

$$= \frac{(-1) + 0 + 0}{\sqrt{1+0+1}\sqrt{1+1+0}}$$

$$= \frac{-1}{\sqrt{2}\sqrt{2}}$$

$$= -50\%$$

Our final answers are then that Kendall's tau is -33% and Spearman's rho is -50%. In this example, Spearman's rho and Kendall's tau share the same sign, but they are not equal.

7. We start by calculating the copula's density function, $c(u, v)$:

$$c(u, v) = \frac{\partial^2 C(u, v)}{\partial u \partial v} = \frac{\partial^2}{\partial u \partial v} uv = \frac{\partial}{\partial u} u = 1$$

We next calculate the expected value of the copula:

$$\int_0^1 \int_0^1 C(u, v) c(u, v) du dv = \int_0^1 \int_0^1 uv \, du dv$$

$$= \int_0^1 \left[\frac{1}{2} u^2 v \right]_0^1 dv$$

$$= \frac{1}{2} \int_0^1 v dv = \frac{1}{2} \left[\frac{1}{2} v^2 \right]_0^1 = \frac{1}{4}$$

Substituting into our equation for Kendall's tau,

$$\tau = 4 \int_0^1 \int_0^1 C(u,v)c(u,v)dudv - 1 = 4\frac{1}{4} - 1 = 0$$

Not surprisingly for something called the independent copula, Kendall's tau is zero.

8. To calculate Spearman's rho, we first integrate the copula, $C(u,v)$, function with respect to u:

$$\int_0^1 C(u,v)du = \int_0^1 uv[1 + \alpha(1-u)(1-v)]du$$

$$= \int_0^1 [u(v + \alpha v(1-v)) - u^2\alpha v(1-v)]du$$

$$= \left[\frac{1}{2}u^2(v + \alpha v(1-v)) - \frac{1}{3}u^3\alpha v(1-v)\right]_0^1$$

$$= \left[\frac{1}{2}(v + \alpha v(1-v)) - \frac{1}{3}\alpha v(1-v)\right] - [0-0]$$

$$= \left(\frac{1}{2} + \frac{1}{6}\alpha\right)v - \frac{1}{6}\alpha v^2$$

Next, we integrate this result with respect to v:

$$\int_0^1 \int_0^1 C(u,v)dudv = \int_0^1 \left[\left(\frac{1}{2} + \frac{1}{6}\alpha\right)v - \frac{1}{6}\alpha v^2\right]dv$$

$$= \left[\frac{1}{2}\left(\frac{1}{2} + \frac{1}{6}\alpha\right)v^2 - \frac{1}{18}\alpha v^3\right]_0^1$$

$$= \left[\frac{1}{2}\left(\frac{1}{2} + \frac{1}{6}\alpha\right) - \frac{1}{18}\alpha\right] - [0-0]$$

$$= \frac{1}{4} + \frac{1}{36}\alpha$$

Finally, we use this result to calculate Spearman's rho:

$$\rho = 12 \int_0^1 \int_0^1 C(u,v)dudv - 3$$

$$= 12\left(\frac{1}{4} + \frac{1}{36}\alpha\right) - 3$$

$$= \frac{1}{3}\alpha$$

9. The daily log returns are independent and identically distributed. Because these are log returns, each annual log return would just be the sum of the 256 daily log returns. For the annual log returns, then, the mean, standard deviation, skewness, and excess kurtosis would be 25.6%, 16%, −0.10, and 0.02, respectively.

$$\mu_A = 256 \times 0.10\% = 25.6\%$$

$$\sigma_A = \sqrt{256} \times 1\% = 16\%$$

$$S_A = -\frac{1.6}{\sqrt{256}} = -0.10$$

$$K_{Ex,A} = \frac{5.12}{256} = 0.02$$

CHAPTER 7

1. The VaR of the portfolio would be approximately $10.6 million. Using Equation 7.5:

$$d(\text{VaR}) = \frac{dw_i}{w_i}\text{iVaR}_i = \frac{\$1.2 \text{ million} - \$1.0 \text{ million}}{\$1.0 \text{ million}}\$3 \text{ million} = 0.2 \times \$3 \text{ million}$$

$$d(\text{VaR}) = \$0.6 \text{ million}$$

The total VaR would then be approximately $10.6 million, $10 million + $0.6 million = $10.6 million.

2. The iVaR of Position B is −$100. For the portfolio as a whole, the iVaR is equal to the VaR, so the iVaR of this portfolio must be $1,000. For any portfolio the sum of the iVaRs must be equal to the total VaR or iVaR. In this case $300 + (−$100) + $800 = $1,000. Remember, unlike VaR, iVaR can be negative. The fact that the iVaR of Position B is negative tells us that increasing the size of Position B, at least at the margin, will actually lower the overall risk of the portfolio.

	VaR	iVaR
Position A	$500	$300
Position B	$400	−$100
Position C	$650	$800
Portfolio	$1,000	$1,000

3. In order to calculate the variance of the portfolio we first calculate the expected value of r_p:

$$E[r_p] = E[\alpha] + E[\beta r_{Index}] + E[\varepsilon]$$

$$= \alpha + \beta E[r_{Index}] + E[\varepsilon]$$

The portfolio variance, σ_p^2, is then

$$\sigma_p^2 = E[(r_p - E[r_p])^2] = E[(\alpha + \beta r_{Index} + \varepsilon - \alpha - \beta E[r_{Index}] - E[\varepsilon])^2]$$

$$= E[(\beta(r_{Index} - E[r_{Index}]) + \varepsilon - E[\varepsilon])^2]$$

$$= E[\beta^2(r_{Index} - E[r_{Index}])^2 + 2(r_{Index} - E[r_{Index}])(\varepsilon - E[\varepsilon]) + (\varepsilon - E[\varepsilon])^2]$$

$$= \beta^2 E[(r_{Index} - E[r_{Index}])^2] + 2E[(r_{Index} - E[r_{Index}])(\varepsilon - E[\varepsilon])] + E[(\varepsilon - E[\varepsilon])^2]$$

$$= \beta^2 \sigma_{Index}^2 + 2 \times 0 + \sigma_\varepsilon^2$$

$$= \beta^2 \sigma_{Index}^2 + \sigma_\varepsilon^2$$

In the last line we have expressed the total portfolio variance as a linear combination of the variance of the index, σ_{Index}^2, and the variance of the error term, σ_ε^2. As anticipated, for variance the sum of systematic and idiosyncratic risk equals the total portfolio risk.

For standard deviation, the total portfolio risk is generally less than the sum of the systematic and idiosyncratic risk. They are only equal in the degenerate cases when the systematic risk, the idiosyncratic risk, or both are zero. Mathematically,

$$\sigma_p \leq \beta\sigma_{Index} + \sigma_\varepsilon$$

We can prove this by completing the sum of squares under the square root. Standard deviation must be positive; therefore, if β is positive, then $\sigma_{Index}\sigma_\varepsilon > 0$, and

$$\sqrt{\beta^2 \sigma_{Index}^2 + \sigma_\varepsilon^2} \leq \sqrt{\beta^2 \sigma_{Index}^2 + 2\beta\sigma_{Index}\sigma_\varepsilon + \sigma_\varepsilon^2}$$

or,

$$\sqrt{\beta^2 \sigma_{Index}^2 + \sigma_\varepsilon^2} \leq \beta\sigma_{Index} + \sigma_\varepsilon$$

From our previous result, the left-hand side is equal to the portfolio standard deviation, so

$$\sigma_p \leq \beta\sigma_{Index} + \sigma_\varepsilon$$

4. $h = 0.50$ or 50%.

$$h = 1 - \frac{30}{10 + 20 + 30} = 1 - \frac{30}{60} = 0.50$$

5. $N = 2.45$

$$N = e^{-[0.60 \times \ln(0.60) + 0.30 \times \ln(0.30) + 0.10 \times \ln(0.10)]} = e^{0.90} = 2.45$$

6. If you can borrow at the risk-free rate, then applying leverage will not impact the Sharpe ratio. The Sharpe ratio of the 3× version of the ETF will also have a Sharpe ratio of 0.80.

The expected return of the levered product is 50%. Rearranging Equation 7.14, we have

$$R_i = S_i\sigma_i + R_{rf}$$

For the ETF,

$$R_{ETF} = 0.80 \times 20\% + 2\% = 18\%$$

To create the levered product, for each $1 invested, we need to borrow an additional $2, so that we can buy $3 of the ETF. The return would then be three times the return of the ETF minus two times the risk-free rate:

$$R_{3\times} = 3 \times 18\% - 2 \times 2\% = 50\%$$

We can double check this using Equation 7.14. The standard deviation of the 3× product would be three times the standard deviation of the ETF, or 60%, therefore,

$$S_{3\times} = \frac{50\% - 2\%}{60\%} = 0.80$$

As required, the Sharpe ratio of the levered product is the same as for the ETF.

In practice, any return, positive or negative, will change the leverage ratio of a levered product. In order to maintain a constant level of leverage, a levered product would need to be rebalanced from time to time. The standard deviation of the underlying, how often the product is rebalanced, and the cost of rebalancing will all impact the actual performance of a levered product.

7. Using Equation 7.15, we calculate an incremental Sharpe of 0.50 for Alice and 0.20 for Bob,

$$S_A^* = 0.80 - 0.30 \times 1.00 = 0.50$$

$$S_B^* = 1.10 - 0.90 \times 1.00 = 0.20$$

Both managers would improve the Sharpe ratio of the fund at the margin, but Alice would improve the Sharpe ratio more.

CHAPTER 8

1. The present value is $1,092.97. Using Equation 8.1, we have

$$V_0 = \frac{10\% \times \$1,000}{(1 + 5\%)} + \frac{10\% \times \$1,000}{(1 + 5\%)^2} + \frac{\$1,000}{(1 + 5\%)^2}$$

$$= \$95.24 + \$90.70 + \$907.03 = \$1,092.97$$

2. If there is no default, the bondholder will receive $104 at the end of the year, the $4 coupon plus the $100 notional. If the bond defaults, the bondholder will receive 20% of this amount. The risk-neutral value of the bond is just the weighted average of these two values discounted back at the risk-free rate:

$$V_0 = 88\% \frac{\$104}{1.04} + 12\% \frac{20\% \times \$104}{1.04}$$

$$= \frac{\$104}{1.04}(88\% + 12\% \times 20\%)$$

$$= \$100(88\% + 2.4\%)$$

$$= \$100 \times 90.4\%$$

$$= \$90.40$$

The risk-neutral value is $90.40.

3. This setup is simple enough that we can find an explicit solution for the yield. The yield, Y, must satisfy the following equation:

$$V_0 = \$85 = \frac{\$10}{(1+Y)} + \frac{\$110}{(1+Y)^2}$$

Rearranging, we have

$$\$85(1+Y)^2 - \$10(1+Y) - \$110 = 0$$

This is a quadratic equation. The solution can then be found as

$$(1+Y) = \frac{\$10 \pm \sqrt{\$10^2 + 4 \times \$85 \times \$110}}{2 \times \$85}$$

$$= \frac{\$10 \pm \$193.65}{2 \times \$85} = 5.88\% \pm 113.91\%$$

$$= 119.79\%$$

In the last line, we selected the positive root, which gives us a yield of 19.79%. The negative root, while a solution to the quadratic equation, does not make much sense for the yield. The yield is 19.79%.

4. The discount rate used by investors, R, must satisfy the following equation:

$$\$72 = (1 - 19\%)\frac{\$100}{1+R} + 19\%\frac{(1 - 100\%)\$100}{1+R}$$

Rearranging, and solving for R:

$$\$72 = (1 - 19\%)\frac{\$100}{1+R} = \frac{\$81}{1+R}$$

$$R = \frac{\$81}{\$72} - 1 = \frac{9}{8} - 1 = \frac{1}{8} = 12.5\%$$

Compared to the risk-free rate of 5%, the investors are asking for an additional 7.5% to accept the credit risk of this bond. The correct answer is 7.5%.

5. The enterprise value is equal to $4,000 = $1,924 + $2,076. (The value of the equity is equal to the market capitalization.) Using Equation 8.15,

$$\Delta = \frac{-\ln\left(\frac{V_E}{B}\right) - \left(r - \frac{\sigma_V^2}{2}\right)T}{\sigma_V \sqrt{T}} = \frac{-\ln\left(\frac{\$4,000}{\$2,076}\right) - 0}{40\%\sqrt{1}} = -1.64$$

The distance to default is -1.64 standard deviations. Plugging this into the standard normal cumulative distribution, we get our final answer for the probability of default, 5%.

6. There is a 9.01% probability that exactly four bonds default:

$$P[K = k] = \binom{n}{k} p^k (1 - p)^{n-k}$$

$$P[K = k] = \binom{40}{4} 5\%^4 95\%^{36} = 9.01\%$$

CHAPTER 9

1. In terms of shares, the 15-day average trading volume based on the mean is 28.9 million shares. Based on the median, the average is 22 million shares.

To calculate the average dollar volume, we first need to calculate the dollar volume each day. We do this by multiplying the price and volume figures each day, as in the following table. Based on this new column, the 15-day mean volume is $4.4 billion. Based on the median, it is $3.4 billion.

In both cases, the mean and median are considerably different. You can get a sense of how much the volume varies by comparing the volume on June 8th and 12th.

	Volume (millions of shares)	Price ($)	Volume ($millions)
5/23/2017	20	153.80	3,076.00
5/24/2017	19	153.34	2,913.46
5/25/2017	19	153.87	2,923.53
5/26/2017	22	153.61	3,379.42
5/30/2017	20	153.67	3,073.40
5/31/2017	24	152.76	3,666.24
6/1/2017	16	153.18	2,450.88
6/2/2017	28	155.45	4,352.60
6/5/2017	25	153.93	3,848.25
6/6/2017	27	154.45	4,170.15
6/7/2017	21	155.37	3,262.77
6/8/2017	21	154.99	3,254.79
6/9/2017	65	148.98	9,683.70
6/12/2017	72	145.42	10,470.24
6/13/2017	34	146.59	4,984.06

2. You own 0.5 days' volume of IBM:

$$2 \text{ milllion shares} \frac{\text{day}}{4 \text{ million shares}} = 0.5 \text{ days}$$

3. Because we are assuming 20% of average daily volume, we can sell 0.8 million shares of IBM and cover1.2 million shares of MSFT each day. At current market prices this is equal to $64 million per day of IBM and $60 million per day of MSFT. Our current portfolio contains a total of $160 million of IBM and −$150 million of MSFT. The complete liquidity schedule is as follows:

	Per Day			Cumulative	
Day	IBM ($MM)	MSFT ($MM)	Total ($MM)	Total ($MM)	% Liquidated
1	$64	$60	$124	$124	40%
2	$64	$60	$124	$248	80%
3	$32	$30	$62	$310	100%

4. If there are 256 business days in the year, and the annualized volatility is 16%, then the daily volatility is $1\% = 16\%/\sqrt{256}$. If returns are normally distributed, then we need to multiply this daily standard deviation by 1.645. Using Equation 9.2, we have

$$\text{LVaR}_{ABC} = 1{,}000 \times 1 \times 1\% \times 1.645 + 1{,}000 \times 0.01 = 26.45$$

$$\text{LVaR}_{XYZ} = 1 \times 1{,}000 \times 1\% \times 1.645 + 1 \times 1 = 17.45$$

The LVaR of $1,000 invested in ABC or XYZ are $26.45 and $17.45, respectively. You could also have expressed your answer as a percentage of total market value, in which case the answer would be 2.64% and 1.74%, respectively.

The VaR of both positions is the same, but the LVaR of the ABC is greater. This is because the bid-ask spread, even though it is less in dollar terms, is greater in percentage terms.

5. We can rearrange Equation 9.3 to get the approximate change in price:

$$dP = \frac{1}{\lambda}\frac{dQ}{Q}P = \frac{1}{-4}\frac{2.5 \text{ million}}{10 \text{ million}}\$64 = -\frac{1}{4}\frac{1}{4}\$64 = -\$4$$

Trying to sell an additional 2.5 million shares will cause the price to fall by approximately $4, giving us a final price for XYZ of $60. For the sale, you can assume you will get a price close to the mean of the starting price and the final price, or $62. The total proceeds would then be $155 million.

In reality, Equation 9.3 is only true for infinitesimal changes. In this case, though, the approximation is very close. We could have used Equation 9.4 to calculate the exact price change. If we had done this, rather than $60, the exact final price would have been $60.53.

CHAPTER 10

1. Using Bayes' theorem,

$$P[\text{GDP} \downarrow | \text{unemployment} \uparrow] = \frac{P[\text{unemployment} \uparrow | \text{GDP} \downarrow] P[\text{GDP} \downarrow]}{P[\text{unemployment} \uparrow]}$$

$$P[\text{GDP} \downarrow | \text{unemployment} \uparrow] = \frac{40\% \times 20\%}{10\%} = 80\%$$

2. The answer is 32.14%. By applying Bayes' theorem, we can calculate the result

$$P[\text{actual} = D | \text{model} = D] = \frac{P[\text{model} = D | \text{actual} = D] P[\text{actual} = D]}{P[\text{model} = D]}$$

$$P[\text{actual} = D | \text{model} = D] = \frac{90\% \times 5\%}{90\% \times 5\% + 10\% \times 95\%} = 32.14\%$$

Even though the model is 90% accurate, 95% of the bonds don't default, and of those 95% the model predicts that 10% of them will default. In other words, within the bond portfolio, the model identifies 9.5% of the bonds as likely to default, even though they won't. Of the 5% of bonds that actually default, the model correctly identifies 90%, or 4.5% of the portfolio. This 4.5% correctly identified is overwhelmed by the 9.5% incorrectly identified.

		Actual		
		D	No D	
Model	D	4.5	9.5	14.0
	No D	0.5	85.5	86.0
		5.0	95.0	100.0

3. We can start by summing across the first row to get W:

$$W + 5\% = 15\%$$

$$W = 10\%$$

In a similar fashion, we can find X by summing across the second row:

$$45\% + X = 65\%$$

$$X = 20\%$$

To calculate Y, we can sum down the first column, using our previously calculated value for W"

$$W + 45\% + Y = 10\% + 45\% + Y = 60\%$$

$$Y = 5\%$$

Using this result, we can sum across the third row to get Z:

$$Y + 15\% = 5\% + 15\% = Z$$

$$Z = 20\%$$

The completed probability matrix is:

		Equity		
		Outperform	**Underperform**	
	Upgrade	10%	5%	**15%**
Bonds	**No Change**	45%	20%	**65%**
	Downgrade	5%	15%	**20%**
		60%	**40%**	**100%**

The last part of the question asks us to find the conditional probability, which we can express as, P[downgrade|underperform].

We can solve this by taking values from the completed probability matrix. The equity underperforms in 40% of scenarios. The equity underperforms and the bonds are downgraded in 15% of scenarios. Dividing, we get our final answer, 37.5%. Mathematically,

$$P[\text{downgrade}|\text{underperform}] = \frac{P[\text{downgrade and underperform}]}{P[\text{underperform}]}$$

$$= \frac{15\%}{40\%}$$

$$= 37.5\%$$

4. The prior probabilities are

$$P[p = 0.55] = 50\%$$

$$P[p = 0.50] = 50\%$$

The probability of the strategy generating 10 positive returns over 20 days if the analyst is correct is

$$P[10 + |p = 0.55] = \binom{20}{10} 0.55^{10} \times 0.45^{10}$$

The unconditional probability of 10 positive returns is

$$P[10+] = P[10 + |p = 0.55]P[p = 0.55] + P[10 + |p = 0.50]P[p = 0.50]$$

$$= \binom{20}{10} 0.55^{10} 0.45^{10} \cdot 0.50 + \binom{20}{10} 0.50^{10} 0.50^{10} \cdot 0.50$$

$$= 0.50 \binom{20}{10} (0.55^{10} 0.45^{10} + 0.50^{10} 0.50^{10})$$

To get our final answer, the probability that $p = 0.55$ given the 10 positive returns, we use Bayes' theorem:

$$P[p = 0.55|10+] = \frac{P[10 + |p = 0.55] \times P[p = 0.55]}{P[10+]}$$

$$= \frac{\binom{20}{10} 0.55^{10} \times 0.45^{10} \times 0.50}{0.50 \binom{20}{10} (0.55^{10} \times 0.45^{10} + 0.50^{10} \times 0.50^{10})}$$

$$= \frac{0.55^{10} \times 0.45^{10}}{(0.55^{10} \times 0.45^{10} + 0.50^{10} \times 0.50^{10})}$$

$$= \frac{1}{1 + \left(\frac{100}{99}\right)^{10}}$$

$$= 47.49\%$$

The final answer is 47.49%. The strategy generated a profit in only 10 out of 20 days, so our belief in the analyst's claim has decreased. That said, with only 20 data points, it is hard to tell the difference between a strategy that generates profits 55% of the time and a strategy that generates profits 50% of the time. Our belief decreased, but not by much.

5. The final answer is 92.31%. Use + to signify the procyclical index being up, G to signify that the economy is up (growing), and $\overline{G}$ to signify that the economy is down or flat

(not growing). We are given the following information:

$$P[+|G] = 75\%$$

$$P[+|\overline{G}] = 25\%$$

$$P[\overline{G}] = 20\%$$

We are asked to find $P[G|+]$. Using Bayes' theorem, we have

$$P[G|+] = \frac{P[+|G]P[G]}{P[+]}$$

We were not given $P[G]$, but we know the economy must be either growing or not growing; therefore,

$$P[G] = 1 - P[\overline{G}] = 80\%$$

We can also calculate the unconditional probability that the index is up, $P[+]$,

$$P[+] = P[+|G]P[G] + P[+|\overline{G}]P[\overline{G}]$$

$$= 75\% \times 80\% + 25\% \times 20\%$$

$$= 60\% + 5\% = 65\%$$

Putting it all together, we arrive at our final answer,

$$P[G|+] = \frac{P[+|G]P[G]}{P[+]} = \frac{75\% \times 80\%}{65\%}$$

$$= \frac{60\%}{65\%} = 92.31\%$$

6. The prior beliefs for beating the market in any given year are:

$$P[p = 0.40] = \frac{1}{4}$$

$$P[p = 0.50] = \frac{1}{4}$$

$$P[p = 0.60] = \frac{1}{4}$$

$$P[p = 0.80] = \frac{1}{4}$$

The probability of beating the market three out of five years is

$$P[3B|p = p_i] = \binom{5}{3} p_i^3 (1 - p_i)^2$$

Given a constant, c, the posterior probability can be defined as

$$P[p = p_i|3B] = cP[3B|p = p_i]P[p = p_i]$$

$$= c \times \binom{5}{3} p_i^3(1 - p_i)^2 \times \frac{1}{4}$$

We know that all of the posterior probabilities must add to one; therefore,

$$\sum_{i=1}^{4} P[p = p_i|3B] = 1$$

$$c \times \binom{5}{3} \times \frac{1}{4} \sum_{i=1}^{4} p_i^3(1 - p_i)^2 = 1$$

$$c = \frac{4}{\binom{5}{3} \sum_{i=1}^{4} p_i^3(1 - p_i)^2}$$

The posterior probabilities are then

$$P[p = p_i|3B] = \frac{4}{\binom{5}{3} \sum_{i=1}^{4} p_i^3(1 - p_i)^2} \times \binom{5}{3} p_i^3(1 - p_i)^2 \times \frac{1}{4}$$

$$= \frac{p_i^3(1 - p_i)^2}{\sum_{i=1}^{4} p_i^3(1 - p_i)^2}$$

To get the final answer, we simply substitute in the four possible values for p_i. For example, the posterior probability that the manager is an underperformer is

$$P[p = 0.40|3B] = \frac{0.40^3(1 - 0.40)^2}{\sum_{i=1}^{4} p_i^3(1 - p_i)^2}$$

$$= \frac{0.40^3 \times 0.60^2}{0.40^3 \times 0.60^2 + 0.50^3 \times 0.50^2 + 0.60^3 \times 0.40^2 + 0.80^3 \times 0.20^2}$$

$$= \frac{4^3 \times 6^2}{4^3 \times 6^2 + 5^3 \times 5^2 + 6^3 \times 4^2 + 8^3 \times 2^2}$$

$$= \frac{2{,}304}{10{,}933}$$

$$= 21.1\%$$

The other three probabilities can be found in a similar fashion. The final answer is that the posterior probabilities of the manager being an underperformer, an in-line performer, a star, or a superstar are 21.1%, 28.6%, 31.6%, and 18.7%, respectively. Interestingly, even though the manager beat the market 60% of the time, the manager is almost as likely to be an underperformer or an in-line performer (49.7% probability) as a star or a superstar (50.3% probability).

7. The answer is 10%. You are given the following:

$$P[+|Bull] = 75\%$$

$$P[+] = 50\%$$

$$P[Bull] = 60\%$$

You are asked to find $P[Bear|+]$. A direct application of Bayes' theorem will not work. Instead we need to use the fact that the Federal Reserve's statement must be either bearish or bullish, no matter what the market does. Therefore,

$$P[Bear|+] = 1 - P[Bull|+]$$

$$= 1 - \frac{P[+|Bull]P[Bull]}{P[+]}$$

$$= 1 - \frac{75\% \times 60\%}{50\%} = 1 - \frac{\frac{3}{4}\frac{3}{5}}{\frac{1}{2}}$$

$$= 1 - \frac{9}{10}$$

$$= 10\%$$

8. Because the prior distribution is a beta distribution and the likelihood can be described by a binomial distribution, we know the posterior distribution must also be a beta distribution. Further, we know that the parameters of the posterior distribution can be found by adding the number of successes to the first parameter, and the number of failures to the second. In this problem, the initial distribution was $\beta(4, 4)$ and there were 60 successes (up days), and $100 - 60 = 40$ failures. Therefore, the final distribution is $\beta(64, 44)$. The mean of a beta distribution, $\beta(a, b)$, is simply $a/(a + b)$. The mean of our posterior distribution is then

$$\mu = \frac{a}{a + b} = \frac{64}{64 + 44} = \frac{64}{108} = 59.26\%$$

We therefore believe there is a 59.26% probability that the strategy will be up tomorrow.

9. There are 27 possible states for the network: $3^3 = 27$. The minimum number of probabilities needed to define the network is 22. As an example, we could define $P[A = up]$, and $P[A = unchanged]$ for node A, which would allow us to calculate $P[A = down] = 1$

$-P[A = \text{up}] - P[A = \text{unchanged}]$. Similarly, we could define two probabilities for node B. For node C, there are nine possible input combinations (each of three possible states for A can be combined with three possible states from B). For each combination, we can define two conditional probabilities and infer the third. For example, we could define $P[C = \text{up} \mid A = \text{up}, B = \text{up}]$ and $P[C = \text{unchanged} \mid A = \text{up}, B = \text{up}]$, which would allow us to calculate $P[C = \text{down} \mid A = \text{up}, B = \text{up}] = 1 - P[C = \text{up} \mid A = \text{up}, B = \text{up}] - P[C = \text{unchanged} \mid A = \text{up}, B = \text{up}]$. This gives us a total of 22 probabilities that we need to define: $2 + 2 + 9 \times 2 = 22$.

10. The correlation matrix for the first network is:

Network 1

	E	*S1*	*S2*
E	100%	49%	20%
S1	49%	100%	10%
S2	20%	10%	100%

11. The correlation matrix for the second network is:

Network 2

	E	*S1*	*S2*
E	100%	49%	7%
S1	49%	100%	15%
S2	7%	15%	100%

CHAPTER 11

1. The expected value of the option is $50: $60\% \times \$100 + 40\% \times (-\$25) = \$60 - \$10 = \$50$. A risk-averse investor would only purchase the option for less than $50. A risk-neutral person would purchase the option for $50 or less. A risk-seeking person would pay more than $50, but how much more is unclear from the information we have been given.

2. The consumer's current consumption can be described by a uniform distribution, $f(C)$,

$$f(C) = 1 \quad 0 \leq C \leq 1$$

The consumer's expected utility is then equal to

$$E[U] = \int_0^1 f(C) \times U dC = \int_0^1 1 \times (1 - e^{-\alpha C}) dC$$

Solving, we find

$$E[U] = \int_0^1 (1 - e^{-\alpha C}) dC = \left[C + \frac{1}{\alpha} e^{-\alpha C} \right]_0^1$$

$$= \left(1 + \frac{1}{\alpha} e^{-\alpha} \right) - \left(\frac{1}{\alpha} \right)$$

$$= 1 - \frac{1}{\alpha} (1 - e^{-\alpha})$$

If we give the consumer $\overline{C}$ with certainty, the consumer's utility will be

$$U = 1 - e^{-\alpha \overline{C}}$$

This will be equal to the current utility when

$$1 - e^{-\alpha \overline{C}} = 1 - \frac{1}{\alpha} (1 - e^{-\alpha})$$

$$e^{-\alpha \overline{C}} = \frac{1}{\alpha} (1 - e^{-\alpha})$$

$$\overline{C} = -\frac{1}{\alpha} \ln \left[\frac{1}{\alpha} (1 - e^{\alpha}) \right]$$

Using the value of 5 for α, we find our final answer,

$$\overline{C} = 0.32$$

In other words, rather than their current uncertain consumption level with an expected value of 0.50, the consumer would be just as happy with a certain consumption of 0.32. This is another example of risk aversion.

3. If π_N is the earnings when there is no flood (in the first case $100), then the expected utility without insurance is

$$E[U] = 0.99 \frac{(\pi_N + 1)^{1-\theta} - 1}{1 - \theta} + 0.01 \frac{(0 + 1)^{1-\theta} - 1}{1 - \theta}$$

$$= 0.99 \frac{(\pi_N + 1)^{1-\theta} - 1}{1 - \theta}$$

If we buy insurance and the cost of the insurance is x, then we would earn $(\pi_N - x)$ whether it floods or not. The expected utility with insurance is then

$$U_I = \frac{(\pi_N - x + 1)^{1-\theta} - 1}{1 - \theta}$$

We would be willing to pay for the insurance if it leaves us better or as well off as we are without insurance. We will be indifferent to either having insurance or not having insurance when $E[U] = U_I$:

$$0.99\frac{(\pi_N + 1)^{1-\theta} - 1}{1 - \theta} = \frac{(\pi_N - x + 1)^{1-\theta} - 1}{1 - \theta}$$

Solving for x, we have

$$x = \pi_N + 1 - \left[0.99(\pi_N + 1)^{(1-\theta)} + 0.01\right]^{1/(1-\theta)}$$

For $\theta = 0.50$, we would be willing to pay \$1.81 for insurance. For $\theta = 2.00$, we would be willing to pay \$50.50.

4. If earnings were expected to be \$1,000 instead of \$100, assuming no flood, and $\theta = 0.50$, we would be willing to pay \$19.29 for insurance.

   You might expect a factory owner to pay exactly 10 times as much to ensure 10 times as much earnings. It depends on the shape of the factory owner's utility function. With the particular utility function we are using, this is almost the case. Compared to the previous question, our earnings are 10 times as much, but we are willing to pay slightly more than 10 times as much for insurance.

5. Because we already have three years of history, we'll consider this year to be year 4 and next year to be year 5. The habit level this year is then

$$H_4 = \frac{4}{7}C_3 + \frac{2}{7}C_2 + \frac{1}{7}C_1$$

$$= \frac{4}{7}105 + \frac{2}{7}95 + \frac{1}{7}90$$

$$= 100$$

If we invest in GRW, utility this year will be

$$U_{4,\text{GRW}} = \sqrt{\frac{110}{100}} \approx 1.05$$

Next year, the habit level will be

$$H_{5,\text{GRW}} = \frac{4}{7}110 + \frac{2}{7}105 + \frac{1}{7}95 = \frac{745}{7}$$

and the utility will be

$$U_{5,\text{GRW}} = \sqrt{\frac{120}{745/7}} \approx 1.06$$

If instead, we invest in DCL, the utility this year will be

$$U_{4,\text{DCL}} = \sqrt{\frac{120}{100}} \approx 1.10$$

The habit level next year will now be

$$H_{5,\text{DCL}} = \frac{4}{7}120 + \frac{2}{7}105 + \frac{1}{7}95 = \frac{785}{7}$$

and the utility will be

$$U_{5,\text{DCL}} = \sqrt{\frac{110}{785/7}} \approx 0.99$$

The combined utility over two years for an investment in GRW is approximately 2.11, and 2.09 for DCL. Even though the total consumption is the same, the investor would prefer the investment in GRW, where consumption continues to grow each year.

In this question, we assumed a discount factor of zero. Interestingly, though, habit formation tends to push in the opposite direction of discounting. If the discount rate was not zero, then the present value of $120 this year and $110 next year would be greater than the present value of $110 this year and $120 the following year. Habit formation can lead us to reverse our normal preference for current consumption over future consumption.

6. As a risk manager, it is not necessarily your job to second guess investment decisions, but style drift—when managers make significant changes to their investment style—is considered by many to be a risk in itself. Also, to the extent that moving the portfolio from lots of large retailers toward small technology companies impacts the risk of the portfolio, you may want to discuss the change in the risk profile with the portfolio manager. In discussing the decision, you may be able to uncover potential risks that might otherwise be overlooked.

In this particular case, the portfolio manager may be influenced by the availability bias. Because they are easy to recall, the recent store closings and the recent article on technology companies, might make it seem more likely that retail companies will fail and tech companies will succeed.

You may also want to consider representativeness bias. All successful technology companies were once small companies, but not all small technology companies go on to become large successful companies.

You may also want to consider the endowment effect. Even though the manager is talking about making a significant change to the portfolio, the endowment effect might make her reluctant to actually make that change.

REFERENCES

Artzner, P., F. Delbaen, J.-M. Eber, and D. Heath (1999). "Coherent Measures of Risk," *Mathematical Finance*, 9(3): 203–228.

Benartzi, S., and R. H. Thaler (1995). "Myopic Loss Aversion and the Equity Premium Puzzle," *Quarterly Journal of Economics*, 110(1), 73–92.

Henrich, J., S. Heine, and A. Norenzayan (2011). "The WEIRDest people in the world?" *Behavioral and Brain Sciences*, 33, 61–135.

Kahneman, D. and A. Tversky (1974). "Judgment under Uncertainty: Heuristics and Biases," *Science*, 185, 1124–1131.

Kahneman, D. and A. Tversky (1984). "Choices, Values, and Frames," *American Psychologist*, 34, 341–350.

Koenker, R. and G. Bassett, Jr. (1978). "Regression Quantiles," *Econometrica*, 46, No 1, January 1978, 33–50.

Levitt, S. D. and J. A. List (2007). "What Do Laboratory Experiments Measuring Social Preferences Reveal About the Real World?" *Journal of Economic Perspectives*, 21, 153–174.

Mehra, R. and E. C. Prescott (1985). "The Equity Premium: A Puzzle," *Journal of Monetary Economics*, 15, 145–161.

Meucci, A. (2009). "Managing Diversification," *Risk*, 22, May, 74–79.

Miller, M. B. (2014). *Mathematics and Statistics for Financial Risk Management*. 2nd ed. Hoboken, NJ: John Wiley & Sons.

INDEX